Ahmed Al-Nahhas studied law at Brunel University and the College of Law. He commenced his training contract as a solicitor with a firm in the City of London in 2005 and qualified in May 2007. He joined Bolt Burdon Kemp solicitors in 2011, where he is now a Partner and the Head of the military claims department. In 2015 he obtained his higher rights of audience as a Solicitor Advocate.

# A Practical Guide to Military Claims

# A Practical Guide to Military Claims

Ahmed Al-Nahhas LLB Hons,
Solicitor Advocate (civil proceedings),
Partner and Head of the Military Group,
Bolt Burdon Kemp solicitors

Law Brief Publishing

Published 2019 by Law Brief Publishing, an imprint of Law Brief Publishing Ltd
30 The Parks
Minehead
Somerset
TA24 8BT

www.lawbriefpublishing.com

Paperback: 978-1-912687-27-5

*To my wife and family.*

# PREFACE

I have practiced as a Solicitor and Advocate acting exclusively for service personnel and their families for the majority of my career. Being a 'claimant' lawyer, my experience comes from bringing civil claims against the Ministry of Defence, not defending them. The purpose of this book is to provide a concise and practical guide to those claims, and to identify the peculiarities and challenges that they may bring to your practice.

I have not covered all types of civil claims that could be brought by service personnel, just the common ones. By civil claims I mean primarily those brought in common law negligence and some brought under statute.

For the sake of brevity, any potential claimant will simply be referred to in this book as "*your client*". We will focus on the Regulars, Reservists and Veterans, and refer to these collectively as *"service personnel"*, although in doing so I do not mean to ignore the distinctions between these groups.

I have assumed that most readers will have a grasp of the litigation process, the Civil Procedure Rules and some fundamental principles of tort law; although this knowledge will not be entirely necessary. At the end of most chapters you will find a number of bulleted "*points for practice*". These lists are never exhaustive, but aim to encourage reflection and further enquiry.

I hope you find this book a helpful introduction to this niche field, which is stimulating, challenging and fulfilling.

The law referred to in this book is believed to be correct as at 1st October 2019.

Ahmed Al-Nahhas
October 2019

# ACKNOWLEDGEMENTS

I would not have been able to write this book without the support of my partners, colleagues and friends at Bolt Burdon Kemp solicitors, as well as my associates from Forces Law and the Bar, with whom I have worked over the years.

There are too many people for me to mention and thank here, but I would like to identify a few in particular. My sincere thanks to Laura Collignon, John Sephton, Keir Hirst and Tean Butcher for proof reading elements of this book, their guidance and helpful suggestions.

My thanks also to Lynne Burdon, Jonathan Wheeler, Rhicha Kapila, Jonathan Dingle, Debra Fox and Jeremy Fitzgibbon for their endless support.

To my editors, Tim Kevan and Garry Wright of Law Brief Publishing: I was flattered and humbled that you asked me to write this book. Thank you both for the opportunity, your encouragement and your patience.

# CONTENTS

# CHAPTER ONE
# INTRODUCTION

*"I do not ask the wounded person how he feels, I myself become the wounded person."*

Walt Whitman

## 1.1 Know your client

As lawyers, we must try to understand our clients if we are ever going to have a chance of acting in their best interests. To do this, we must discover their motivations and values. But this is not a simple process and you might start by unlearning what you already know. There is a great deal of misunderstanding about what military life entails, and perhaps tabloids, films and television dramas have some part to play in this. Equally, they may have had some influence on the attitudes towards lawyers working in this field.

Whilst I have never served in the armed forces, I have come to know that community fairly well. My understanding must be skewed by the specific nature of my work, and the fact that most of my clients come to me in times of crisis, but for my part acting for service personnel has been a privilege. They are, on the whole, well mannered, widely travelled, organised, professional, loyal, honest to a fault and able to see the funny side in almost any (and often the very worst) of situations.

In my practice I will typically come across a service person who has been seriously injured and is in the process of being medically discharged from their military service. This transition may have occurred with little warning, and they may find themselves moving from a life of being a supremely fit individual with a career path and future, to one of physical, psychological and financial uncertainty. They may have a young family in tow and will present with issues constructed of their own ego; damaged pride and anger at the thought of not being able to provide for their loved ones.

Your client may come to you with a similar story. They may have chosen a military life because of a firm belief that they wanted to serve their country. Perhaps the prospect of combat beckoned to them, or maybe enlisting was simply their best option at the time. The lengthy engagement, plethora of benefits, decent salary and exceptional pension would have enticed them further. Whatever their reasons for joining, your client would soon have become indoctrinated into a new family, and that camaraderie and sense of belonging will stay with them for the rest of their lives.

As a recruit, they swore allegiance to the Crown and relinquished their civilian status. They then became subject to military law and discipline. They would have been assigned a new home, whether based on land or at sea, living and working alongside a number of their peers. All would undergo rigorous training, both physically and mentally. They may not have seen combat, but they would have challenged themselves, and been challenged, to their very limits. Throughout their service, they lived in the knowledge that they may be called on to perform their duty, which may involve putting their own life at risk, or taking the lives of others. Often, for these same reasons or perhaps because of things they have witnessed or done during their service, your client may also present as one of the most troubled individuals that you will encounter in your professional life.

At some point, perhaps as a result of negligence, their military career was brought prematurely to an end. Once they entered civilian life (or 'civvy-street' as they will term it), they became frustrated by everyday things that they had taken for granted. They are surprised when they have to wait weeks for a medical appointment to see their civilian GP. Their outgoings, no longer subsidised, are scandalously high. Their family no longer feels safe now that they are living outside of military camp. Their children are no longer entitled to school bursaries. They may then have struggled to integrate into civilian life and to find work. Their old friends, who they trained and served with, are elsewhere, pre-occupied with their own careers and duties. They now fear that they no longer belong and that the service community, their armed forces 'family', has forgotten them. They feel lost and grow bored. Without proper support, and along with the pressure of dealing with their injuries, they may become depressed. Their family life suffers too. As their situation starts to unravel, they turn to you for help.

As a claimant lawyer, you will probably be meeting your client whilst they are in the midst of this extremis. You will seek to place them in the position they would have been in *but for* the negligence; to try to turn back the clock. Unfortunately, you will probably fail to meet their expectations, because their greatest challenge will be accepting the reality that their military career is over. Of course not all military careers end so bleakly, in fact the vast majority of service personnel successfully transition into civilian life. Equally, the vast majority of veterans have positive views of their time in service. But as lawyers, we rarely get involved in the stories with happy endings. Managing your client's expectations will therefore be, as ever, a priority.

Service personnel revere loyalty and in my experience their loyalty is directed towards their comrades first. But your client is likely to maintain some loyalty to their particular service and, by association, to the Ministry of Defence. For this reason, they may find it challenging to engage in the litigation that you are steering them through. They will have doubts, even though they may have suffered injuries and losses as a result of negligence on the Ministry's part. You should tread carefully. To you the Ministry of Defence might simply be another defendant, but to your client they are, or were, family. In fact, it may have been the only organisation that has ever truly believed in them, and nurtured them. Your client will struggle, for example, to comprehend why the Ministry, now represented by solicitors, is denying their claim in its entirety. Or worse, why they seek to make allegations of contributory negligence, besmirch their character and belittle their career. What to you may seem only a part of the 'game' of litigation will leave your client feeling angry and confused. Suddenly things will get very personal for them, and they will find it difficult to dissociate the various issues in the case from their years of service and what they feel is their 'due'. Perhaps in this way service personnel are no different to any other litigant, but it will serve you to remember the special relationship that existed between the parties. It will inform a large part of what you do and underpins much of the law in this niche field.

When you start your work, the nature of this close-knit military community may make things challenging for you also. Witnesses will not come forward. Disclosure will be fruitless. You will need to know where to look, and to understand the language, hierarchy and bureaucracy of the military first, only then will your avenues of enquiry open up before you. In the meantime, start with the fundamentals, and get to know your client.

## 1.2 Know your opponent

The administration of the armed forces used to lay under the powers of the Royal Prerogative. By the 20th Century, this responsibility was shared amongst several government bodies. The Defence (Transfer of Functions) Act 1964 transferred these functions and responsibilities primarily to the Secretary of State for Defence, who manages all military business through their government department; the Ministry of Defence (the "MoD").

The MoD is today a large government body and has approximately 56,920 civilian staff. Its overriding mission is to protect the nation and its values and interests abroad. It does this primarily by managing, maintaining and when necessary deploying an effective military force.

The MoD Common Law Claims and Policy Division is the department responsible for handling civil claims against the Ministry. Its figures published in November 2018 provide the following statistics for civil claims in the financial year 2017/2018 alone:

- The MoD paid out approximately £130 million in respect of civil claims and claimant legal costs.

- The highest value claim settled was approximately £2.97 million.

- 3,754 new claims were made.

These statistics are as interesting as they are instructive. The MoD faces a high volume of claims and defending them is an expensive business. You are not facing an organisation that is unused to litigation and there will be policy behind the hurdles that you face as a claimant lawyer. Ultimately the MoD, like any other government body, has an obligation to preserve 'the public purse', and like any insurer or company, it will be looking to:

- reduce risk;
- reduce financial exposure; and
- achieve certainty.

The MoD will have the added objective of maintaining public confidence in the armed forces. This obligation is far reaching and is tied to issues of national security and fulfilling the nation's obligations to service personnel. It is sometimes in these areas of policy that the most interesting pressure can be applied.

### 1.3 Questions for you

- What are your client's motivations and values?
- What support is in place for them?
- What problems do they face in their day-to-day life?
- What are the issues that are relevant to your work?
- What are their objectives and how will you achieve them?
- How will you manage their expectations?

# CHAPTER TWO
# THE ARMED FORCES COMMUNITY

## Introduction

In 2014 the British armed forces community, including personnel, veterans and their families, was estimated to number between 6.5 and 6.7 million people; a significant section of the population. In this chapter we will introduce the main constituents of this community, its structure and the rules that govern it. We will also consider some of those groups which support the armed forces at home and abroad.

## 2.1 The British Armed Forces

The British Armed Forces defend the United Kingdom. Their strength as at January 2019 was circa 190,750 personnel. They are formed of the three single 'Services':

- The Royal Navy
- The British Army
- The Royal Air Force

Collectively these are referred to as the British Armed Forces or 'Tri-Services'. Within each of these Services there are a variety of specialisms or 'trades' that personnel can train in, as well as a myriad of rules, regulations, traditions, etiquettes and even clubs. Their history and stories can be fascinating, if sometimes a little bewildering.

In addition to serving the interests of the UK and its allies, these forces often take part in missions and training for the United Nations and NATO. The Commander-in-Chief of the British Armed Forces is the current monarch, Queen Elizabeth the Second. In reality, the Command lies with the Prime Minister.

Like the military of other nations, the British Armed Forces are organised hierarchically and split into progressively smaller 'units'. There is no one definition of a 'unit', save that it is a defined group within the larger military structure.

Each service person is assigned to a particular unit and placed under the command of the officer in charge of that unit or "Officer Commanding" (OC). This home unit is primarily responsible for that service person's training, welfare and healthcare.

The OC is distinct from the "Commanding Officer" (CO) who is often at the pinnacle of the management structure within the military. For example, they are usually in charge of many units or a military establishment. They can be responsible for hundreds if not thousands of personnel.

Below is a short summary of the constituents of each Service, including their objectives, values and standards. These differ between each Service, but the themes are similar.

### 2.1.1 **The Royal Navy**

The Royal Navy is termed the 'senior' Service, being the oldest of the military forces. Today it includes approximately 32,380 service personnel (including the Royal Marines) plus some 3,780 volunteer reserves and 2,380 other personnel. It has recourse to some 75 commissioned ships, including 10 nuclear powered submarines.

The functions of the Royal Navy are various and include:

- Preventing conflict.
- Providing security at sea.
- Developing international partnerships.
- Preparing to fight.
- Protecting the UK economy.

- Providing humanitarian assistance.

The Royal Navy is further divided into several smaller services or 'Arms':

- Surface Fleet
- Submarine Service
- Royal Marines (the amphibious fighting force of the Royal Navy)
- Royal Fleet Auxiliary
- Fleet Air Arm

Royal Navy personnel can specialise in a variety of different branches, including Warfare, Engineering and Logistics, amongst others. The Special Boat Service (SBS) are the Special Forces of the Royal Navy.

The Core Values of the Royal Navy are commitment; courage; discipline; respect for others; integrity; loyalty; tradition; leadership; teamwork; morale; can-do attitude; sense of humour and humility.

### 2.1.2 The British Army

The British Army can trace its roots as far back as 1707, and further back to the Restoration in respect of England alone. The Bill of Rights imposes an obligation on Parliament to approve the existence of the British Army during peacetime, which is now done every five years by passing successive Armed Forces Acts. The British Army today comprises 78,360 regular personnel, some 3,070 Gurkhas, 29,600 volunteer reserves and 4,230 other personnel.

The primary role of the British Army is to defend the interests of the UK. It has a Regimental and Corps system; large groups of fighting soldiers traditionally recruited from and trained in one geographical area. Some examples are:

- The Army Air Corps
- The Royal Regiment of Artillery
- The Corps of Royal Engineers
- The Royal Logistics Corps

The Special Air Service (SAS) and the Special Forces Support Group (SFSG) comprise the Army's Special Forces.

The values of the British Army are:

- Selfless commitment
- Courage
- Discipline
- Integrity
- Loyalty
- Respect for others

The standards of the British Army are:

- lawful;
- appropriate behaviour; and
- total professionalism.

### 2.1.3 The Royal Air Force

The RAF emerged out of the success of the First World War. It was founded in 1918 and has since played a vital part in the United Kingdom's military capability, including of course its contribution to the Battle of Britain during World War II. Today it comprises some 32,690 regular personnel, 3,040 volunteer reserves and 1,210 other personnel, as well as many hundreds of operational aircraft. The role of the RAF includes:

- Defending of the nation
- Control of the air
- Mobility in the air
- Providing intelligence
- Offensive capabilities

There are various trades in the RAF, including:

- Pilots
- Weapon system operators
- Intelligence
- Engineering
- Logistics
- Medical & Dental

The core values of the RAF are:

- Respect – mutual and self-respect.
- Integrity – moral courage, honesty, responsibility and justice.
- Service – physical courage, loyalty, commitment, teamwork.
- Excellence – personal excellence, discipline and pride.

## 2.2 **Personnel**

Your client may be a service person, reservist, veteran or civilian employee. You will need to determine this at an early stage by asking them for their service agreement or contract of employment respectively. Their rights and remedies will depend on their legal status and terms of engagement.

### 2.2.1 **Regulars**

Service personnel are servants of the Crown; they do not have an enforceable contract of employment. They do not cease to become civilians simply because they serve, but they do take on additional responsibilities because, by agreeing to serve, they are also agreeing to become subject to service law. As such they are subject to the provisions of the Armed Forces Act and the Queen's Regulations (for their particular Service), mentioned below.

For operational and security reasons, service personnel are bound by the Official Secrets Act (1989) and are required to sign a declaration to that effect. In many senses, their freedom of expression is highly restricted and often monitored. This Act exposes them to the threat of prosecution in the event that they disclose or fail to keep safe any official and sensitive material. They are also not permitted to:

- Join a trade union or political organisation
- Stand for election in public office
- Speak to the media (without express permission)

Regular service personnel may also be referred to simply as the 'Regulars', which distinguishes them from the Reserve Forces.

### 2.2.2 **Reservists**

The British Reserve Forces consist of the Royal Naval Reserve, Royal Marines Reserve, Army Reserve and Royal Air Force Reserves. In essence, Reservists are everyday people who volunteer to give up their spare time to train and serve with the regular forces in exchange for service pay, allowances and pension. They are normally committed to up to 35 days of mandatory training per year, which takes place on weekends with a lengthier training period of up to 15 days occurring annually. They are also obliged to respond to any request to be 'mobilised', which normally is for a period of six to 12 months and may be to serve in operations at home or abroad.

From a legal perspective, you should treat Reservists in much the same way as Regulars, albeit they will have a different length of engagement, working frequency and pay structure; which may all influence quantum. They are subject to the provisions of the Reserve Forces Act and the Queen's Regulations (mentioned below), but only so long as they are on duty.

### 2.2.3 Veterans

Technically, a veteran is anyone who has served for at least a day, whether as a Regular or a Reservist. Most of the clients you act for will be veterans who have been medically discharged. Some may have started their career as a Regular and then became Reservists, or vice versa.

### 2.2.4 Employees

The MoD employs a variety of civil servants and other civilian personnel, in the same way as any other large government body or corporation. If your client is a civilian employee, they will be employed under terms of a contract of employment. They will be entitled to make a variety of claims in the employment tribunal, such as unfair dismissal, as well as claims for breach of contract in the civil courts. As mentioned in the preface to this book, we will focus on the Regulars, Reservists and Veterans, and refer to these collectively as 'service personnel' below.

### 2.2.5 Rank structure

Service personnel (including Reservists) are primarily divided into two categories:

- Officers – these are the managers and leaders of the military and comprise any rank above Warrant Officer Class 1 (see table below). Officers for each service undergo specialist training in how to be an officer, which includes amongst other things tactics and strategy, how to command and how to apply military discipline. They also receive specialist training in their chosen field, whether it is engineering, warfare or a plethora of other specialties.

- Other ranks (ORs) – these are the 'workforce' of the military, but this is not meant in any derogatory way. Other ranks are taught leadership, management and a variety of other skills which make them an invaluable resource. Other ranks in the Royal Navy are called 'Ratings'.

Non-Commissioned Officers (NCOs) are a special type of other rank and this term denotes a service person who does not yet have a Commission but is senior amongst the other ranks. NCOs are further subdivided:

- Senior Non-Commissioned Officers (SNCOs) are those holding the rank of Sergeant up to and including Warrant Officer (or the Royal Navy or RAF equivalent).

- Junior Non-Commissioned Officers (JNCOs) hold the rank of Corporal or equivalent.

Other ranks are selected on merit for promotion and, if successful work their way up to become a JNCO and then potentially progress to SNCO. Those who show real promise and development can then transfer to become an officer and 'Commission'. Very few in fact achieve this (broadly around 3% depending on their Service).

The chain of command in the military is an essential concept to maintaining order, discipline and effectiveness. Lower ranks must follow the orders of their superiors and going above the head of your immediate superior is strictly frowned upon. Disobeying commands and/or undermining the chain of command can result in serious disciplinary consequences.

The table below sets out the rank structure in descending order for each Service plus the Royal Marines (which whilst part of the Royal Navy hold a different rank structure):

| **Royal Navy** | **Royal Marines** | **British Army** | **Royal Air Force** |
|---|---|---|---|
| Admiral of the Fleet | - | Field Marshal | Marshall of the Royal Air Force |
| Admiral | General | General | Air Chief Marshall |
| Vice Admiral | Lieutenant General | Lieutenant General | Air Marshall |
| Rear Admiral | Major General | Major General | Air Vice-Marshall |
| Commodore | Brigadier | Brigadier | Air Commodore |
| Captain | Colonel | Colonel | Group Captain |
| Commander | Lieutenant Colonel | Lieutenant Colonel | Wing Commander |
| Lieutenant Commander | Major | Major | Squadron Leader |
| Lieutenant | Captain | Captain | Flight Lieutenant |
| Sub Lieutenant<br>Midshipman | Lieutenant<br>Second Lieutenant | Lieutenant<br>Second Lieutenant | Flying Officer<br>Pilot Officer |
| Warrant Officer | Warrant Officer Class 1 | Warrant Officer Class 1 | Warrant Officer<br>Master Aircrew |
| - | Warrant Officer Class 2 | Warrant Officer Class 2 | - |
| Chief Petty Officer<br>Master at Arms | Colour Sergeant | Staff Sergeant<br>Staff Corporal | Flight Sergeant<br>Chief Technician |

| | | | |
|---|---|---|---|
| Petty Officer | Sergeant | Sergeant<br><br>Corporal of Horse | Sergeant |
| Leading Hand | Corporal | Corporal<br><br>Bombardier | Corporal |
| - | Lance Corporal | Lance Corporal<br><br>Lance Bombardier | Lance Corporal (RAF Regt) |
| Able Rate 1<br><br>Able Rate 2 | Marine | Private Class 1-3 (Alternatively: Trooper, Ranger, Sapper, Rifleman, Fusilier or Guardsman) | Junior Technician<br><br>Senior / Leading Aircraftman<br><br>Aircraftman |
| - | - | Private Class 4 | - |

Rank may be "acting" or "substantive." Acting rank is generally awarded when there is no one of substantive rank available to fill a particular role or post. Acting rank is paid at the higher rate but it does not accrue seniority. It allows an individual the opportunity to show potential for promotion.

### 2.2.6 Engagements and commissions

The potential length of your client's service will often be a live issue for the purposes of any negligence claim, as this may directly correlate to loss of earnings, benefits and pension. Whilst 55 is still deemed to be the 'normal' retirement age for service personnel, careers can extend to age 60 (which is the compulsory retirement age). It is important that you ascertain the commission or engagement upon which your client is serving and the options they may or may not have to extend their service.

Officers serve under the terms of a 'Commission'; a formal document issued to appoint a person to high office and giving authority to the officer from the Sovereign. Across the UK Armed Forces commissioned officers receive their commission at the end of their initial officer training, marked by a passing out parade; it is a significant moment for an officer and their family. There will be a number of requirements which they will have to meet depending on their particular Service and any specialisation, including age limits and academic requirements.

The length of a commission will normally be for an initial 12-year period, which can be extended to 20 years' service or their 40th birthday (whichever is the latter). Following this, extensions may be obtained to the age of 55 (or 60 in exceptional circumstances), depending again on whether they meet certain criteria and the needs of their particular Service and specialisation.

Other ranks serve under the terms of a service agreement (an 'Engagement'). Entry requirements vary but are less stringent than for officers, normally involving a recruitment test for basic numeracy, language and reasoning skills. The length and terms of an Engagement will depend on the Service. Traditionally, long-term engagements of up to 22 years' service were offered, but changes made in the last decade have introduced a number of different engagements.

In 2008 the British Army introduced the Versatile Engagement (VEng) with three sub-categories of service. A soldier progresses through each of the categories subject to meeting the requisite standards and depending on vacancies and manning considerations:

- Short – 12 years.
- Full – 24 years.
- Long – 30 years.

Since 2015, The Royal Navy and Royal Marines have offered three engagements. Again, the service person must progress through each stage:

- Engagement Stage 1 (ES1) – service to 12 years;
- Engagement Stage 2 (ES2) – service to 20 years; and
- Engagement Stage 3 (ES3) – initially either for 5, 10 or 15 years and thereafter in 5-year blocks to age 60.

RAF recruits are normally enlisted on a 12-year Notice Engagement which is followed by a period of six years' service in the RAF Reserves. Extensions of service can be sought up to age 60.

As for officers, for other ranks passing out following the completion of their initial training is a significant achievement shared with family and friends. They then progress their engagement and continue to their training.

Transitional provisions exist for those service personnel who transferred to new terms of engagement, as well as single-Service regulations governing terms of service for both officers and other ranks.

Service personnel have a statutory right to leave service. The termination process, notice period and requirements will depend on the Service, your client's age and the stage of their career. For example, in the British Army a service person is able to 'discharge as of right' within the first three months of service. Beyond this they must have served for at least four years and must give 12 months' notice to terminate.

The commission and engagement process allows the Armed Forces to plan their workforce requirements to meet the prevailing needs of each service, whilst affording officers and other ranks choice in their length of service subject to individual performance and potential.

## 2.3 Useful rules and reference

There are some distinct statutes and regulations which may help you better understand the working lives of service personnel, as well as being a source of guidance for your investigations. The key sources and some guidance on terminology are set out below.

### 2.3.1 The Armed Forces and Reserve Forces Acts

The Armed Forces Act came into force in 2006 and replaced three previous and separate Acts which accounted for discipline in all three Services; bringing all military discipline under one Act. The Act provides for the jurisdiction of the Court Martial, which is empowered to try any service offence under the Act.

The Reserve Forces Act 1996 sets out the rules governing the organisation and maintenance of the Reserve Forces, including their terms of service. In a similar vein to the Armed Forces Act, it sets out a number of service offences. In addition, the Act created a new category of 'Sponsored Reserves', which are civilians specifically authorised by the MoD to carry out tasks on its behalf. Examples of this are the Royal Fleet Auxiliary, which supplies the Royal Navy with supplies at sea, and the Mobile Meteorological Unit, which provides weather data to the Armed Forces. All Reservists are subject to military discipline when they are serving.

### 2.3.2 The Queen's Regulations

The Queen's Regulations were first published in 1731 (what was then the 'King's Regulations'). These regulations have developed over time and by the mid-19th Century there existed separate editions for each branch of the armed forces:

- The Queen's Regulations for the Royal Navy (1997)
- The Queen's Regulations for the Army (1975)
- The Queen's Regulations for the Royal Air Force (1999)

The Queen's Regulations are comprehensive to say the least. They are a helpful source of guidance to and governance of the military, including:

- Structure and duties

- Guidance for commanders
- Appraisals and reporting
- Values, standards and discipline

### 2.3.3 **Joint and single-Service publications**

Throughout this book you may find reference to Joint Service Publications (JSPs). These regulations are published and controlled by the MoD and are intended to apply to all three services. JSPs might be treated in the same way as an employee handbook for a private company or corporation, save that JSPs are usually far more extensive both in respect of technical detail and guidance.

JSPs are designed to assist personnel and their commanders in the proper procedure and fulfillment of their duties. They will provide you with insight about everything from health and safety issues through to risk assessments and complaints procedures, as well as making reference to applicable law and terminology. For virtually every task that your client may have been required to do, there will probably be a corresponding JSP. Where service personnel have disregard of the JSPs and any recommended practice, they may well be subject to disciplinary action.

Most but not all JSPs are available online on the Government website, although some are not for security reasons. You may have to make an application under the Freedom of Information Act for copies of JSPs that are no longer published or are unavailable online.

In addition to JSPs, each service will regularly produce and update its own 'single-Service' guidance, especially where it is difficult to formulate rules that would apply easily to all three services.

### 2.3.4 Terminology

If you are going to act for service personnel, you will need to understand their language. You will also need to interview witnesses, traverse records and consider statements. In doing so, you will discover a world of acronyms, nicknames and shorthand references which may have little or no meaning in a civilian context, but which might tip your understanding of the facts in a particular case. Helpfully, the MoD publishes a list of formally recognised acronyms and terms which is available online and over 400 pages long! Most JSPs will also include a glossary of terms relevant to those specific regulations.

## 2.4 The Armed Forces Covenant

The Armed Forces Covenant is a promise between the nation and its armed forces. It is rooted in legislation that sought to guarantee welfare to the families of fallen service personnel. Today, it seeks to set out the way the armed forces community, including personnel and their families, expect to be treated and compensated for their service. It also encourages understanding and commitment from various levels of society, increasing public awareness of the sacrifices that service personnel and their families make. Despite its long and noble history, the Armed Forces Covenant is a rather nebulous concept and remains a non-legal 'contract'. The MoD treats the covenant as a binding agreement, albeit the terms of which are fairly broad-brush. It can prove helpful in framing your client's pleadings and/or when engaging in settlement discussions, and is often under-used in military claims.

## 2.5 Service families and federations

The military has long since recognised the pivotal role that service families have in supporting personnel. Service families have unenviable tasks, often required to move with their serving spouses either around the Country or abroad, with little notice. They are by their nature versatile and stoic. However, like service personnel, they can become reliant on the armed forces community.

There are a number of benefits provided to service families, including subsidised accommodation and utilities, as well as financial support for education. Where families are stationed at home their healthcare needs are normally provided through the NHS. When stationed abroad, they may be provided with access to military primary healthcare.

Each Service has an independent Federation which offers service families support and advice, as well as canvassing local authorities and Government on issues of welfare for service personnel and their families. Each Service also has a network of 'HIVEs', which provide information services and act as a point of contact between the chain of command and service families.

## 2.6 Cadets

The Cadet forces are community based organisations run and attended on a voluntary basis. They promote positive social and personal development of young people in the community (i.e. those aged 12 – 18), largely by introducing them to military structure and a range of related activities, sports and exercises. They are usually staffed by trained volunteers, who are often former service personnel.

## 2.7 Military charities

There are many military charities, some have been established for many years and have long histories of supporting the services. When acting for injured service personnel, a charity's involvement in supporting your client may become apparent in their records, and also relevant to a number of issues in the claim. Some charities provide emotional support and financial assistance, whilst others may become actively involved in referring and/or providing treatment (sometimes to their own specialist centers across the UK). As such, a duty of care my arguably arise, depending on the facts.

Many new charities were created in response to the wars in Iraq and Afghanistan and increasing concern over the welfare of veterans returning home. By 2018, there were approximately 1,888 armed forces charities in the UK. In recent years there has been much scrutiny and some criticism levelled at Government for the fact that many service leavers are forced to rely on charities for support.

## 2.8 Points for practice

- The armed forces community is large, tight-knit and, at least historically, has been very inward looking. The uninitiated may find it daunting. Developing your network within the armed forces community will be crucial to your practice and understanding.

- Ask your client for a copy of their service agreement or contract of employment (if they are an employee). Their rights and remedies will depend on their legal status and terms of engagement or commission.

- Understanding your client's service background, where they have served, there trade and skill set. This will all come into play when progressing their case.

- Check what organisations or charities may have supported your client. There may be relevant records for you to obtain and/or witnesses available who may buttress your client's claim.

- JSPs are invaluable sources of information. They usually begin with a policy statement which explains the purpose of the guidance and cross references other applicable regulations. There may be differences in practice between Services.

- Always ensure that the version of the JSP or guidance you are considering covers the relevant period of the accident or negligence. You may have to make an FOI request for those JSPs that are not immediately available online.

- Rely on your client to help guide you and be prepared to ask them questions about the regulations and guidance. Often there will be manuals that are not available online. Make a list of these and ensure that they form part of your disclosure enquiries.

- Understanding the language of service personnel does not mean adopting their vernacular. Many of the third parties you work with, experts for example, may not be familiar with this terminology.

- All service personnel are prohibited from speaking to journalists and/or the media without authorisation from their chain of command. Their social media is also increasingly scrutinised. Clients may need to be warned not to court the press and to behave online!

# CHAPTER THREE
# THE EMPLOYER'S DUTY OF CARE

## Introduction

In this Chapter we will explore the legal rights of service personnel, the types of claims they may bring and consider some developments in the law. As we shall see, although their rights are heavily curtailed when compared to civilians, they are still owed a duty of care by the State which is analogous to that owed by employers to employees, and they have the means to enforce that duty in the civil courts.

## 3.1 Actions against the Crown

Previously the Crown (i.e. the State) enjoyed immunity from claims in tort, which meant that service personnel could not sue the MoD in negligence. This doctrine derived from times when the Crown could do no wrong. The Crown Proceedings (Armed Forces) Act 1987 abolished that immunity prospectively from 15th May 1987. This meant that Section 2 of the Crown Proceedings Act 1947 applied to actions against the Crown by service personnel:

> *Section 2. Liability of the Crown in tort.*
>
> *(1) Subject to the provisions of this Act, the Crown shall be subject to all those liabilities in tort to which, if it were a private person of full age and capacity, it would be subject:—*
>
> *(a) in respect of torts committed by its servants or agents;*
>
> *(b) in respect of any breach of those duties which a person owes to his servants or agents at common law by reason of being their employer; and*

*(c) in respect of any breach of the duties attaching at common law to the ownership, occupation, possession or control of property:*

*Provided that no proceedings shall lie against the Crown by virtue of paragraph (a) of this subsection in respect of any act or omission of a servant or agent of the Crown unless the act or omission would apart from the provisions of this Act have given rise to a cause of action in tort against that servant or agent or his estate.*

*(2) Where the Crown is bound by a statutory duty which is binding also upon persons other than the Crown and its officers, then, subject to the provisions of this Act, the Crown shall, in respect of a failure to comply with that duty, be subject to all those liabilities in tort (if any) to which it would be so subject if it were a private person of full age and capacity.*

What this means is that:

- Claims in tort for breaches of common law and/or statutory duties can proceed against the Crown as if it were a private individual and/or vicariously for breaches of Crown servants, agents or employees.

- Your client can pursue claims in respect of torts that occurred from 15th May 1987. Obviously, they may be precluded from doing so because of the limitation of claims in negligence (normally three years from the date of injury) and depending on any arguments that they may have under Section 33 of the Limitation Act 1980, which might allow them to bring a claim out of time (see **12.2**).

- The Secretary of State does have powers to under Section 2 of the Crown Proceedings (Armed Forces) Act 1987 to revive the old immunity provisions in cases where it is "*necessary or expedient*" to do so, which may be by reason of any imminent national danger or great emergency. There are currently no known plans to revive the immunity.

## 3.2 Domestic health and safety legislation

MoD policy expressly stipulates that it will adhere to domestic health and safety legislation as far as possible. This is your starting point. For our purposes it is also worth noting that the following Acts will bind the Crown as well as any regulations made under them: the Health and Safety at Work Act 1974, the Occupier's liability Act 1957 and the Highways Act 1980. In many senses the MoD should be treated like any other employer, but there are some exceptions and a few general points to bear in mind:

- There are specific health and safety regulations from which the MoD are exempt (an example is the Carriage of Dangerous Goods etc. Regulations 2007, Regulations 3 and 4, which otherwise would have regulated the ability of the military to transport ammunition and explosives for military exercises). The Secretary of State for Defence also has powers to claim exemption from domestic health and safety legislation in the interests of national security, but this power is rarely exercised.

- In respect of deployments overseas, the MoD's policy is to apply UK health and safety standards where reasonably practicable, and to take into account the legislation of host nations. But importantly, the MoD will not normally be bound by domestic legislation in relation to overseas deployments. This would not preclude a claimant from arguing that an exercise abroad was negligent on common law principles, or identifying breaches of domestic regulations which may help to prove unsafe working practices.

- Whilst MoD policy requires it to comply with all domestic health and safety legislation, Section 69 of the Enterprise Act 2013 now prohibits civil claims from being brought for breaches of the regulations under the Health and Safety at Work Act 1974 (for all accidents occurring after 1st October 2013). The practical effect of this Act has been fairly limited so far. It has reduced claims involving reliance on strict liability provisions and has generally shifted the burden on claimants to prove common law principles of negligence to succeed in civil claims against their employers.

- The MoD has a memorandum of agreement with the Health and Safety Executive ("HSE"), which is the government agency responsible for regulating and enforcing health and safety practice in the United Kingdom. This provides for the HSE to have a number of operational investigators who, in agreement with the MoD, inspect a number of its activities and assess them for health and safety practice.

- Military personnel from other States which are stationed in the UK, termed 'visiting forces', are exempt from domestic health and safety legislation. The Visiting Forces Act 1952 provides, amongst other directives, for the Secretary of Defence to have recourse to settle civil claims brought for negligent actions or omissions of service personnel from States privy to reciprocal agreements under the Act.

- A number of military regulations exist which supplement and explain the MoD's common law and statutory duty of care (see **Chapter 5**).

## 3.3 Combat immunity

The doctrine of combat immunity provides that the State shall not be responsible for acts or omissions which result in death or injury to service personnel in 'combat'. The public policy arguments in favour of combat immunity are varied and include that:

- There would be unfair pressure applied to personnel and commanders if they had to second guess themselves in the heat of battle out of fear of becoming personally liable to civil claims.

- Commanders may become too cautious in planning operations.

- Combat effectiveness would be undermined and this might threaten national security and the lives of service personnel.

These arguments might at first appear compelling but they are not supported empirically. Some argue that service personnel and their families should be provided with a remedy where negligence has resulted in injury or death, bearing in mind that negligence in this context would not mean decisions made in the heat of battle, but reckless mistakes made outside of combat and which could have reasonably been avoided.

But what does the term 'combat' mean and how might it influence your client's prospects in bringing a claim? There have been some important cases which have examined this doctrine and the legal definition of 'combat', as well as exploring the boundaries of the civil claims that might follow. Below we chart the development of this case law. Some cases are not strictly relevant to the issue of combat immunity, but rather deal with rights under the European Convention on Human Rights (ECHR). It is arguably these cases which have contributed most to recent developments in this field.

In ***Mulcahy v MoD* [1996] EWCA Civ 1323**, Mr Mulcahy was serving in the Gulf War as a Gunner in the artillery when he suffered an injury. Mr Mulcahy had been ordered to fetch some water in front of a Howitzer gun, which was fired, exposing him to damaging noise which resulted in significant damage to his hearing and the loss of his military career. Mr Mulcahy brought a claim in negligence against the MoD, claiming that the gun was fired negligently and/or that systemic failings in safety contributed to or caused his injury. He accepted that he was deployed to a warzone and that he was part of the allied forces deployed during the war, but also pleaded that:

- The gun being fired was located in Saudi Arabia, firing into Iraq, and the risk of retaliation was minimal.
- In the days running up to and immediately after the injury, his unit had not been under any enemy fire whatsoever.
- On the day of the injury his unit was being visited by journalists.

The MoD sought to strike out the claim on the basis that combat immunity applied and therefore that Mr Mulcahy had no cause of action. The application to strike out was refused by Walker J, whose judgment still reflects the issues we grapple with today in relation to combat immunity:

> *"...It has to be established...whether the degree of involvement in warlike activities was such as to allow the Crown to argue that it was in fact a heat of battle situation. The Crown says, 'well, this is precisely the situation where there should be no investigation because it is contrary, in a sense, to public policy to be investigating the circumstances on the field of battle'. The question is was it the field of battle? The plaintiff will seek to argue that it was not the field of battle, although it was firing at the enemy. There are obviously degrees of involvement in warlike activities, some of which have been canvassed by me to counsel on a hypothetical basis. What is the situation of somebody involved in firing a guided missile a hundred miles? What is the situation in somebody arming a bomber? All that had to be determined..."*

The MoD successfully appealed Walker J's decision and Mr Mulcahy's case was struck out by the Court of Appeal. They successfully argued that imposing a duty of care in the circumstances would not be fair, just or reasonable. In the leading Judgment of the Court of Appeal, Neil LJ found that:

> *"I do not consider it necessary to examine whether a duty would be owed when someone was involved firing a guided missile over a distance of a hundred miles or when someone was arming a bomber... The plain facts of this case were that the plaintiff was in a war zone taking part in warlike operations and he was a member of a gun crew which was engaged in firing shells on enemy targets...In my judgment the circumstances in which the plaintiff was injured clearly constituted "battle conditions...As I said earlier, I do not find it necessary to explore the territorial limits of this immunity. It is sufficient to say that in my view it covers the present situation where in the course of hostilities against the enemy a howitzer of the plaintiffs' battalion was engaging the enemy and the plaintiff was a member of the gun team."*

Interestingly, Neil LJ explored the powers of the secretary of State under the Crown Proceedings Act to withdraw liability for tort against the State (mentioned at **3.1** above), and concluded that in the absence of such powers being enacted one must start with the proposition that a duty of care does exist in common law as between service personnel (and indeed no authority exists which would contradict this assumption).

None of the terms "*battle conditions*", "*warlike activities*", "*heat of battle*" or "*warlike operations*" were explored in any depth in ***Mulcahy***. In fact, one might sympathise with the claimant, who faced no real threat of 'combat' in the literal sense, but who having accepted that he was operating in a war zone and firing live shells at enemy targets, was not able to secure a remedy despite clear negligence on the part of his superior (in fact the MoD had accepted that two of the three tests required for a duty of care to be applied, namely proximity and foreseeability of damage, were satisfied).

***Multiple Claimants v MoD [2003] EWHC 1134 (QB)*** comprised two group actions brought by veterans who had suffered psychiatric harm as a result of conflicts. In a wide-ranging judgment, Owen J tried the generic issues between the cases, one of which was the application and scope of the doctrine of combat immunity. The facts of the various claims differed greatly and related to exposures to traumatic events across a range of operations and deployments. In respect of the Falklands War veterans, they claimed that combat immunity did not apply to their claims because the MoD failed:

- to make provision for Field Psychiatry Units (FPUs) during the conflict;
- to brief troops properly in the run up to the deployment; and/or
- to debrief troops after the conflict or arrange any necessary follow-up.

The veterans argued that the doctrine of combat immunity should not apply to their claims because these acts or omissions did not occur in combat, but rather they occurred before and/or after combat. In essence, that combat immunity should only apply to breaches during combat, and that because these particular breaches would have occurred in the planning and preparation for warfare, they were avoidable and actionable. Neil J considered this distinction and concluded that it would be wrong to hold the State to account in such circumstances:

> "[The doctrine of combat immunity] *plainly applies when service personnel are engaged with the enemy in the course of hostilities... does the immunity extend to acts or omissions in the course of planning and preparation for operations in which service personnel may engage in hostilities? Where is the line to be drawn?...In aggressive operations the objective will be to defeat of the enemy; in defensive operations the successful repulse of the enemy. In the planning or and preparation for such operations any more than in their execution. The planning or and preparation for military operations will include decisions as to the deployment of resources. Does the immunity apply to anti-terrorist, policing and peace keeping operations...In my judgment it will apply to operations in which service personnel come under attack or the threat of attack."*

Neil J went on to formulate some guiding principles:

> *"Accordingly in my judgment the application of the immunity can be resolved by reference to the following propositions.*
>
> 1. *A solider does not owe a fellow soldier a duty of care in tort when either (one or other or both) are engaged with an enemy in the course of combat.*
>
> 2. *The MoD is not under a duty to maintain a safe system of work for service personnel engaged with an enemy in the course of combat.*
>
> 3. *In relation to both (1) and (2) the term combat has an extended meaning in that –*
>
>     (a) *The immunity is not limited to the presence of the enemy or the occasions when contact with the enemy has been established. It extends to all active operations against the enemy in which service personnel are exposed to attack or the threat of attack. It covers attack and resistance, advance and retreat, pursuit and avoidance, reconnaissance and engagement.*
>
>     (b) *The immunity extends to the planning of and preparation for operations in which the armed forces may come under attack or meet armed resistance.*
>
>     (c) *The immunity will apply to peace-keeping/policing operations in which service personnel are exposed to attack or the threat of attack."*

Interestingly, Neil J also dismissed out-of-hand the MoD's contention that claims for personal injuries sustained in combat are not justiciable, and so compensation for damage suffered during combat is not recoverable. In so doing he said:

> *"In my judgment that submission is misconceived and confuses the issue of the existence of the duty of care with the causation of injury. The issue is whether the MoD is under a duty of acre in a particular set of circumstances. If the restriction to the duty of care does not arise on the facts, and a claimant is able to demonstrate breach of duty resulting in injury and consequential loss and damage, it is immaterial that the injury was sustained in the course of combat. The question with regard to the injury is then simply one of causation; is it attributable to the breach of duty?"*

The point here is that one should not conflagrate the issues of whether immunity applies with the timing of when damage is occasioned; it does not necessarily follow that an injury caused during combat is not actionable. Rather, applying the principles of causation, one must trace the injury to the breach of duty and it is the point of the breach which is crucial in assessing whether combat immunity would apply.

In ***Bici and another v Ministry of Defence*** [2004] **EWHC 786 (QB),** British soldiers were found to owe a duty to civilians despite having been engaged in peace-keeping operations for the UN. The claimants were both Kosovar Albanians who in July 1999 were passengers in a car travelling through the city of Pristina. Seemingly without provocation, British soldiers fired upon the car and killed two of the occupants. The first claimant suffered an injury when shot in his face. The second claimant, although physically unharmed, claimed to have suffered psychiatric injury as a result of this traumatic event.

The parties agreed that the case should be determined according to English law. It was clear that the soldiers owed a duty of care to the public and the MoD accepted in principle that it would be vicariously liable for any proven wrongs of any of its service personnel, but raised the doctrine of combat immunity and also claimed that the soldiers had acted in self-defence.

Elias J heard evidence from General Sir Mike Jackson, who was in Command of the forces in Kosovo at the relevant time and described the state of anarchy that existed in Pristina after the Serb forces had left the city. He explained that the role of the British forces was to help facilitate the transfer of power to the Kosovo Albanians. Elias J also heard evidence on the rules of engagement stipulated to British Forces on the ground, namely, that anyone thought to be threat should first be challenged and that force should be used as a last resort. Having considered all the circumstances, Elias J found that there was no evidence of threat or provocation to the soldiers which could have necessitated their reaction to fire on the vehicle, nor sensible grounds on which to argue that this was a 'combat' situation. The forensic evidence lay waste to the suggestion of any imminent threat posed to the soldiers by the occupants in the vehicle, whereas the evidence of the British soldiers was far from convincing (two of the three chose not to attend the trial and give evidence). In his judgment, Elias J rejected the contention that the soldiers had acted in self-defence and determined that combat immunity did not apply, stating that:

> *"The defence of combat immunity is not strictly a defence at all, in the sense of rendering lawful what is alleged to be unlawful. Rather, where the doctrine applies its effect is to remove the jurisdiction of the court to decide certain kinds of dispute; they are non-justiciable... I confess that I have considerable difficulty in seeing how the doctrine has any application at all in this case. It is relied upon when a person is injured or their property is damaged or destroyed in circumstances where they are the "innocent" victims of action which is taken out of pressing necessity in the wider public interest arising out of combat. It is not the conduct of the victim which justifies immunity from suit but rather a very pressing public interest."*

The first Claimant succeeded in proving recklessness and negligence, and in securing damages. The second Claimant failed to prove trespass to his person, because there was no evidence of intention to place him in fear of imminent violence. ***Bici*** helps to identify precisely the sort of case to which the doctrine of combat immunity should *not* apply.

***R (on the application of Smith) v Secretary of State for Defence and another*** **[2010] UKSC 29** concerned the death of Private Jason Smith who was deployed to Iraq in 2003. Private Smith was operating in temperatures in excess of 50 degrees Celsius and became ill. He repeatedly complained to medical staff about his symptoms. Eventually, he suffered cardiac arrest and died of hyperthermia (see **Chapter** 7). An inquest was held into his death but which was wholly inadequate in respect of its breadth and transparency. Private Smith's mother, Catherine Smith, challenged the Coroner's decision by way of judicial review proceedings on the basis that crucial documents were not made available to the family. She wanted another inquest to be held which would accord with the requirements of Article 2 ECHR: the right to life. This is known as an 'Article 2 Inquest'; essentially a broader and more thorough exploration of the circumstances of death.

At first instance, the High Court determined that, inter alia, the Human Rights Act (and therefore Article 2 of the ECHR) applied to service personnel both on and off base i.e. *wherever they may be deployed in the world*. This would have meant that in the future, wherever and whenever systemic failures were suspected to have caused loss of life, and those systems where the responsibility of a public body, then an inquest into the death would have to be fully compliant with Article 2.

The MoD appealed this decision on the basis that this would open the 'floodgates' to litigation and that decisions of commanders in operational situations will be scrutinised under the ECHR. But the Court of Appeal upheld the decision. Its reasoning was that service personnel remain subject to British military and civil law wherever they are in the world, and that therefore they should enjoy the same protections.

The MoD appealed a second time, this time to the Supreme Court. By that stage, the MoD had conceded that an Article 2 inquest was warranted and the Supreme Court directed that the new inquest would necessarily have to take place. However, on the jurisdictional point, the Supreme Court held that for the purposes of the ECHR, service personnel would only be considered within the jurisdiction of the State *when on a British military base*. This meant that the obligations on the State under the convention ceased when service personnel were 'off-base', for example in transit, on operations or other duties. In overturning the decision of the Court of Appeal, the Supreme Court limited geographically the applicability of human rights to service personnel abroad.

The decision in ***R (on the application of Smith)*** was subsequently overruled by the Supreme Court in ***Smith and Others v the Ministry of Defence [2013]***, which determined that the protections under the ECHR *could* extend to service personnel operating outside of a military base. The case which contributed to that eventual about-turn was ***Al-Skeini v United Kingdom (2011) 53 EHRR 589***. This case concerned claims brought by the relatives of six Iraqi civilians who were all killed during the Gulf War whilst British and American forces occupied Iraq. The relatives had exhausted domestic recourse for compensation and had lost their cases at the House of Lords, which determined that the ECHR did not apply to the actions of British Soldiers occurring outside of the British Army base. The Grand Chamber of the European Court of Human Rights disagreed and overturned this decision. It determined that the UK *did* have a duty to investigate the deaths because, regardless of the fact that they occurred outside of a British Army base, the UK had assumed responsibility for the security of Basrah and Southern Iraq, and so was exercising 'control and authority' over Iraqi civilians at the time. It determined that:

> "*...the United Kingdom (together with the United States) assumed in Iraq the exercise of some of the public powers normally to be exercised by a sovereign government. In particular, the United Kingdom assumed authority and responsibility for the maintenance of security in South East Iraq. In these exceptional circumstances, the Court considers that the United Kingdom, through its soldiers engaged in security operations in Basrah during the period in question, exercised authority and control over individuals killed in the course of such security operations, so as to establish a jurisdictional link between the deceased and the United Kingdom for the purposes of Article 1 of the Convention.*"

Having determined that the UK had jurisdiction within the meaning of Article 1 ECHR (i.e. the general obligation to respect human rights) for all six deaths, the court then considered whether an effective investigation into the deaths had been carried out in accordance with Article 2. It found that there had been no adequate inquiry in accordance with Article 2 and awarded 17,000 Euros to five of the six applicants plus 50,000 Euros towards their costs jointly. The decision in ***Al-Skeini*** extended the MoD's duty of care under the ECHR to civilians in a warzone. What this also achieved was to extend geographically the duty of care owed by the MoD to service personnel i.e. outside of British bases. The most recent guidance on combat immunity has been provided in the cases of ***Smith and others v Secretary of State for Defence; and two other cases [2013] UKSC 41***, which involved several claims arising out of the deaths of three soldiers and injuries caused to another two soldiers during military operations in Iraq between 2003 and 2006:

- The 'Challenger' claims concerned the death of Corporal Albutt and injuries caused to Trooper Julien and Lance Corporal Twiddy in 'friendly fire' incidents. The Claimants argued that technology and training was available which would have reduced the risk of such incidents when operating Challenger tanks.

- The 'Snatch Land Rover' claims arose from the deaths of Private Philip Hewett and Private Lee Ellis, who were both killed in separate incidents of Improvised Explosive Devices ('IEDs') and allegedly as a result of inadequate planning and provision in respect of the Snatch Land Rover's that were provided by the MoD for patrolling and other duties. Primarily, it was argued that (i) the MoD was in breach of its Article 2 obligations (i.e. to protect life) and (ii) that the vehicle or systems in place provided no adequate counter-measure to the likelihood of IED devices. Essentally, that the MoD should have provided better armoured vehicles or stipulated that those available vehicles that were armoured would have to travel at the front of any patrol.

These cases are sometimes referred to colloquially as the '*Snatch Land Rover*' cases and, whilst all the claims comprised different facts, they were all related because the claimants (and/or their dependants) all alleged that the MoD failed to provide adequate equipment and/or training *prior* to deployment and/or combat. The MoD argued that the claims should be struck out on the basis of combat immunity and that it would not be fair, just or reasonable to impose a duty of care. They also sought to strike out any claim under the ECHR for any deaths that occurred outside of the jurisdiction of the UK.

At first instance in the High Court, Owen J struck out the Article 2 aspect of the Land Rover claims on the basis that the Claimants had not been within the jurisdiction of the United Kingdom when they died (i.e. following ***R (on the application of Smith)*** above). On appeal by the claimants, the Court of Appeal made similar conclusions, and the cases proceeded to the Supreme Court, which had to consider three main issues:

1. Whether Hewett and Ellis were at the time of their deaths within the jurisdiction of the United Kingdom for the purposes of Article 1 ECHR.

2. Whether the State owed a positive duty under Article 2 ECHR to preventing the death of its own soldiers in active operations against the enemy.

3. In respect of the negligence claims, whether it would be fair, just and reasonable to impose a duty of care in the circumstances (i.e. the question of combat immunity).

The Court found:

- Unanimously that Hewett and Ellis were within the United Kingdom jurisdiction for the purposes of Article 1 of the ECHR. In so doing, the Court overruled its own decision in ***R (on the application of Smith*** in line with the developments in ***Al-Skeini***, extending the protections of the ECHR to service personnel 'off-base'.

- By majority, that the claims could proceed to trial because they fell within the scope of Article 2 ECHR.

- That in respect of the claims in negligence, these could proceed to trial because the facts indicated that a duty of care *could* be imposed, despite arguments that the doctrine of combat immunity applied.

In making its determinations, the Supreme Court allowed these cases to proceed to trial and we await those further decisions, which may cast more light on the factual circumstances in which claims brought in 'combat' may still proceed. In the meantime, the following general points are offered in summary of the current position:

1. A duty of care normally exists between the MoD, service personnel and civilians.

2. The duty of care cannot normally exit in "combat". What will be termed combat will depend on the facts of the case. The more risks there are of hostilities and engagement with the enemy, the more likely that any given situation will be termed one of "combat".

3. Just because an injury occurred in combat, does not mean that "combat immunity" will apply. What is important is *when and where* the breach of duty occurred. For example, a failure to provide training before deployment which results in injury may be actionable in principle.

Whilst the ECHR has played a significant part in recent developments in combat immunity, there are current plans for the UK to opt out of the ECHR on future military operations (depending on the nature of the operation). The potential danger here, advocated by some, is that opting out of the ECHR would result in protections for both service personnel and civilians being lost. This remains an area of uncertainty and contention for now.

## 3.4 The Compensation Act

The Compensation Act 2006 was designed to address some specific issues in mesothelioma cases and to regulate claims management companies. In so doing, it summarised some basic legal principles in respect of common law negligence and breach of statutory duty, but there was quite a furor when the Act came into force and personal injury lawyers questioned the construction of the Act. For our purposes, Section 1 may come into play:

> *1. Deterrent effect of potential liability*
>
> *A court considering a claim in negligence or breach of statutory duty may, in determining whether the defendant should have taken particular steps to meet a standard of care (whether by taking precautions against a risk or otherwise), have regard to whether a requirement to take those steps might—*
>
> (a) *prevent a desirable activity from being undertaken at all, to a particular extent or in a particular way, or*
>
> (b) *discourage persons from undertaking functions in connection with a desirable activity."*

Some defendants, and particularly the MoD, have sought to buttress their defences to claims by arguing that training and exercises are a "desirable activity". For example, the MoD will regularly argue that:

- military training exercises are a desirable activity because they seek to create effective service personnel and this contributes to national security; and therefore that
- the courts should give weight to s. 1 of the Compensation Act when determining whether liability should attach in any particular case.

However, the case law suggests that the Act does not in any way expand on the legal or policy considerations that would normally be taken into account by the courts when assessing negligence or breach of statutory duty (see ***Royal Opera House Covent Garden Foundation v Goldshieder** [2019] EWCA Civ 711*).

## 3.5 Points for practice

- The Crown can normally be sued in common law negligence and for breaches of statutory duty as if it were an individual for any torts that occurred from 15th May 1987 (subject of course to considerations of limitation). It can also be sued vicariously for the wrongs of its employees, servants and/or agents.

- MoD policy is to apply and adhere to domestic health and safety legislation wherever possible. The provisions of the Health and Safety at Work Act 1974 and its associated regulations will normally apply to the MoD, save where express exemption is provided.

- Military claims lawyers need to be flexible in their approach and, generally, will need to rely on a combination of the common law, statutory duty and military regulations (JSPs) in proving breach of duty. This process can be challenging when there are relatively few reported cases that address breach of duty in a military context and/or when interpreting and applying domestic regulations to facts involving military activities. More on this in **Chapter 5**.

- Where your client was injured in combat, they may be precluded from bringing a claim because of the doctrine of combat immunity. This doctrine is still being tested in the courts. The majority of military claims relate to accidents and faults in this jurisdiction and outside of combat, whether in training or in respect of management or treatment, and so will not normally engage the doctrine of combat immunity.

- The MoD will raise s.1 of the Compensation Act 2006 wherever possible. This is unlikely to influence the court's approach to the legal principles in a negligence claim, but it acts as a reminder that policy considerations will be a natural haven for defendants in military claims.

# CHAPTER FOUR THE CLINICAL DUTY OF CARE

## Introduction

One of the very challenging aspects of military claims is that practitioners can come across both clinical negligence and personal injury aspects in the same case. Having an understanding of the principles of clinical negligence, particularly the often complex aspects of causation, and the military medical grading system will be crucial to both types of claim. This is because medical grading has a direct bearing on employability within the military and a claimant's long-term prospects, which will impact on their potential losses.

In this chapter we will begin by exploring the medical experts and support staff that are involved in caring for the armed forces. We will then consider the unique medical categorisation and employability system in place for the armed forces.

## 4.1 Defence Medical Services

The MoD provides a system of occupational healthcare which oversees the physical and mental health of service personnel from the day they join through to the day their service terminates. In this way, the MoD can be viewed as a very special employer which undertakes a significant duty of care for its employees. The use of military doctors during military service is mandated to service personnel; they do not have a choice save for certain circumstances where civilian (NHS) medical care may be used.

The Defence Medical Services (DMS) governs military medical care. Its purpose is to protect and restore the health of the armed forces, ensuring that they are medically fit to deploy and carry out whatever their duties require of them. It does this through the support of various services, departments and units. For our purposes, *all* are managed by and the responsibility of the MoD.

UK based medical facilities are inspected by the Care Quality Commission, although there is no statutory requirement for them to be registered under the Health and Social Care Act. There are a variety of military personnel who provide medical care, and some civilians who support them, most are explored below.

### 4.1.1 Primary healthcare

The Medical Officer (MO) is a pivotal figure in the military. Their role will be to treat the sick and injured, including referring to specialist secondary care where necessary. They will also be responsible for determining the medical grading for service personnel.

Most Medical Officers are registered at the time of their service with the British Medical Association as 'occupational health' doctors or alternatively as GPs. They may, subject to whether or not they stay in general practice, later register as a GP and continue to practice in that field. But not all are generalists and there are a plethora of surgeons and other specialists who begin their careers in the military.

Medical Officers have precisely the same ethical obligations as those imposed on civilian doctors and surgeons, and helpful guidance is provided by the British Medical Association for military medical personnel (published online). They are also bound by a duty of confidentiality in respect of their patients and should not normally disclose confidential information unless it is in the patient's best interests or in case of national security. Despite this, it is quite common for discussions to occur between Medical Officers and the chain of command in respect of the health of individual service personnel.

The Medical Officer is not to be confused with the 'Medic', which may mean something entirely different. For example, in the Army, it is fairly rare for a Medical Officer to be required in the field in so far as training and day-to-day duties are concerned there may be a 'Combat Medic' available who would triage injured or sick service personnel and, where appropriate, refer them to a Medical Officer and/or report injuries to the chain of command. You might think of them in a similar vein to civilian paramedics. But the standard of care can vary greatly and will depend on their level and training of the individual. Medics are often important features of military claims, because they may be the first port of call when a service person is injured and in many circumstances they will have an obligation to refer to superiors and/or arrange medical evacuation for injured personnel. The important distinction to make is that Medical Officers have a far higher standard of care given that they are qualified and trained clinicians.

There is normally a medical centre at most military bases (for example in barracks or on board a ship). Depending on the size of the establishment, it will normally be headed by a Senior Medical Officer (SMO) or principle Medical Officer (PMO), usually of high rank. Medical Officers may be deployed and rotate to other medical centres.

A medical centre may also be staffed by civilians, for example, these might be a Civilian Medical Practitioners (CMPs). These civilians are an increasingly normal feature of most military medical centres, and will often work on contract or locum basis; the important point being that the duty of care cannot be delegated solely to them; it will remain with the MoD. CMPs are often retired service personnel themselves, and many will have received some training on service medical policy and reporting procedures.

### 4.1.2 Secondary healthcare

Where appropriate, referrals may be made to civilian hospitals (NHS) and specialist civilian clinicians for treatment. Where such a referral is made then this may complicate claims where there exist several breaches of duty in different establishments. Arguably, the MoD will retain a non-delegable duty of care towards any service person that is referred onwards, but in reality the duty of care is likely to transfer to the NHS unless the decision to refer was a gross error.

### 4.1.3 Mental health

A Defence Centre for Community Mental Health (DCMH) is a specialist establishment that treats the mental health and wellbeing of service personnel. Cases will normally be referred to a Psychiatrist in the first instance, but most treatment will be provided by a Community Psychiatric Nurse (CPN). They will have access to a range of treatments, including medication, as well as involvement with (and referral to) clinical psychologists and mental health social workers.

### 4.1.4 Dentistry

All three Services provide dental care. In addition to dentists, dental hygienists and nurses are engaged to provide support. Military dentists have the same clinical duty of care as civilian dentists and are bound by the professional standards of the General Dental Council. They should be registered to practice as a dentist in their country of residence (normally the UK). They receive officer training and, as Medical Officers, form part of the chain of command.

### 4.1.5 Rehabilitation

An injured service person may be referred for rehabilitation at a number of different care centres:

- Primary Care Rehabilitation Facilities (PCRFs) – These provide physiotherapy and are based at units/stations across the country
- Regional Rehabilitation Unit (RRUs) – These are multi-disciplinary and will take patients with more complex rehabilitation needs, often as inpatients.

Since the Second World War a key centre for rehabilitation for all three Services was the Defence Medical Rehabilitation Centre Headley Court in Surrey (DMRC, or more commonly known as "Headley Court"). The centre ceased operations in 2018 and these have been transferred to the new Defence and National Rehabilitation Centre (DNRC) at Stanford Hall in the East Midlands. The DNRC is set to provide cutting edge rehabilitation services and a multi-disciplinary approach to treating injured service personnel.

There are a number of specially trained personnel who will provide physiotherapy services. Some will specialise in sports and exercise medicine, whilst others may be Physical Training Instructors (PTIs). PTIs play a very important role in the daily exercise regimes, often advising commanders and planning exercises. Their views are generally highly regarded but when ignored may result in excessive or inappropriate exercise and consequent injury to service personnel.

## 4.2 PULHHEEMS

Medical Officers are responsible for assessing the health of service personnel regularly and at various stages of their careers. The purpose of this is to ensure that they remain fit to carry out their specific duties (both physically and mentally). This process includes making a functional assessment in accordance with the military grading system (PULHHEEMS), so that a decision can be made about their employability (the Joint Medical Standard or JMES, discussed below).

*JSP 950: Joint Service Manual of Medical Fitness* (latest version 1.2 Dec 2017) provides over-arching medical guidance for all three Services. However, within each Service you will find regulations that cover specific roles and duties, which may deviate from the norm:

- British Army: *PULHHEEMS Administrative Pamphlet 10 (PAP10)*
- Royal Navy: *Handbook of Naval Medical Standards (BRD 1750A)*
- RAF: *RAF Manual of Medical Fitness (AP 1269A)*

These comprehensive systems are introduced below, but readers are encouraged to read the guidance thoroughly.

### 4.2.1 Why is the assessment made?

The purposes of the PULHHEEMS assessment is to:

- Record accurate information about the medical fitness of personnel.
- Help managers make decisions about the employability of service personnel.
- Ensure that service personnel are not required to carry out duties or be deployed in an unfit state.

The system is designed to allow a sick or injured service person to make a recovery if medically possible. However, if that is not the case consideration will be given to either continued service in a reduced medical category or medical discharge.

### 4.2.2 When is the assessment made?

Assessments are to be carried out by a Medical Officer (or Civilian Medical Practitioner), who may arrange a Medical Board to carry out a fuller review if a change of the service person's employability grading is indicated (discussed below). The guidance provides specific times when an assessment must be made, as well as general reasons for a review. An assessment will normally be made:

- When entering service – a pre-service medical assessment is intended to determine whether a recruit meets the entry requirements for their Service.
- During service – medical assessment will occur routinely during service and the frequency of these reviews may depend on the

nature of the service person's trade and duties. For example, aircrew would tend to have much more frequent assessments. Normally medical assessments are made very five years for personnel aged over 30 and every two years for personnel aged over 50. Assessments are also made when service personnel are being mobilised for deployment, to ensure their fitness.

- Commanders are also obliged to refer service personnel to the Medical Officer in certain circumstances, most obviously when they are sick or injured and cannot carry out their duties, and which may trigger an assessment.

- At the end of service – there is a mandatory medical assessment.

Note that any subsequent re-gradings are referred to as 'medical boarding', whether carried out at unit level (i.e. by a single Medical Officer) or by a formally constituted Medical Board. At each assessment a PULHHEEMS profile is recorded in the medical records and transmitted to the appropriate administrative office for that service person.

### 4.2.3 How is the assessment made?

A code or '**profile**' is given according to whether certain medical conditions are present. The profile refers to different functions, referred to as '**qualities**', which accord to the letters in the acronym PULHHEEMS:

| Quality | Definition |
|---|---|
| Physical capacity<br><br>**P** | This indicates an individual's overall physical and mental development, his or her potential for physical training and suitability for employment worldwide (i.e. the overall functional capacity). The 'P' grading is affected by other qualities in the profile, namely the 'U', 'L', 'HH', 'EE' 'M' and 'S' grading. |
| Upper limbs<br><br>**U** | This indicates the functionality of the hands, arms, shoulder girdle and cervical and thoracic spine. A reduced 'U' grading will also affect the 'P' grading. |

| | |
|---|---|
| Locomotion<br><br>**L** | This refers to the functional efficiency of the locomotor system. This quality must therefore take into account assessment of the lumbar spine, pelvis, hips, legs, knees, ankles and feet. Observation of gait and mobility are also important. Any conditions affecting the function of the locomotor system will result in a reduced 'L' grading which will in turn be reflected in the 'P' grading. |
| Hearing acuity<br><br>**HH** | This quality assesses auditory acuity only. Diseases of the ear such as otitis externa are assessed under the 'P' quality. However, severe loss of hearing will affect the 'P' grading. |
| Visual acuity<br><br>**EE** | This quality assesses visual acuity only. Diseases of the eye such as glaucoma are assessed under the 'P' quality. However, severe loss of visual acuity will affect the 'P' grading. |
| Mental capacity<br><br>**M** | Mental capacity is not subject to formal medical assessment at recruitment. However, the recruit selection procedure, including interviews, and the individual's academic record will allow judgement to be made on this quality. Subject changes are only likely to occur as a result of neurological disease or head injury. |
| Stability (emotional)<br><br>**S** | The 'S' quality indicates emotional stability which grades the individual's ability to withstand the psychological stress of military life (especially operations). Amendments to the 'S' grade are usually required in cases of psychiatric illness but are not restricted to these circumstances. |

Each quality has the potential to be awarded a grade of 1 to 8, but bear in mind:

- Only the 'E' quality uses all 8 possible numerical gradings.
- The HH and EE qualities are graded first for the right and then the left ears and eyes respectively.
- Where a condition is expected to resolve, the letter R (for 'remediable') may be inserted after the quality in question. For example: P3 L3 become P3R L3R. Non-remediable conditions do

not require the R suffix. These grading may be held in a temporary capacity indicated by a T suffix after the degree of P quality (or after the Medical Employment Standard mentioned below). The maximum period for which an individual may hold such a temporary grading is subject to single-Service regulations but should not normally exceed 18 months.

- Where a condition persists beyond 18 months, or it can be predicted that this will be the case at an earlier stage, a definitive standard (permanent) is to be awarded, without the letter R for remedial conditions. Where a temporary condition is changed to permanent, and this may happen if medically indicated, then a Medical Board will be required to determine the new profile.

- *Section 4 of JSP 950* and the separate single-Service guidelines provide guidance on specific conditions and the approach that medical staff should take to these in making an assessment, which may depend on whether the assessment is being made before or during service.

### 4.2.4 Interpreting the medical profile

Readers are encouraged to read the guidance and examine the examples provided in *JSP 950* to develop a full understanding of the system. However, practically you will be most concerned with understanding the 'P' quality, which reflects a service person's overall functional capacity. The degrees for this quality are as follows (including references to the JMES standard that would be applied, discussed further below).

- **P2 – Medically fit for unrestricted service worldwide** – this grade would attract a JMES deployment standard of medically fully deployable (MFD).

- **P3 – Medically fit for duty with minor employment limitations** – this grade indicates a medical condition that prevents the service person undertaking the full range of their military duties.

This grade will normally attract a JMES deployment standard of Medically Limited Deployability (MLD).

- **P4 – Medically fit for duty within the limitations of pregnancy** – pregnant personnel are graded P4 and attract a JMES deployment standard of Medically Not Deployable (MND).

- **P7 – Medically fit for duty with major employment limitations** – this grade is to be used for an individual who is capable of performing useful military duties within the limits of his/her disabilities, expected to give regular and efficient service and not likely to deteriorate if suitably employed and allowed time for regular meals and rest. Individuals may be restricted in their ability to work at night or undertake shift work. They may require regular, continued medical care or supervision and may require regular long-term medication. They may require access to secondary (hospital) medical facilities. They are not normally fit to deploy on military operations. This grade will normally attract a JMES deployment standard of MND, or exceptionally MLD.

- **P8 – Medically unfit for service** - this grade will attract a JMES deployment standard of MND.

- **P0 – Medically unfit for duty and under medical care** – likely to return to duty within a total period of 12 months. This grade will attract a JMES deployment standard of MND.

The following example shows a profile of an individual with a left inguinal hernia, which is considered remediable. The grading P3R will be retained until they are ready to be awarded a permanent grade. This may be P2, assuming full recovery.

<table>
<tr><th>Year of birth</th><th>P</th><th>U</th><th>L</th><th>H</th><th>H</th><th>E</th><th>E</th><th>M</th><th>S</th></tr>
<tr><td>1986</td><td>3R</td><td>2</td><td>2</td><td>1</td><td>2</td><td>1<br>-</td><td>1<br>-</td><td>2</td><td>2</td></tr>
<tr><td>Ht......179.........cm<br>CP......2..............<br>Wt......77...........kg</td><td>P<br>U<br>L<br>S</td><td colspan="8">Relevant clinical details<br>Left inguinal hernia awaiting operation.</td></tr>
</table>

Apart from the 'P' quality, the following definitions for the grades of the U, L, M and S qualities may also help paint a picture of your client's limitations:

| Degree | Definition/functional capacity |
|---|---|
| 2 | Medically fit for unrestricted service worldwide.<br>Average functional capacity. |
| 3 | Medically fit for duty with minor employment limitations.<br>Below average functional capacity. |
| 4 | Medically fit for duty within the limitations of pregnancy. |
| 7 | Medically fit for duty with major employment limitations.<br>Very limited functional capacity. |
| 8 | Medically unfit for service.<br>Severely limited functional capacity. |

## 4.3 The Joint Medical Employability Standard

The PULHHEEMS profile in isolation may say little about what a service person can or cannot do in the workplace. A decision must then be made on that individual service person's employability and Deployability. This decision will be made by an 'Employability Board' in certain circumstances (normally when a medical profile has been changed).

The Joint Medical Employability Standard (JMES) aims to provide information to commanders and career managers about how a service person may be employed at work, if at all, bearing in mind their functional, geographical and specific medical limitations. It includes a specific assessment of whether a service person is deployable.

Prior to 2009 the employability standard for each service differed, but since then a number of steps were taken to harmonise these, which has resulted in the 'joint' standard that is applied today. Again, there remain some differences with specific roles and duties which can be found in the guidance for the separate Services. The system is divided into (four) primary and (two) detailed elements, which constitute a JMES grading.

The **four primary elements** are:

1. **Date of award** – this is the date the JMES assessment took place or the date when the medical assessment was last reviewed.

2. **Date of review** – the next review must take place in accordance with single-Service policy by this date.

3. **Permanency** – when a Medical Board awards a JMES a decision should be made as to whether the JMES is temporary (Temp), permanent (Perm) or not applicable (NA). The maximum period of validity of a temporary JMES is 12 months for the Royal Navy and Army and normally 18 months for the RAF. A permanent JMES may be awarded at any time if clinically indicated. When a temporary JMES is to become permanent, a formal Medical Board will be convened in accordance with

single-Service policy. Permanent does not imply that the JMES can never change but serves to distinguish for personnel staff the longer-term health problems affecting function from the relatively short term, in order to assist with employment decisions.

4. **Medical Deployment Standard (MDS)** – this is an overall deployability summary coding with the sub-categories of either:

- Medically Fully Deployable (MFD) – No limitations for deployment globally. No medical needs beyond primary healthcare when deployed.

- Medically Limited Deployability (MLD) – Limited deployment due to medical condition or risks. Any grade of MND requires a medical risk assessment (MRA) to be carried out that will be specific to any deployment.

- Medically Not Deployable (MND) – Not deployable outside the UK and/or under medical care and/or awaiting medical discharge.

The **two detailed elements** of the JMES are:

| | |
|---|---|
| **Medical Employment Standard (MES)** | This is an alphanumeric code reflecting an individual's fitness to be employed in the Air (A), Land (L) and Maritime (M) environments together with any additional specific Environment and Medical Support (E) considerations.<br><br>JSP 950 provides several tables to help interpret the MES alphanumeric code which includes single-Service guidance notes (i.e. depending on which Service your client is in) |

| **Medical Limitations (MedLims)** | Annex C of the JSP provides for MedLim codes that are applied as necessary and are visible on the medical records. The following are a few examples:<br><br>1209 – *Office duties only*<br>5103 – *Unfit exposure to cold environments*<br>6201 – *No load carrying*<br>8104 – *Restricted lower-limb non-impact physical training*<br><br>JSP 950 provides tables of all available MedLim codes so you can interpret the restrictions placed on your client. |
|---|---|

A typical JMES might read:

| **Date of Award** | **Date of Review** | **Permanency** | **MDS** | **MES** | **MedLim** |
|---|---|---|---|---|---|
| 10 Aug 16 | 10 Feb 17 | TEMP | MLD | A4 L3 M4 E3 | 1206 |

This code means that:

- It was awarded on 10th August 2016.
- It will be reviewed on 10th February 2017.
- The award is temporary.
- MLD – the individual has medically limited deployability.
- A4 – they are fit to be flown in a passenger aircraft.
- L3 – they are fit for limited duties but with some restriction subject to Medical Risk Assessment.
- M4 – they are fit to be carried as embarked forces in transit (the usual grading for Army or RAF personnel without a maritime role).
- E3 – they have restricted employment outside of UK due to medical support or environmental requirements.
- 1206 – they are unfit to work in confined spaces.

It is astonishing how much information will be contained in a relatively simple code like this!

The JMES and the information associated with it is saved and available electronically on the military's Joint Personnel Administration System (JPA), which is the human resources database for the forces. This means that Medical Officers, commanders and career managers should have regular access to this information. In addition, the following documents (depending on Service) may be handed or emailed to your client and they may be asked to relay their employability information to their chain of command (as such they can be important for considerations of knowledge, foreseeability and contributory negligence in claims):

- Royal Navy – *JMES Electronic Signal.*
- Army – *PAP Appendix 9 document.*
- RAF – *Reassessment of Employment Standard – Patient Advice Notice.*

Once notified of the JMES, it becomes the responsibility of the chain of command to decide how to employ or deploy service personnel, or not. *JSP 950* provides express guidance on this, including whether and how a decision can be made to employ or deploy a service person outwith their JMES. In fact, it is made expressly clear that this should only happen: "*in an emergency; in extremis; where there is no other choice and not using that Service Person would result in very serious consequences. Financial reasons or standard manning difficulties would not necessarily be regarded as reasonable considerations. Unless life is at stake, it would be considered unreasonable to task a Service Person with a duty outwith their JMES.*"

In addition, where a service person is employed or deployed outwith of their JMES, then commanders should:

1. obtain the opinion of an Occupational Health Consultant;

2. carry out a risk assessment; and

3. obtain the consent of the service person in question.

Under no circumstances should the JMES be changed in order to facilitate employability or deployment. However, in practice these steps do not always happen and any breach of protocol may buttress a claim in negligence.

## 4.4 Summary: medical profiles and employability standards

The medical grading system is complex and at first confusing. You may find yourself jumping from one guidance document to another in order to interpret your client's medical profile and their limitations. There are some points that may help you get to grips with these systems:

- It is a medical responsibility (i.e. of Medical Officers) to ascertain correct medical profiles. These are not determined in a vacuum; knowledge of the service person's duties will be required to give an accurate grading. Medical Officers are also able to refer to specialists for further investigation of symptoms and to achieve accurate diagnoses.

- Look to the 'P' grade in the medical profile for an overall indication of functional capacity and employability. Ask yourself was/is your client fit, restricted or unfit for service?

- Deployability will also be a determinative factor. Look to the Medical Deployment Standard in the first instance (MFD/MLD/MND). If a service person cannot deploy or is restricted, then they are at more risk of medical discharge and/or will face challenges to their career progression. Where deployability is limited, look for any Medical Risk Assessments (MRAs) in the records.

- It is the responsibility of the chain of command to interpret and apply the JMES. Commanders cannot employ or deploy personnel contrary to their employability standard.

- Good health will generally be important for the career progression of service personnel. Temporary gradings may give a service personnel a reprieve, but still create a risk to their careers. A permanent grading will crystalise that risk and their limitations. Whilst appraisals should not take into account medical condition, the fact that a service person has been sick or injured will be known to their chain of command and can influence decisions on promotion.

- Interpreting the medical profile is only part of the puzzle; this will give you an understanding of the service person's health at that particular time and possibly an indication of likely employability (or a need to review) in the future. You will need to consider the medical grading at key stages of medical treatment. Prepare a chronology to help highlight your client's medical history and trajectory.

## 4.5 How negligence can arise

Military clinical negligence claims may arise in a variety of circumstances. Below are a few examples:

- Failure to diagnose a condition.

- Failure to treat, by either referring to specialist care or, if treating conservatively, a failure to follow-up.

- A negligent operation or procedure.

- Failing to advise the chain of command on restrictions to work and duties.

- Failing to advise a patient about their limitations.
- Failure to medically downgrade or refer to a Medical Board.
- Authorising a deployment for a patient who is 'MND' without carrying out a proper Medical Risk Assessment.
- Treating without consent.

A significant proportion of claims may relate to the failure to diagnose and treat musculoskeletal disorders and injuries (MSKI), which are very common in the armed forces due to high intensity exercise regimes and load carrying. In addition, there will be a number of potential failures by the chain of command, which may precede or follow negligent medical treatment:

- Ignoring medical advice or sick notes.
- Ignoring the JMES.
- Ignoring the service person when they complain of pain, sickness or injury and not referring them to a Medical Officer.

## 4.6 Establishing liability

The principles of establishing liability in clinical negligence claims are complex and cannot be covered here in great detail; the same considerations apply to cases involving military doctors and clinicians. You have to establish that a duty of care existed, that there was a breach of that duty and that the breach caused your client loss.

It is not normally an issue that a duty of care is owed. It is clear that military doctors owe a duty of are to their patients and that the MoD owe a duty of care to service personnel, who are mandated to comply with its occupational health system both at home and when deployed abroad. Whether that duty is delegable or not may depend on the circumstances and can become very complex where service personnel are receiving treatment abroad (see ***A (A child) v MoD [2005] QB 183***). The main question will be whether there was a breach of that duty. In general, you will have to satisfy the ***Bolam*** test i.e. a doctor will *not* be negligent if they acted in accordance with practice which is accepted as proper by a responsible body of similarly skilled doctors.

You will also have to establish causation, which will be a fertile ground for argument in most clinical negligence claims. You will have to consider:

- Whether the breach of duty caused harm i.e. the '*but for*' test
- Whether the harm was too remote.

You will have to be guided primarily by your medical expert on these issues. It will be normal practice for you to obtain at least two reports, one dealing with condition and prognosis (to be served with proceedings) and one dealing with breach of duty and liability (to be served at a later stage of the proceedings, after full disclosure and exchange of evidence).

However, military claims can add a layer of complexity to clinical negligence claims. For example, you would normally be investigating an alleged breach of duty by a Medical Officer. In such circumstances:

- The standard of care, skill and knowledge of a Medical Officer will normally be different to that provided by a civilian GP. You will need to find an expert who is suitably qualified to comment, and these are hard to come by.
- Military medical regulations change often. Expert GPs who are no longer serving may have little experience or knowledge of new practices, standards and regulations.

- A medical expert who is a former service person is more likely to be conflicted in cases, where they may have served with clinicians who you are pursuing in negligence.

- In cases involving the interpretation of medical profiles, the PULHHEEMS system and associated guidance can provide a wide discretion for Medical Officers. This can sometimes lead to less certainty and a greater variety of views between experts.

- There may be a number of intervening acts, often decisions made by your own client and/or their chain of command, which may have led to an exacerbation or further injury.

- You may need multiple experts to address breach of duty/causation and condition/prognosis, including an employment expert with a military specialism to comment on military employability issues.

- Service personnel will often have underlying/pre-existing conditions, whether physical or psychiatric, and which may create difficulties in establishing causation. You may succeed in providing a breach of duty, only to discover that your client was likely to be discharged for some other reason, which will significantly reduce the value of their claim.

## 4.7 Points for practice

- Military clinical negligence claims are complex. Not only do you face the normal challenges and often high hurdles in clinical negligence, but layered on this is a need to interpret the medical categorisation system. As a first step, you will need to take a full history from your client, review the records carefully and prepare a detailed chronology, highlighting any changes to medical profile or employability grading, as well as any potential breaches of duty.

- Familiarse yourself with *JSP 950* and any associated guidance, bearing in mind any separate guidance specific to your client's Service and/or particular duties.

- It is the duty of the Medical Officer to assess and grade (medically), but the duty of commanders to take the JMES on board. Where errors by both medical staff and managers have occurred, then a case may include multiple claims and different standards in respect of the duty of care.

- Your choice of expert will be crucial. Military occupational health and/or GP experts often find that they are not familiar with the latest regulations because these change quite frequently in the military sphere. This may mean that your expert is not willing to report. They may also be conflicted if they have previously treated your client or know their treating clinicians.

- Where a case hinges on a client's presentation, and what was said and done during a medical appointment, you may want to proceed with caution. It is quite common for service personnel to downplay their symptoms, sometimes in the eagerness of deploying. Be conscious of the fact that the court will tend to give a lot of weight to contemporaneous medical records.

# CHAPTER FIVE
# ACCIDENTS AT WORK

## Introduction

In this chapter we explore some of the circumstances in which service personnel may be injured during work, training and deployment, and what to look out for when investigating and progressing a claim. Some of the issues already explored in **Chapter 3** in relation to the general duty of care that the MoD owes towards its service personnel will be relevant here.

## 5.1 Health and safety at work

Service personnel are, depending on their particular trade, required to do a number of tasks and duties throughout their working day. These may include driving, using machinery, operating aircraft, manual handling and working in an office environment, to name a few. In many ways their everyday tasks will be indistinguishable from employees working in heavy industry, for example, driving an HGV. At other times, their tasks are far removed from what might be envisaged in the civilian sector, for example, the requirement to board and search a vessel at sea during anti-piracy operations. During training, they may be required to undertake extraordinary feats of physical and mental endurance. For these reasons, it is sometimes challenging to find comparators from civilian industry and/or safety regulations which would necessarily help the military claims lawyer. Thankfully, the military maintain detailed health and safety regulations which can assist. There are some essential regulations that come as recommended reading and which you should treat as a starting point:

| | |
|---|---|
| DSA01.1 | *Defence Policy for Health, Safety and Environmental Protection* |
| JSP 375 | *Management of Health and Safety in Defence* |
| JSP 392 | *Management of Radiation Protection in Defence* |
| JSP 418 | *Management of Environmental Protection in Defence* |
| JSP 419 | *Joints Services Adventurous Training (JSAT) scheme* |
| JSP 800 | *Defence Movement and Transport Regulations* |

The Secretary of State's policy statement for Health Safety and Environmental Protection in the military provides a helpful introduction:

> "[This policy statement] *applies to everyone and all organisations within Defence and who conduct activities on behalf of Defence, including contractors and MoD's partner organisations... they are required to describe their management arrangements, including the delegations to those managing activities on their behalf and ensure that at every level, both military and civilian, are suitably and sufficiently trained and provided with relevant information and access to resources to ensure compliance* [with health and safety policy]"

This policy statement is an important document because it underpins a number of supportive military regulations and gives direction to how health and safety should be managed across the Tri-Services. The MoD's comprehensive health and safety manual, DSA01.1 (which replaces the older JSP 815), expands on this policy broadly in four areas:

- Risk management
- Safety checking and reporting
- Training
- Regulation

Perhaps most relevant to the military claims lawyer in addition to DSA01.1 will be *JSP 375: Management of Health and Safety in Defence*, which guides commanders on risk assessments, amongst other things, and is discussed in detail below. When considering the duty of care owed to your client, bear in mind that:

- The systems that are in place to manage and implement military health and safety policy mimic those required under domestic health and safety legislation (and often refer to it).
- Beyond the main military regulations above, there will be further JSPs and single-Service Publications which relate to specific tasks and duties. Look to the preamble or 'directive' in JSPs and in the footnotes for reference to associated guidance.
- There may exist other guidance documents such as orders, memoranda and communications from the chain of command which supplement the guidance within the regulations.

## 5.2 Terminology

For service personnel a large proportion of accidents at work will occur during training and deployments. In this respect, there are some terms that practitioners may come across which may need explanation.

| **Term** | **Definition** |
|---|---|
| Adventurous training | Challenging outdoor training for service personnel in specified adventurous activities, involving controlled exposure to risk, to develop leadership, teamwork, physical fitness, moral and physical courage, among other personal attributes and skills vital to operational capability. Adventurous training is governed by its own set of regulations (*JSP 419*). |

| | |
|---|---|
| Beasting | A physical punishment which is unlawful. Whilst military policy forbids these punishments, in practice they do occur. |
| Deployed | Personnel are deployed when they are positioned or stationed in a particular location, establishment or theatre of war. An 'operational deployment' is a deployment of personnel on an operation. |
| Exercise (Ex) | When the armed forces practice what they might have to do on an Operation. It would not normally include any risk of actual combat but may try as much as possible to simulate the risks and pressures of engagements with the enemy, for example. |
| Fitness test (FT) | There are a variety of fitness tests applicable to service personnel, which may vary depending on their particular service, trade, duties and/or medical category. Where a service person is unable to pass the required fitness test this may have serious consequences on their career and lead to their discharge. |
| Operation (Op) | Service personnel undertake operations to achieve specific objectives, whether defeating the enemy in combat or peace keeping duties, for example. Most of the armed forces operate globally in a number of places, not always in hostile environments. Operations are authorised at the highest level and normally involve bringing military force to bear. An operation may also involve highly classified activity in support of the national interest /national security. For example, a Trident Nuclear Submarine at sea is on an "Op." |

| | |
|---|---|
| Order of Battle (ORBAT) | A list of Army forces, units, sub-units, personnel etc. involved in a particular exercise or operation. |
| Order | A command given in whatever format by a superior. Service personnel must follow orders or risk disciplinary action. |
| Promotional course | Throughout each year personnel may be selected to attend promotional courses. These tend to be more difficult that regular training and can comprise both physical elements, tests of technical competence and application of theory in examinations. Promotional courses are essential for career progression and can help indicate a service person's potential. |
| Physical training (PT) | All service personnel need to maintain a good level of physical and mental fitness to perform and to pass the requirements of their regular medical checks. It is not safe to assume that just because your client is in the Army, for example, that they would be doing more in respect of physical exercise. However, in respect of the infantry soldiers and Royal Marines, for example, they will tend to have more regular physical exercise which is mandated and planned by specialised training staff (often Physical Training instructions or "PTIs"). Service personnel are not normally allowed to miss training, unless they are sick, but it can be tailored to suit them depending on whether they are medically downgraded and according to any restrictions on their employability. |

| | |
|---|---|
| Rest and relaxation (R&R) | A break from duties and obligations to allow for recovery, sometimes at the conclusion of prolonged training, exercises or operational deployment. |
| Standing orders | There may exist written standing orders provided by or for military Establishments, Commanding Officers and/or specific departments. These will detail everyday practice and may be general in nature or specific to the way that the Commanding Officer would like a particular unit to operate. |
| Tour (of duty) | An operational 'tour' of duty is a deployment into a combat zone and/or a hostile environment for a specified amount of time. |
| Training | Training is a general term that might encompass a number of different things. During selection and initial training for example, recruits are required to undergo fitness and other evaluations according to the requirements of their service. Some evaluations will be technical, such as weapons handling. Beyond the physical training regimes, there are a plethora of professional courses delivered to service personnel. Some of these will be carried out annually across the board. An example of this is the Army's Military Annual Training Tests (MATTs), which comprise various elements from health and safety training to equality and diversity in the workplace. |

There are more terms that you will need to become familiar with and further guidance can be found in the Queens Regulations for each Service.

## 5.3 Risk assessments

The MoD is obliged to adhere to domestic health and safety standards, including the need to provide risk assessments. Risk assessments may provide you with insight into why your client was injured and whether there were any failures to assess particular risks or otherwise provide a safe system of work. They will vary greatly depending on the task or training being assessed, but there are some general considerations that might apply whatever the circumstances. They should include consideration of:

- Personal protective equipment.
- Equipment, weapons, vehicles and machinery.
- The safety and reliability of systems and processes.
- How risks are reported and audited.

In respect of training, when defending claims and/or the accuracy of risk assessments the MoD will argue that:

- For public policy reasons (i.e. national security) it is obliged to carry out realistic training and in the military context this will necessarily involve risk (and for the same reasons section 1 of the Compensation Act 2006 should encourage the courts to find that liability should not attach)
- It is also in the interests of the health and safety or service personnel that they are provided with realistic training, otherwise when they are required to deploy they may not be able to carry out their tasks safely, or may become a danger to themselves and others.

The HSE helpfully provides a statement on its website which addresses the value of 'realistic training'. This helps illustrate the dangers involved in the training and exercises that service personnel have to undertake but also the challenge that the MoD faces in providing a safe system at work:

> *"...realistic training is that which:*
>
> - *is necessary to properly prepare military personnel for combat or other work in combat zones;*
> - *deliberately includes exposing staff to appropriate degrees of risk, possibly on a progressive basis, for the purposes of their training, but*
> - *is delivered under managed conditions.*
>
> *Realistic training options may also include simulation exercises – which enable participants to experience decision making in hazardous operations without endangering life or assets. This may be particularly relevant in the early stages training when exposure to fully realistic risks is too dangerous, and when access to the real thing is too expensive or impractical. Such applications include landing aircraft and parachute drops, for instance."*

When assessing the safety provisions that should have been in place for your client, it helps to consider this statement and ask whether any safety precautions would have in any way reduced the 'realism' of the training. More specifically, *JSP 375* provides guidance on specific risk factors in different working environments (see *JSP 375 Part 2: Guidance*). The separate chapters of this document will introduce personnel to the safety considerations of everything from manual handling to working with animals. Find the chapter most relevant to your client's work and study it.

Primarily, just as managers are in the civilian sector, military commanders are required to arrange activities so that the risk of injury is As Low As Reasonably Practicable ("ALARP"). They must:

1. Identify the hazards.

2. Decide who or what environment might be harmed and how.

3. Evaluate the risks and decide on precautions.

4. Record their significant findings and implement them.

5. Review their risk assessments and update them if necessary.

There are a number of issues to bear in mind:

- A number of standard risk assessments will be available to commanders which they may adopt for particular exercises. In fact, many forms are available to them which help them record and assess risk in different situations. You should treat the generic risk assessments with some caution, however. Are they addressing the specific risks or are they paying lip service to them?

- Guidance on whether a particular risk has in fact been reduced to ALARP is provided in DSA01.1. This informs commanders that they must take reasonably practicable steps to lower the risks and references the following quote from the judgment in the case of ***Edwards v National Coal Board [1949] 1 All ER 743 (CA)***: *'Reasonably practicable' is a narrower term than 'physically possible' ... a computation must be made by the owner in which the quantum of risk is placed on one scale and the sacrifice involved in the measures necessary for averting the risk (whether in money, time or trouble) is placed in the other, and that, if it be shown that there is a gross disproportion between them – the risk being insignificant in relation to the sacrifice – the defendants discharge the onus on them." In Edwards, the defendant had given the* *risk which resulted in the death of the claimant little or no thought at all, and so had not discharged the burden on them.* ***Edwards*** provides little practical guidance to commanders but does help remind practitioners that each case will turn on its facts.

- If the work is complex (e.g. an aircraft, ship or other complex platform) a simple risk assessment will not be sufficient to assess the health and safety implications. Commanders should then prepare a 'Safety Case', which is in essence a much more detailed risk assessment supported by arguments in favour of certain precautions. The military's definition of a safety case is *"a structured argument, supported by a body of evidence that provides a compelling, comprehensible and valid case"*.

- MoD policy requires the appointment of 'Duty Holders' where it has been assessed that there is credible and reasonably foreseeable risk to life. When appointed, a Duty Holder is accountable for mitigating that risk to ALARP and to a level that is tolerable for those involved in the activity and anyone affected by it, including the public. Importantly, military Duty Holders can be held formally to account for their actions (i.e. disciplined).

- Commanders should not be tied to formal/written risk assessments and should be making dynamic risk assessments when situations change. For example, the weather is an ever-changing factor and may preclude the use of certain equipment or influence the risk profile of outdoor exercises. Commanders should not be blind to these changing factors, which may render a well thought out risk assessment useless.

In addition to finding failures to risk assess, you should also explore the safety culture that existed at the time your client was injured. Here are some signs of poor safety culture:

- Reactionary steps taken to address risks including, for example, an immediate change of equipment, systems or PPE made following an accident. This would indicate that proactive steps were not being taken to reduce risks.

- Irregularity or inaccuracy in audits and/or reporting.

- A history of similar accidents and/or routine procedural violations.

- Orders from superiors that appear consistently to put results before safety considerations.

Paramount for you will be to check with your client (and ideally any witnesses in support) the systems and precautions in place 'on the ground' as opposed to what may be documented. You may discover that an establishment with rigorously documented health and safety protocols had been under management of a lax superior officer who allowed safety concerns to become secondary. Similarly, you may find that at the stage of disclosure you receive volumes of health and safety records, only to discover from your client that none were made available to them and/or in fact implemented in any way. In other words, do not be discouraged by the existence of policies alone; the factual question is whether or not those policies were adhered to.

Another issue which is often overlooked is your client's own training. If they have not been provided with training in the tasks they are required to undertake and the associated safety protocols, then this can go a long way to proving negligence. Their training records should be checked thoroughly and the syllabus for training also inspected as, depending on the nature of the activity, the training provided can sometimes be light-touch and inadequate.

## 5.4 Fatal accidents

Where training accidents have resulted in loss of life the Estate and/or dependents of the deceased may be entitled to bring civil claims. The nature and scope of the civil claims that can follow a fatal accident is beyond the scope of this book. The following is a summary of the key claims:

1. A claim by the Estate of the deceased under the Law Reform (Miscellaneous Provisions) Act.

2. A claim by the dependents of the deceased under the Fatal Accidents Act 1976.

3. A claim for a bereavement award for a specified group of dependents under the Fatal Accidents Act 1976.

4. A claim for damages under the Human Rights Act (Article 2: right to life).

The MoD also has its own provisions for investigating serious injuries, fatalities and incidents which raise serious health concerns (regardless of whether any injury or harm was caused). These may include:

- Service Inquiries (SIs)
- Internal Reviews
- Board of Inquires (BOIs)
- Military Aircraft Accident Summaries (MAAS)
- Non-Statutory Inquiry Reports

In addition, the MoD has a memorandum of agreement with the Health and Safety Executive ("HSE"), which provides for the HSE to have a number of operational investigators who, in agreement with the MoD, inspect a number of its activities and assess them for health and safety practice. Where the MoD are found to have breached safety standards, the HSE will report and provide recommendations. The HSE will almost always investigate incidents where there has been loss of life. The MoD enjoys Crown immunity from prosecution, and so avoids the most severe consequences of health and safety breaches, namely, criminal prosecution (military activities are also expressly excluded from the provisions of the Corporate Manslaughter and Corporate Homicide Act 2007). But the MoD can be issued with Crown Notices and Censures, the latter of which is so serious as to indicate that a prosecution would have been likely.

The HSE will become helpful to the military claims lawyer in a number of ways:

- Its website provides safety guidance in a downloadable format for a range of activities at work, which can be used to bolster claims where breaches in health and safety practice can be identified.

- Its previous investigations, Notices and Censures will act as a fertile background to claims. Where your client has been injured in a similar way, these notices can provide you with guidance for your enquiries and in identifying breaches of duty.

- It will investigate in cases involving fatal accidents and its reports may form part of the evidence considered by the Coroner in an inquest.

## 5.5 How negligence can arise

Negligence at work can manifest in a number of ways for your client. The following are a few examples:

- They may have been injured because of faulty or unsafe equipment.

- They may have been provided with the wrong or inadequate personal protective clothing (PPE).

- They may have been tasked with something inherently dangerous that was not properly risk assessed (unsafe working practices or systems).

- They may not have been provided with sufficient or appropriate training before or during the exercises.

- They may have been medically unfit for the specific exercise and/or tasks which they were required to complete. This may have been because a Medical Officer did not medically downgrade them.

- They may have been correctly medically downgraded, but the restrictions applied to their downgrade were incorrect (for example they were cleared to carry load or to march despite the fact that they were suffering with a musculoskeletal injury).

- They may have been correctly medically downgraded with appropriate restrictions, but these were not properly relayed to their chain of command i.e. your client's superiors were oblivious.

- They may have been correctly medically downgraded with appropriate restrictions, and these may have been properly relayed to their chain of command, but the restrictions were ignored either negligently or deliberately.

- They may have suffered an innocent/non-negligent accident during exercises which is subsequently not diagnosed or treated by their Medical Officer and which becomes exacerbated. An example is compartment syndrome – a condition that can be caused by excessive exercise. damage to muscles may result in these tissues swelling and bursting out of the surrounding tissues that hold them (the fascia). This very serious and painful condition must be treated promptly and normally by way of a fasciotomy; literally slicing through the muscle tissue to release the internal pressure. This will leave significant and unsightly scars. The condition is sometimes not diagnosed by Medical Officers and, where it has been diagnosed and a referral made to a hospital, delays are sometimes encountered with treatment. Another example is not referring or following up a musculoskeletal injury that requires specialist assessment and/or imaging.

## 5.6 Establishing liability

For most accidents, whether what was being done was inherently dangerous and whether appropriate measures were taken to ameliorate the risk will be questions of fact to be determined by the court. However, the nature of these exercises can sometimes be difficult to envisage and/or may be highly technical in nature. The court may therefore benefit from the input of expert opinion. You may need experts in several different fields, here are a few examples:

- Health and safety
- Engineering
- Maritime
- Aviation
- Military training

You will also need to deal with two issues of importance. Firstly, whether the MoD will be held vicariously liable for the injury, which is discussed at length at **10.4** in relation to intentional torts. In the context of accidents at work and/or during training, establishing vicarious liability will not normally be a hurdle because your client would have been undertaking something as part of their duties and/or under instruction from a superior. But this is not always clear cut – see the case of ***Radclyffe*** below.

Secondly, you will need to consider to what extent your client may have contributed to their injury. There are few cases which have determined contributory negligence in the military context and little guidance available to us in this specific field. But we can apply some general principles and bear in mind some factors which may influence the Court's view:

- The rank and seniority of your client.
- The knowledge of their chain of command of the situation and the risks.
- Whether your client complained or raised awareness of the risk/danger.
- Whether your client took the correct kit.
- Whether your client had received sufficient training and/or disregarded safety protocols.

In ***Radclyffe v MoD (appeal judgment - [2009] EWCA Civ 635)*** Mr Radclyffe had been Second Lieutenant in the First Battalion of the Irish Guards. He was 24 years old at the relevant time and on Adventurous Training in Germany following operational deployment in Iraq. He was under the Command of Captain Jones. On 8th August 2003, Mr Radclyffe's unit was relaxing by swimming in a reservoir. Some of the men asked Captain Jones for permission to jump into the reservoir from a bridge around 65 feet high. Captain Jones asked them to check the height of the bridge and the depth of the water, before authorising them to proceed. Captain Jones also suggested to Mr Radclyffe that they should both join in; it would not be proper for the officers to be seen to be afraid and/or not taking part with the other men. Mr Radclyffe, who was new to the unit, was hesitant but agreed. Captain Jones was his superior and had insisted that he take part. He joined in with the other soldiers and jumped from the bridge. They were uninjured.

The following day, on 9th August 2003, Mr Radclyffe was asked by another group of soldiers if they could jump off the same bridge. He agreed and indicated that he should show them how it was done. Unfortunately, the level of the water had dropped considerably and he suffered catastrophic injury, resulting in paraplegia. He brought a civil claim against the MoD for his injury, claiming that it was vicariously liable for the actions of Captain Jones, who had directly encouraged him to jump in the first instance and whose suggestions had pressured him to dive again the following day. At first instance he was successful but subject to a finding of 40% contributory negligence.

The MoD appealed this decision and argued that Captain Jones could not be responsible for the decision made by Mr Radclyffe to jump the following day from the bridge. They argued that Mr Radclyffe had been off-duty and entirely responsible for his own actions, and that what Captain Jones had done the previous day was not done in the course of his employment (the test for vicarious liability taken from ***Lister v Hesley Hall Ltd*** – see **10.4**).

The court of appeal refused the MoD's appeal and upheld the decision below. In respect of vicarious liability, it was satisfied and whilst Mr Radclyffe was off duty at the time of his injury, the actions of Captain Jones the preceding day were sufficient to attach a duty of care and had influenced his decision to jump a second time. Mr Radclyffe regarded himself as on duty at the time, having been taught at Sandhurst (The Officer's Academy for the British Army) that he was responsible for his men 24 hours of the day:

> *"In the present case, the judge considered that the defendants sought to draw too hard and fast a line between being on and off duty. It was not a simple employment context. The swimming and jumping from the bridge were not part of the organised Adventurous Training Exercise and the men did not have to go swimming. The question was whether those who went to the lake were under military discipline. The judge had no doubt but that they were. In asking permission to jump, the men recognised that there were things which they should not do without their officers' express authority. In giving permission, Captain Jones was authorising what would not otherwise have been authorised. That was understood by the men. There would have been disciplinary consequences if Captain Jones had refused permission, but the guardsmen had jumped. That was inconsistent with*

> *the men being off duty in the sense of being outside the scope of military discipline. The judge further held that it was Captain Jones' duty to look out for his men's safety, and to prevent them from undertaking risky activities for no adequate reason. The judge accordingly held that Captain Jones was acting in the course of his employment. He further owed the men under his command, who included Mr Radclyffe a duty of care, it being fair, just and reasonable so to hold."*

In respect of contributory negligence, the court found that judge's decision should remain intact:

> *"the judge assessed Mr Radclyffe's contributory negligence at 40%. He disregarded a risk which he considered. He adopted Captain Jones' assessment as his own. What should have been obvious to Captain Jones should have been obvious to him. But Captain Jones was more senior to him and must be more to blame for his injuries... Mr Radclyffe took an ill-judged decision to face an obvious risk but he was under great pressure from what Captain Jones, his senior officer, had said, done and not done on the previous day. An attribution of 40% is not plainly too little and I am not persuaded that this finding of fact by the judge should be disturbed on appeal."*

In ***Vaughan v Ministry of Defence [2015] EWHC 1404 (QB)*** Mr Vaughn, a Royal Marine, had also been taking part in Adventurous Training. This was taking place in Gran Canaria. The purpose of the exercise was to provide Mr Vaughn and his colleagues with the opportunity to crew a yacht in offshore sailing around the Canaries. On the final day of the training, he and his colleagues were instructed by their superior, Colonel Sanders, that they had some free time and could do what they wished until the afternoon, there having been insufficient wind for the sailing exercise. Mr Vaughan and a number of others chose to go swimming in the sea that morning. The beach was one regularly visited by tourists and manned by lifeguards. Whilst waist deep in water, he executed a shallow dive which unfortunately resulted in him hitting a sand bar head-first. He suffered catastrophic injury; a fracture of his cervical spine and incomplete tetraplegia. He brought a claim against the MoD.

Davis J had to determine whether or not Mr Vaughn had suffered his injury 'in the course of his employment'. He considered the JSPs in relation to Adventurous Training, which were in force at the relevant time and which defined "*on duty*" for the purposes of adventure training expeditions as "*participating in an activity recognised under the (adventure training scheme) and required to meet the aims of the expedition*". "*Off duty*" was defined as "*participating in other activities not required to meet the aims of the expedition such as social events*". He concluded that Mr Vaughn was not on duty at the relevant time. But this did not wholly answer the question of whether Mr Vaughn had been injured during the course of his employment, because Mr Vaughn had also argued that he was taking part in physical exercise, which was a requirement of his service as a Royal Marine (and indeed military policy indicates that they must maintain their fitness). Corporal Sanders, who was not present at beach, had no knowledge of the Marines' decision to go swimming, whether for exercise or recreational purposes. Davis J found that (i) even if Corporal Sanders had been present, the Marines would probably not have asked his permission to go into the sea or to execute a shallow surface dive on their own free time, (ii) that the purpose of the visit to the beach was not one of physical exercise but rather a personal choice and a recreational "*dip in the sea*", (iii) that it would be onerous to impart on Corporal Sanders (or vicariously on the MoD) the duty to have inspected and risk assessed the beach and (iv) there was an obvious risk to diving in shallow water and, in any event, a warning would have made no difference to the unfortunate outcome. The claim was dismissed.

***Vaughn*** might be distinguished from ***Radclyffe***, where the presence of a senior officer and the pressure he had levied on acting in a certain way was a crucial element of attaching a duty of care. In the former, no liability attached, in the latter, there was a significant finding of contributory negligence.

## 5.7 Points for practice

- The MoD must comply as far as it can with domestic health and safety legislation and regulations. This includes a duty to reduce the risk of injury at work to ALARP. Bear in mind that a civil judge may not be entirely familiar with the rules and regulations that we have explored above, but many will mimic and refer to domestic legislation.

- Defendants will stress where argument allows that (i) accidents happen, (iii) military life is tough and (iii) the task that your client was obliged to carry out was necessary and in the interests of maintaining an effective fighting force. There are a number of ways to counter these arguments, not least by indicating the correlation between risk and risk management; the higher the risk in any exercise the more detailed a risk assessment should be. Equally, realistic training will necessitate realistic risk assessment. The MoD's own health and safety policies can be used to buttress your client's pleadings on these issues.

- Obtaining early disclosure of liability evidence will be crucial. In addition to regulations you will need to consider risk assessments, written orders, and any internal guidance specific to the activity. You will also need to rely heavily on your client and their witnesses to explain the dynamics on the ground. What was the hierarchy? What was their understanding of the tasks involved and the risks? Was this communicated - both up and down the chain of command?

- A significant proportion of military claims will involve excessive or inappropriate physical training when a service person is medically downgraded or on 'light duties'. Consider the interplay between your client's medical category and what they were required to do. Were they fit for the task?

- Discipline and the chain of command is paramount in the military. Subordinates will follow orders and the example of their superiors. These dynamics may be important when assessing issues of liability and contributory negligence. Whether or not your client was technically 'on duty' at the time of their injury may be a factor but is not determinative.

- Even if your client can establish liability, depending on their own seniority, training, knowledge and circumstances they may be found to have contributed to their injury and this may impact significantly on quantum and risk profile of their case.

# CHAPTER SIX
# COLD INJURIES

## Introduction

In **Chapters 6 and** 7 we will explore the climatic injuries that service personnel may encounter during their careers. **Chapter 6** will deal with cold injuries, and **Chapter** 7 will deal with heat illness.

Service personnel are exposed to extreme conditions during their training and deployment; hot, dry, humid and cold environments, which often test them to the very limits of their physical and mental endurance. Training may help prepare them for such extreme conditions, but the balance between realistic training and serious harm is a very precarious one. The risk of injury can be high and the outcome for those injured can be long-term, disabling and in some circumstances, fatal.

Thankfully, the methods for minimising the risks of climatic injury are often simple and effective; they are largely preventative in nature and focus on thorough planning for exercises and education for those taking part. Unfortunately, the evidence suggests that lessons are not being learned and cultural attitudes towards the way that exercises are managed are sometimes to blame for this.

There are some similarities in the way that claims involving cold injuries and heat illness should be approached, particularly when applying the guidance in the MoD's regulatory document: *"Climatic illness and injury in the armed forces: force protection and initial medical treatment"* (also known by its official name: *JSP 539*), which is the 'bible' for all such climatic injury claims.

*JSP 539* provides a guide to the type of climatic injuries that might be sustained, the steps that commanders must take in order to minimise the risks and the protocols that Medical Officers must follow when diagnosing and treating them. It is an excellent starting point. The latest version (v 3.1, April 2019) is available online. The references made below in respect of the steps that should be taken in managing the risk of climatic injury and in the event of one occurring can all be found within *JSP 539*.

## 6.1 Freezing and non-freezing cold injuries

There are a variety of 'cold injuries', which is a collective term for systemic and localised conditions that can be caused to the body as a result of cold exposure.

Generalised cold injuries are the type of injury you might find in a group of mountaineers who have strayed off their path and spent a night out in the cold, or in someone who has been rescued from sea. Their core body temperature drops and we say they suffer from '*hypothermia*'. This can in prolonged cases lead to organ failure and death. Individuals recover fully so long as they are rewarmed properly.

Localised cold injuries happen when specific parts of the body are damaged because of exposure to the cold. They can be freezing cold injuries (FCI), such as frostbite or frostnip, the latter being less severe and reversible. Freezing cold injuries can happen during exposure to sub-zero temperatures and/or when the body comes into contact with certain chemicals (e.g. liquid nitrogen) or freezing objects. When this happens, the water inside our tissues freezes and the tissues die (*necrosis*). The extremities are normally targeted first and blistering can also occur. You may sometimes hear of mountaineers who have lost digits, noses or ears to frostbite, for example. It is rare to come across freezing cold injuries in the context of military claims, although quite common for those adventurous personnel who undertake expeditions in extreme conditions. Often such exercises are carried out by the participants with full knowledge of the risks and are not mandated by the MoD, so these will rarely result in a civil claim.

The vast majority of cold injuries in a military context are 'non-freezing cold injuries' (NFCI), which is why we will focus on them here. NFCI have a long history, having been recognised widely in the First World

War, when the condition was termed 'trench-foot'. It is sometimes also referred to as 'immersion foot (or hand) syndrome'. The condition was particularly debilitating during the Falklands War, where it was the most common type of non-battle casualty. In fact, following the Falklands War the Institute of Naval Medicine ('INM') was established in Gosport, which became a centre of excellence in diagnosing and treating climatic injuries.

It is possible that those who have suffered extreme exposure to the cold present with a mixture of freezing and non-freezing cold injures.

### 6.1.1 What are NFCIs and how are they caused?

A NFCI is a combination of vascular and neurological injury. They normally occur after several hours of exposure to cold and/or wet conditions. Cold in this context usually means a few degrees above freezing, but not always. NFCI have occurred in fairly moderate temperatures (generally anything below 15 degrees Celsius). You can also suffer NFCI in dry conditions, but being both wet and cold will increase the chances of an injury. The key ingredient is the length and nature of the exposure.

When exposed to the cold for a prolonged period of time, the vascular system to the extremities of the body constricts (*vasoconstriction*); this is the body's natural defence as it seeks to keep the core organs, essential for life, warm and working well. When this happens, and if the exposure is prolonged enough, then the extremities may succumb to damage. This happens most often to the feet, commonly to the hands and sometimes to the genitals. It is thought that this damage is caused as the body rewarms the affected organ (what is known as a 'reperfusion injury'), but frankly there remain a lot of unknowns about NFCI, both in respect of the mechanism of injury and the prognosis of those who suffer them. Clinical interest in the condition has been increasing over the years and a body of research is developing.

For service personnel, NFCI can be very common because of a number of factors. Firstly, the weather in Britain for most of the year is wet and cold. Secondly, the exercises that service personnel (particularly soldiers) carry out will often involve prolonged outdoor activities.

There are other factors which may affect the likelihood of NFCI, mentioned below, including poor nutrition, hydration and PPE (i.e. cold weather clothing and footwear). There is also some research to suggest that service personnel of African, Caribbean or Pacific-Island descent have an increased risk of suffering NFCI for genetic reasons. This may be an important and underestimated factor because there is a disproportionate number of commonwealth service personnel who have suffered with NFCI.

There are some symptoms that are associated with NFCI:

- *Cyanosis* – a bluish discolouration to the hands or feet, usually the fingertips and toes, which is caused as a result of lack of blood flow and Oxygen to the periphery.

- *Hyperaemia* – swelling/flaking of the skin will occur when the body is rewarming after exposure to the cold.

- *Proprioception* – damage to nerves may result in difficulty with fine motor function.

- *Hyperaesthesia* – excessive perception of pain or sensitivity.

- *Paraesthesia* – numbness and/or a sensation of pins and needles.

- *Hyperhidrosis* – the body's thermoregulatory system can be affected and this may result in excessive sweating, often in the limbs which have been affected.

Some patients can exhibit with a mix of symptoms, which can vary with severity and over time. Your client may tell you that after several hours of training out in the field their hands and feet started to appear pale and/or mottled, as if their skin had just come out of a bath (i.e. wrinkled). They may have felt numbness and/or 'pins and needles', caused by a lack of blood to the nerves. When they returned to a warm environment, they probably experienced pain and swelling as their body was warmed and the blood flooded back into their extremities. This normally occurs whilst having a hot shower after the exercise in question, and actually exacerbates the condition. This swelling and associated pain can last between two weeks and three months.

Following this and depending on the severity of their exposure, your client will be left with a NFCI that is largely invisible but no less disabling than an obvious physical injury. They will react poorly to the cold, experiencing pain, and will have inflammatory responses which may include swelling of their afflicted limbs, flaking of their skin and a number of ongoing conditions mentioned below.

### 6.1.2 Condition and prognosis

Typically, a diagnosis of NFCI will be made soon after the return (or evacuation) from an outdoor exercise. But this assumes that the afflicted service person knows that they have been injured and reports to medical staff. This does not always happen. They may be unaware that they have suffered an NFCI or even of what an NFCI is, depending on whether they have received any adequate training on the condition.

If they do report to a Medical Officer, and a NFCI is suspected, the Medical Officer should make a note in the records and provide a sick note (sometimes referred to as a 'chit). They may also complete a light duties pro-forma, excusing that service person from further outdoor duties, and arrange for a follow-up appointment to review the patient. Where the injury is suspected to be minor, no referral to for specialist assessment is normally needed, though it is preferable.

In moderate to severe cases, the service person should be referred for assessment at a specialist clinic. This normally is the INM in Gosport. Alternatively there is at least one other military cold injury clinic, based in Catterick, and a handful of other NHS clinics that specialise in diagnosing and treating peripheral neuropathy i.e. the nerve damage that is most closely associated with NFCI.

The service person should not be rewarmed too quickly as they may well experience excruciating pain. More importantly, the mechanism of the body rewarming the affected limb(s) too quickly may result in further damage. The initial pain suffered following a NFCI is often treated with pain killers, normally Amitripyline, but not everyone reacts well to this drug. It can leave some feeling groggy and nauseous. There are a range of other drugs used to treat the symptoms of NFCI, and doctors will usually cycle through these to find the best balance between symptom relief and side effects. If unresolved, this neuropathic pain can become chronic.

At the INM, for example, the service person will normally undergo a physical examination and thermal imaging of the afflicted area. The physical examination involves palpation of the affected area by the clinician, to see if it is excessively cold or clammy. They will then have the afflicted area made cold, for example, by being asked to immerse it in cold water or to hold a cold object, and then imaged using special thermal cameras to measure the response of the body on rewarming over time. These thermal images show a spectrum of colour, yellow being the warmest and black the coldest. Images showing dark feet and hands may be indicative of an injury, because the patient's vascular system is not rewarming the affected area as expected. However, some patients with established chronic pain may present with fairly standard thermography. Equally, there exists differing opinion on what biopsies and nerve conduction studies might establish with respect to NFCIs. In fact, most experts will say that there is no one determinative diagnostic method, but these tests may contribute to a diagnosis only after an examination by a suitably trained medical expert has been carried out and a full and detailed medical history taken.

When instructing a suitable expert to prepare your client's medical evidence, they may come from various specialities. In respect of assessing the NFCI, this might be done by:

- A Vascular Surgeon.
- A Neurologist.
- A GP or occupational health expert with a specialism in climatic injuries or background in the military.
- A Consultant in tropical and/or sports medicine.

Whichever expert you approach, it is best practice to ensure that they have the requisite experience in diagnosing and treating NFCI.

In respect of the primary conditions that may persist following a NFCI (i.e. the *sequelae*), these are commonly:

- Increased risk of cold injury
- Increased cold intolerance/sensitivity
- Chronic neuropathic pain – this is thought to occur in more than 70% of NFCI cases

The claimant's prognosis is best left to the medical expert to determine, but there have been very few studies made of the long-term recoverability from NFCIs. Certainly in respect of minor cold injuries there is some evidence to suggest that recovery can happen after several years, but there seems to be little guarantee or consensus. In fact there are no recognised studies to give guidance here.

Many military claims practitioners will say anecdotally that they rarely if ever have come across a former client who has completely recovered from a NFCI. Claimants often do, over significant time and with support, adapt to the pain and limitations. But this does not negate the impact on their careers or day-to-day activities, and those with moderate to severe injuries will drastically change their living and working habits so as to avoid and/or limit cold exposure. They will often remain cold sensitized and more susceptible to cold injuries in the future.

In addition to the conditions mentioned above, some clients may face other problems as a result of their NFCI:

- Altered gait – those who have suffered NFCI to their feet may develop biomechanical issues when they alter their gait to prevent pressure on affected parts of their feet. Over time, these issues may lead to overuse injuries and an altered gait when walking. They may require assessment by a podiatrist or in serious cases by an orthopaedic lower limb specialist.

- Excessive sweating – NFCI can affect the body's ability to thermoregulate and claimants may sweat excessively. This can become more than a minor irritation and, in addition to being embarrassing, can result in additional costs being incurred for replacement clothing (because clothes must be washed more regularly), deodorants and/or antiperspirants. Sweating can also induce pain especially in feet afflicted by a NFCI, because it cools them, and so some claimants will purchase and use regularly talcum powder, to keep their feet dry. In serious cases they may need to be referred to a dermatologist.

- Lack of sleep – many claimants experience serious problems sleeping. They will often wake up in pain and with swollen or 'prickly' feet. Many will resort to pain killers to help manage these symptoms, which in turn may make it difficult for them to concentrate during the day.

- Peripheral nerve damage – claimants may be left with symptoms of numbness, pins and needles and/or erectile dysfunction. They may also have a diminished sense of temperature.

- Cold extremities – particularly hands and feet. This can cause difficulties with intimacy and your client's partner may complain about having to share a bed with someone whose hands and/or feet are constantly cold.

- Psychiatric injury – as a result of the disabling effect of a cold injury, the consequent pain and the impact on their sleep, life and military career, some claimants can also develop psychiatric conditions such as adjustment disorders, anxiety and/or depression. They may need assessment by a psychiatrist.

Given the additional conditions that may follow a NFCI, you may also need to rely on other medical experts:

- A Consultant in Pain Medicine or Anesthesia – to assess any suspected chronic pain and review medication.

- A Consultant Psychiatrist – to asses any psychiatric injury.

- A GP or Occupational Health expert with a military background – to comment on medical downgrade issues i.e. continued employability within the forces and/or in respect of clinical negligence.

Unfortunately, a diagnosis of NFCI is career limiting for service personnel and, more often than not, career ending.

## 6.2 How negligence can arise

As mentioned above, NFCI most often occur to soldiers during their training and/or promotional courses. This is probably because of the nature of the exercises in the Army's promotional courses, which will require soldiers to sleep outdoors and/or carry out 'stag' (i.e. guard) duty for prolonged periods in cold and wet conditions. When prone and unable to rewarm or stay dry, these soldiers become prime targets for NFCI.

Most service personnel, who may be concerned about their careers and also wishing not to let their superiors or comrades down, will struggle on in the cold. At some point the symptoms of NFCI will become difficult to bear and they will complain to their superiors. This stage is crucial for the purposes of establishing liability. The superior will not necessarily have been expected to take action until this point, but once a NFCI is suspected, that service person should be evacuated and assessed by a Medical Officer. Where such an assessment is impossible, they should be taken out of the cold immediately and rewarmed slowly. Stopping the cold exposure there and then is the only way to limit the damage.

Negligence can manifest in a number of ways for your client:

- They may have been tasked with an outdoor exercise in cold and wet conditions without sufficient training, shelter, clothing (PPE), risk assessment and/or any opportunity to dry themselves and their kit.

- Their commanders may have failed to follow the specific guidance in *JSP 539*. For example, they may have failed to carry out or follow a proper risk assessment, or to carry out periodic foot inspections, to spot early symptoms of NFCI.

- They may have already been medically downgraded for an NFCI and restricted from outdoor exercises, or they may have been medically restricted for other reasons, but were cleared negligently by their chain of command to attend an outdoor exercise.

- They may have suffered symptoms of NFCI but those symptoms were ignored and they were not immediately protected from the cold, evacuated from the exercise and/or referred to a Medical Officer in accordance with the procedure set out in *JSP 539*.

- They may have suffered a NFCI on an exercise where all necessary precautions were taken including an immediate evacuation from the field and appropriate rewarming, only to be misdiagnosed or negligently treated (e.g. not followed-up, not assessed at the INM or similar clinic and/or not medically downgraded). They may then have had to carry on serving ignorant of the nature or severity of their condition, which may become exacerbated.

- Subsequent to suffering a NFCI on outdoor exercises and, despite being medically downgraded or having been placed on light duties, they may nevertheless be required by their chain of command to continue with outdoor duties (e.g. guard duty, parades etc.). This is often seen with young soldiers whose commanders may ignore their medical restrictions either purposefully or by error, leading to an exacerbation of their NFCI.

The above are only a few example scenarios, aspects of which are explored in more detail below.

### 6.2.1 Risk assessments

Commanders are required to prepare thoroughly for exercises, to include having a detailed written risk assessment prior to any exercise that takes into account the risk of NFCI; these injuries are almost always a risk for outdoor exercises. In fact, *JSP 539* states: *"The key to the prevention of cold related injuries is the commander's awareness of the risk that their personnel are being exposed to. Any outdoor activity undertaken in adverse cold environments constitutes a risk."*

Commanders will have to reduce the risk to 'As Low as Reasonably Practicable' or 'ALARP' (see **Chapter 5**). There are a number of factors that may pre-dispose an individual to suffering a NFCI, which should also be considered by commanders:

- Constrictive clothing and footwear

- Lack of food
- Dehydration
- Fatigue
- Being prone or restricted in movement
- Gender and ethnic background

In respect of gender and ethnic background, genetically some people are more disposed to cold injuries than others. Not much can be done to screen such differences. However, some research has shown that those of African, Caribbean and Pacific-Islander descent are more susceptible to cold injury (it is thought at least 30% more susceptible). Of these, women are thought to be more resilient to cold injury than men. This is a consideration that may well influence the preparation of a risk assessment or the action that might be taken when a service person complains of the cold on exercise.

In addition to the individual risk factors that may apply and the specific risks of the exercise or task, commanders are required to check the weather conditions and plan appropriately whenever conducting exercises outdoors. Military meteorological stations exist for this very reason and can provide commanders with accurate and localised weather data. *JSP 539* places an onus on commanders to obtain an up to date weather report before embarking on any outdoor exercises. They can do this through the Joint Operational Meteorology and Oceanographic Centre (JOMOC) and/or the Met Office. Commanders must also assess the risk dynamically i.e. as this develops and according to the circumstances and prevailing conditions. You might come across cases involving an exercise that began in moderate conditions, but which becomes untenable because of a change in weather conditions. Whilst a change in the weather cannot be blamed on a commander, their failure to plan for it or cancel the exercise may result in a breach of duty.

*JSP 539* provides commanders with additional assistance and guidance for formulating their risk assessments:

- Table 2 – this provides a 'wind-chill' chart. Wind chill is the cooling effect of the wind and gives a better understanding of the actual temperatures to which anyone may be exposed and insight into 'cold stress', which is the rate at which heat is lost. Wind chill can have an astonishing effect on any considerations of temperature, in fact, the body will lose more heat in +10 degrees Celsius in 20mph wind than at -10 degrees Celsius in still air.

- Annex A – This provides a cold injury risk assessment aide memoire which covers the vast majority of risks in the form of a checklist. It should not replace a full and detailed risk assessment, nor does it take into account the need to make dynamic risk assessments as exercises progress. You will need to seek disclosure of this risk assessment, but may be surprised to discover how rarely it is completed or considered.

The biggest challenge for service personnel is usually the wet conditions and staying dry. If exercises are not managed so as to allow them to change out of wet clothes and into dry clothes, or if the conditions are so bad that they are forced to sleep when wet and cold, then the chances of a NFCI occurring rise significantly.

### 6.2.2 Personal protective equipment

Service personnel are normally issued with a 'kit list' for particular exercises. This is a list of clothing and equipment which is mandated for that particular exercise, and determined by the commander who is in charge of the exercise. There are a few important points about kit lists:

- Service personnel must take what is on their kit list otherwise they may face disciplinary action. It is unusual for service personnel to attend exercises without their kit because they know this will have consequences.

- Experienced soldiers will sometimes take additional items to protect against cold and wet conditions.

- Commanders must normally carry out a kit check before every exercise. This involves physically inspecting kit for everyone attending the exercise.

You should make enquiries about whether a kit list was provided and what it stipulated. These are normally provided in the written orders handed to participants before an exercise. For exercises involving an outdoor element, appropriate kit would normally consist of a variety of cold weather and wet weather clothing. Bear in mind that these can sometimes be mutually exclusive.

Having the correct kit will not necessarily protect service personnel from injury, nor the MoD from a negligence claim. The following may be helpful examples.

- Service personnel are provided with some Gore-Tex items of clothing. Gore-Tex is a patented fabric which is used in shoes and garments to make them water resistant. It does not necessarily keep you warm and other fabrics are sometimes preferred for heat retention. It can also be noisy, for example, some Gore-Tex trousers will rub and make a noise when walking in them. For this reason, service personnel are sometimes instructed not to wear Gore-Tex on certain exercises, for example, during reconnaissance when they need to 'spy' on opposing teams and avoid detection. This means that invariably they will get wet on these particular exercises.

- Gore-Tex boots can be helpful in keeping out water from your feet and socks, but may not be appropriate for marching or running. Where service personnel are required to march for prolonged periods, then they are likely not to have had the benefit of waterproof or water resistant boots and their feet may be sodden and cold for a prolonged period of time.

- Gloves are essential to keep your hands warm and dry, but they cannot normally be worn when using a rifle or weapon. Equally, and increasingly, service personnel are required to carry out highly technical operations using computers whilst on exercise. For example, for targeting weaponry or relaying messages. Often they are unable to use machinery or operate a keyboard whilst using gloves. If they have to operate this way for a prolonged period of time, then they may suffer an NFCI to their hands regardless of the fact that they have gloves available to them.

The above are only a few examples of how important it is to give careful consideration to the detail of your client's kit and the actual tasks they were required to carry out.

### 6.2.3 Training and education

Whether your client received relevant training, its content and frequency may contribute to your view on contributory negligence if it is alleged that your client had the knowledge and means to mitigate their injuries.

All service personnel undergo regular training in health and safety. For example, the Army's health and safety training forms part of their Military Annual Training Tests (or 'MATTs'), which should include presentations about climatic injuries. Where suitable training has been provided to a claimant, defendants will often argue that they exhausted their duty of care in providing it and insist that any injury was as a result of the claimant not paying attention to their training or adhering to the guidelines.

*JSP 539* is mandatory guidance and should be referenced by commanders in training guidelines and written orders. The prospects of a young recruit or non-commissioned officer reading the entirety of *JSP 539* and absorbing its complexity, might be considered very unlikely. But there are a number of DVDs and pamphlets referred to in *JSP 539* which should form part of their regular health and safety training. These documents will normally form part of the 'generic disclosure' that might be served on your client by the MoD during the disclosure phase of their case. You must treat this disclosure with some caution and seek instructions from your client:

- The reality might be that the training wasn't delivered or your client never attended.
- The training may have been inadequate.
- The training may have been so infrequent so as to have lost any meaningful affect.

More often than not, any training provided formed part of a much longer training session and did not provide adequate guidance to personnel about the symptoms, causes and risks. Briefings provided immediately before an exercise should also be scrutinised. These are rarely documented, and you will need to uncover what useful information and guidance was provided before the exercise began, if any. Where such a briefing does not include reference to the risk and management of cold injuries, then the value of such a brief needs to be questioned.

### 6.2.4 Clinical negligence

*Chapter 5 of JSP539* provides detailed guidance to medical officers on the diagnosis and treatment of cold injuries (not just NFCI), including specific instructions on when and how to refer these climatic injuries to the INM. Some aspects to bear in mind are:

- Medical Officers must be familiar with NFCI. A clinician who fails to recognise the symptoms when these are present and especially when they are proximate to prolonged exposure to the cold will struggle to defend a claim in clinical negligence. They should also, where the injury is serious enough and warrants it, make a referral for assessment at the INM and make appropriate (temporary) medical downgrade.

- Civilian GPs employed by the MoD may have less experience in climatic injuries and establishing negligence against them may be trickier because of the standard of care.

- Symptoms of NFCI are similar to and often mistaken for Raynaud's syndrome (or sometimes referred to as Raynaud's phenomenon), which is the most common differential diagnosis. Raynaud's is caused by spasms in the arteries which results in an effect on blood flow, and can often be identified by a marked change in colour of the fingertips and toes (which turn pale or white). It can be triggered or exacerbated by cold conditions, but can also occur all year around. A clinician who does not pay attention to the symptoms or your client's history, and instead insists in the differential diagnosis of Raynaud's may be negligent. This will of course depend on the facts and an expert's opinion.

## 6.3 Establishing liability

Your client will have to prove that there was a breach of duty. They will be assisted by (and should directly reference) the obligations under *JSP 539* and you may wish to consider some of the examples of negligence at **6.2** above. The most salient point to take away from *JSP 539* is that MoD policy acknowledges that climatic injuries are largely a management issue; they should *not* occur when exercises are managed appropriately. This is the foundation of any claim for climatic injury.

Obtaining weather data in the period running up to and during the exercise will also be helpful (and fairly straightforward using online databases). You must establish the conditions that were likely to result in an increased risk of NFCI occurring. Your medical expert will need to address medical causation of injury having been provided with the medical records, a background of the nature of the exercise and details of the weather conditions.

In respect of factual evidence, NFCI claims tend to occur in clusters and usually when an outdoor exercise has been poorly planned or managed. In such circumstances several service personnel may be injured on the same exercise. Exploring witnesses in support of your client's claim may come with the added benefit that additional clients will come to you for advice and representation. Equally, this can cause problems when a service person is reluctant to assist your client because they have their own negligence claim underway and, for whatever reason, they would prefer not to endanger that claim. More often than not the reluctance comes from witnesses who are still serving and are afraid to come forward.

One has to bear in mind that service personnel are geared to work on adverse conditions. They tend to develop an attitude for this and are expected (often ordered) to carry out their duties regardless of pain and/or conditions. They may also be disciplined if they complain and/or may be treated differently by their peers. Most often, they simply do not want to let their comrades down. It is also quite typical to hear of service personnel who complain about symptoms to their chain of command but are simply told to "*man-up*" and "*soldier on*". This often creates an environment where orders are followed without question and this is an aspect that should be borne out in the witness evidence.

One of the problems with NFCIs is that they are notoriously under-reported and one might sympathise with a claimant who decides not to report their symptoms to either their chain of command or a Medical Officer because of the likelihood that a diagnosis will end their careers. Those with minor injuries may struggle on but of course their increased susceptibility to these injuries means that each time they go on outdoor exercises they may be exacerbating their condition and reducing their long-term prospects of recovery. You might also encounter clients who suffered injuries years ago, only to have them come to you for advice after their careers have ended. These cases will face hurdles of limitation and contributory negligence, which may increase the litigation risk significantly. But bear in mind that depending on when they were first diagnosed with the condition and/or informed of its long-term nature and significance, they may have strong arguments in respect of their date of knowledge for the purposes of determining limitation and/or equally in respect of those factors relevant under section 33 of the Limitation Act 1980 (extending time to bring a claim).

## 6.4 Damages

There are only a few cases which have determined PSLA in NFCI cases:

- ***Hope v MoD [2003] 1 QR 11*** – this involved a severe NFCI to hands and feet. The Court approved an agreement that general damages be awarded at £25,000 in November 2001.

- ***Leeson v Siemens Plc [2008] CLY 2902*** – this non-military claim involved a severe NFCI to hands and feet. The Claimant was awarded £20,000 in September 2007

- ***Billett v MoD – [2014] EWHC 3060 (QB)*** – this involved a minor NFCI to feet only. The Claimant was awarded £12,500 in September 2014.

In respect of special damages, your client may have a very significant claim for loss of earnings, benefits and pension. You should consider a claim based on the disabled reduction factors in Ogden Tables B and D. Following ***Billett***, above, it will often be straightforward to establish that your client is "disabled" for the purposes of those Tables, though the court has considerable discretion as to whether or how to apply the disabled reduction factors. For more, see **Chapter 13**.

NFCI will affect your client's ability to withstand the cold and outdoor environments, putting them at risk of suffering further injury. NFCI in the hands may also affect motor ability and preclude your client from being able to carry or fire a weapon. Any such restrictions will likely affect their ability to deploy. In the circumstances, it is no wonder that most service personnel with NFCI are medically discharged. Those suffering with minor injuries may be able to continue to work in a medically downgraded capacity. This is largely dependent on their Service, trade and manning considerations. But they may also suffer a significant and adverse impact on their career progression because they are not able to undertake training or qualifications in an outdoor capacity. For these reasons, some service personnel who suffer with NFCI decide to leave the forces, because they can foresee a very limited career ahead of them.

When establishing your client's loss of career and ongoing disadvantage or disability, you should ensure that an appropriate employment expert is instructed and appreciates the disabling nature of the condition. This may greatly reduce your client's earning capacity and almost certainly will restrict them to indoor work, potentially for life. Given that the skill sets of some service personnel primarily involve outdoor activities, they may also need to retrain. In addition, they may have miscellaneous further losses. Below are a few examples:

- Additional heating expenses – to avoid symptoms of pain client will invariably spend more on heating.

- Additional clothing – cold weather clothing, jackets, thermals and gloves. Clients who sweat excessively and have problems with their thermoregulation will tend to change their clothes more regularly and purchase additional pairs of socks and underwear.

- Medication and sundries – pain killers, antiperspirant, deodorant, talcum powder (to keep their feet dry and therefore warm).

- Care – given the limitations on their day-to-day activities, particularly in outdoor activities, clients will often rely on a loved one or family member to undertake chores and activities that they would normally have undertaken themselves.

- Travel – client's may find it difficult to drive, either because the pain in their feet is exacerbated by using pedals or because gripping the steering wheel can cause them pain in their hands. Of course they may also avoid going outdoors all together. They may rely on others to drive or pay for transport more regularly.

- Household maintenance – clients may avoid chores around the home. They will usually avoid any task that involves hot or cold temperatures or handling hot, cold or wet items, as this will put them at risk of further injury (e.g. burning themselves when cooking) or exacerbate their symptoms (e.g. when coming into contact with cold water). It is common for someone with a NFCI to avoid, for example, cooking, handling items from the fridge or freezer, handling wet laundry, washing dishes, mowing the lawn and/or washing the car.

- Adaptations to the home – for example, thermostatic control for taps in the kitchen and bathroom.

## 6.5 Points for practice

- There are a variety of cold injuries, including freezing and non-freezing cold injuries. The vast majority of claims in a military context are non-freezing in nature.

- *JSP 539* provides guidance on all issues regarding climatic injuries, including the steps that commanders have to take to minimise the risk. Familiarise yourself with *JSP 539*. Let it lead your enquiries and form the basis of your pleadings. You may need to consider the version of *JSP 539* that existed at the time of the negligence, though the content has not changed drastically over the years.

- Clinical negligence is sometimes a factor in these claims and can lead to NFCI being left undiagnosed or untreated, resulting in an exacerbation. More often than not the clinical negligence is not the primary claim because the long-term damage to your client would probably have been done at the point of the initial cold exposure.

- When requesting your client's medical records, you must ensure that these include any treatment records (almost always from the INM but not necessarily). These records will provide the confirmation of diagnosis and comments on severity of injury, which will be crucial to the case.

- NFCI are normally long-term injuries. Where any medical expert, including your own, suggests that your client may recover from their NFCI, you are duty bound to explore this in detail. Given the paucity of data on the long term prognosis of the condition, there is a possibility that your client will suffer with their symptoms for life.

- Clients may come to you having been medically discharged and after assessment at the INM, which will exclude where appropriate the possibility of Raynaud's syndrome. At other times, or in any event, you may face a defence to a NFCI claim alleging that your client suffers from Raynaud's syndrome instead of or as a secondary diagnosis to NFCI. Given that Raynaud's syndrome can occur without injury and/or explanation, it is no wonder that this is sometimes pleaded because, if proven, this will reduce the claim to one of an exacerbation of a pre-existing condition. You should treat these defences with caution as there may be no medical evidence to support the assertion. You may also need to instruct a Consultant Rheumatologist to exclude the possibility of Raynaud's.

- Explore your client's losses carefully. A home visit, where possible and justifiable, will be the best method to do this. Consider in particular the plethora of outdoor activities that your client could have done *but for* their NFCI.

- Modern attitudes towards NFCI remain somewhat unsympathetic and this stems from a lack of understanding of the condition and the fact that it is 'invisible'. Some tabloids, for example, would have you believe that service personnel who suffer with these injuries are malingerers. Your client may face adverse media attention and should be appropriately advised.

# CHAPTER SEVEN
# HEAT ILLNESS

## Introduction

On the hottest day of 2013 three Reservists died undertaking an SAS selection course in the Brecon Beacons in Wales. The tragedy of their deaths attracted a great deal of media attention and the public wondered how such supremely fit individuals could lose their lives as a result of a training exercise, and how such a catastrophe could occur in the UK, which is not renowned for its extremes of temperature. As we will see, heat illness is a misunderstood and greatly underestimated condition. In fact, according to *JSP 539* heat illness is a "*serious problem*" for the armed forces and during the period October 2015 to September 2016 alone 333 personnel were identified as having suffered the condition.

As with the previous chapter, the references made below in respect of the steps that should be taken to identify and manage the risk of heat illness can also found within *JSP 539.*

## 7.1 What is heat illness and how is it caused?

Heat illness is a condition caused by a rise in body temperature (*hyperthermia*), often as a result of or in tandem with a failing thermoregulatory system. It is sometimes used as a catch-all term when discussing two conditions, namely heat exhaustion and heat stroke:

- Heat exhaustion – this results from a lack of salt and water in the body. It will be a pre-cursor to heat stroke.
- Heat stroke – this is considered to be the more serious condition and is associated with an increase in core body temperature, an altered mental state and tissue damage.

The distinction between the two conditions has been debated. For our purposes they form a spectrum of what is collectively referred to as "heat illness" below.

If the internal temperature of the body rises too much, this can begin to play havoc with the biological mechanisms that are temperature dependent. For example, the chemical reactions in the body required for respiration to occur will happen in an ideal temperature range, but outside of this range these reactions will slow or fail completely. The result can be catastrophic and end in organ damage, organ failure and ultimately death.

The body regulates its temperature through a number of mechanisms. Primarily, the evaporation of sweat from the skin will gradually reduce body temperature. But a dangerous situation can arise when the body's ability to regulate its temperature becomes retarded, or if the climatic circumstances are so extreme that this cooling system is insufficient of itself.

Generally:

- When in a high temperature environment the body will gain heat.
- When wearing heavy clothing (for example PPE), the body will retain more heat.
- When undertaking physical exercise the body's temperature will rise and its demand for water will also increase.
- When sweating excessively, the body will lose salt, which is crucial for biological function.
- When dehydrated, the body will lose its ability to sweat and cool itself.

- When in a humid environment, sweat does not easily evaporate and this will also adversely affect the efficiency of the body's cooling system.

For service personnel, heat illness will tend to occur as a result of a combination of environmental conditions and excessive exercise. In respect of the latter, this 'exertional' heat illness happens when body temperature rises as a result of physical exercise as opposed to the prevailing weather conditions alone. In fact, 86 of the 333 service personnel who suffered heat illness over the period October 2015 to September 2016 did so whilst in the UK during the winter months. There are a number of signs that may indicate an underlying or perhaps impending heat illness:

- Thirst
- Nausea and/or vomiting
- Diarrhoea
- Pain (*myalgia*)
- Fainting or dizziness (*syncope*)
- Fatigue
- Headache
- Visual disturbance and loss of coordination
- Hysteria
- Agitation and anxiety
- Hyperventilation
- Numbness (*parasaetheia*)
- Muscle spasms (*tetany*) and cramps
- Swelling (*edema*)
- Heat rash – this can sometimes be caused to the skin as a result of excessive sweating.
- Sun burn – this does not necessarily indicate any underlying illness, but it will indicate that a patient has been exposed to the sun for an excessive period of time without adequate protection.

*JSP 539* warns that not everyone will present with symptoms in a typical fashion; these symptoms may appear on their own or in combination. At other times, the afflicted service person may appear normal but show only transient signs of symptoms. A treating Medical Officer will have to bear these symptoms in mind when making a diagnosis.

Some of the specific conditions associated with heat illness are:

- Organ failure – this can result in coma and death.

- Organ damage – in serious cases this can be permanent and may include damage to the cerebellum (causing problems with co-ordination), the lining of the heart and/or the liver (which may necessitate a transplant).

- Tissue damage – particularly damage to muscles (*rhabdomyolysis*), which will cause these tissues to be released into the bloodstream. This can lead to kidney damage, which may necessitate treatment by dialysis.

- Compartment syndrome – damage to muscles may also result in these tissues swelling and bursting out of the surrounding tissues that hold them (the fascia). This very serious and painful condition must be treated promptly and normally by way of a fasciotomy; literally slicing through the muscle tissue to release the internal pressure. This will leave significant and unsightly scars.

- Physical intolerance to hot conditions – for example, as a result of destruction of sweat glands or other tissue.

## 7.2 Condition and prognosis

Once heat illness is identified, usually through observing symptoms and/or taking the patient's temperature, treatment involves immediate cooling and rehydration. A patient should be taken to a shaded place and stripped. Cold water should be dabbed or sprayed onto them. They should be closely monitored and if their condition does not stabilise or in any event in severe cases, they should be evacuated to a hospital.

Most who survive heat illness will make a full recovery, but this recovery can take time. During that recovery their immune system will be retarded and they may suffer infection. For service personnel, such a period of medical downgrade may necessarily lead to a referral to a medical board and discharge. So whilst recovery may be possible, the impact on their career might still be significant.

The other aspect that should not be underestimated is the psychological harm that might be caused. Surviving a heat illness can be traumatic process. Patients might be hysterical, confused and anxious, and experience a sense of 'impending doom' (akin to a heart attack). Your client may suffer with a number of psychiatric conditions following a heat illness, such as an adjustment or anxiety disorder.

Where your client may develop a physical intolerance to heat or a psychological aversion to hot environments, this will affect their ability to deploy and their medical category. In some cases it is the psychiatric sequela that may persist longer than the physical harm of a heat illness.

When instructing a medical expert to assess the heat illness suffered by your client, you may wish to instruct:

- A Consultant Anaesthetist.
- A GP or Occupational Health specialist with experience of climatic injuries.
- A Consultant in tropical or sports medicine.

You may also need a number of other experts from different fields:

- A Consultant Psychiatrist – to comment on any psychiatric condition.

- A GP or Occupational Health expert with a military background – to comment on medical downgrade issues i.e. continued employability within the forces and/or in respect of clinical negligence.

Depending on the extent of your client's injuries, you may need specific experts to comment on organ function and/or life expectancy.

## 7.3 How negligence can arise

*JSP 539* provides helpful and clear guidance for commanders and Medical Officers on how to avoid heat illness on military exercises and manage its treatment respectively. Where these steps are not followed, negligence can manifest in a number of ways for your client and below is a non-exhaustive list of examples:

- They may have been tasked with an outdoor activity in hot and/or humid conditions without sufficient shelter, appropriate clothing, rest, water or any appropriate period for acclimatization.

- Their commanders may have failed to follow the specific guidance in *JSP 539*. For example, they may have failed to carry out or follow a proper risk assessment.

- That any climatic injury training provided to your client either generally, annually or specifically before the exercise was inadequate, too infrequent or non-existent. Or that your client was not supervised properly.

- They may have already been medically downgraded and restricted from outdoor exercises, but may have been cleared negligently by their chain of command to attend an outdoor exercise. Their pre-existing condition or any medication they take may make them more susceptible to heat illness.

- They may have suffered symptoms of heat illness but those symptoms were ignored by their chain of command and they were not immediately cooled, rehydrated and/or referred to a Medical Officer. The first aid treatment guidelines for commanders are set out at *Annex B to Section 1 of JSP 539 Part 2.*

- That the medical plan in place for treatment or evacuation was inadequate, or no plan existed.

- They may have been referred to a Medical Officer by their chain of command, or having presented to the medical centre themselves, but their symptoms may have been missed or ignored. Alternatively they may have not have been followed-up or referred for specialist assessment (which, like cold injuries, would normally take place at the INM).

The above are only a few example scenarios, aspects of which are explored in more detail below.

### 7.3.1 Risk assessments

Importantly, as with cold injuries, heat illness is a preventable condition and focus is placed in *JSP 539* on thorough risk assessment and planning. *Annex A of Section 1 in JSP 539 Part 2* provides commanders with a heat illness risk assessment checklist. Commanders are required to reduce the risk to ALARP. In fact, any activity involving the use of PPE (especially heavy or impermeable PPE) *or* in hot environments should be considered as one bearing risk of heat illness. Notice that this means there is a need to carry out a satisfactory risk assessment even where an activity is not taking place in hot conditions.

In respect of individual risk factors, the following may predispose a person to heat illness (i.e. make them more likely to suffer the illness):

- Being obese and/or unfit

- Being male
- Having (or having recently had) an infection
- Lack of sleep, water or food
- Having a skin disease
- Having a thyroid condition
- Lack of acclimitisation
- Having taken alcohol or drugs
- Having recently travelled by air
- Having previously suffered heat illness
- Genetics

In respect of the nature of the exercise being planned, obviously the type, intensity and duration of the task, and whether any rest periods are planned, will be important in limiting the exertional 'load' on personnel. The tasks can vary for personnel so, for example, Gunners who are tasked with loading and firing weaponry might in addition to the ambient heat be affected by the heat from their weapons and/or machinery. *Annex D to Section 1 in JSP 539 Part 2* provides commanders with a table showing maximum work rate examples. Where the risk of heat illness is high, adaptations to work and schedules should be made:

- Work rates – the 'loaded' (i.e. weight carrying) exercises that service personnel often engage with increase the risk of heat illness.

- Rest periods – these should be provided to allow personnel to cool down and rehydrate, ideally in shaded areas.

- Scheduling of activities – where personnel are required to undertake physical tasks, these should be restricted to the cooler times of the day.

- Supervision – commanders will need to ensure that there are enough staff to supervise personnel and that this supervision is in fact taking place regularly.

Where the risk of heat illness is very high then the commander must consider whether or not to halt or reduce physical activity completely. This is where dynamic risk assessment will become relevant, for example, when ambient heat conditions rise considerably or water supplies are cut short.

Commanders are also required when risk assessing any activity to develop a medical plan to include cover by an appropriate number of qualified first aiders and/or medical doctors. This includes preparing for casualty evacuation in the event of an emergency. When operating abroad in arduous conditions or where medical assistance may be less accessible, these plans may mean the difference between life and death.

### 7.3.2 Personal protective equipment

In dealing with heat illness it is not normally the need for more clothing (as opposed to cold weather clothing and waterproofs in NFCI claims), but rather the need for *less* equipment, load and clothing, particularly heavy and impermeable clothing, that can influence risk. There are a number of things for commanders to bear in mind:

- Sunscreen – can be provided to protect against sun burn. When minor, sunburn affect performance but serious cases may require hospitalisation.
- Clothing – light clothing is preferred and commanders are required to encourage personnel to wear layers so that these layers can be gradually lost as temperatures increase during the day. Hats can also be provided to shade the face and head from the sun. Chemical, Biological, Radiological and Nuclear (CBRN) protective equipment, such as Hazmat suits, will significantly increase heat retention and consequently the risk of heat illness.
- Equipment and load – body armour, helmets and other equipment will increase heat retention. These should be reduced

where necessary. Hydration bladders might be used to encourage regular hydration.

- Shade/cover – should be provided where possible, particularly in rest areas.
- Fans – where possible and especially in conditions that are humid or where airflow is limited, fans could be provided to promote air movement.

Where personnel have joined an exercise and require acclimatisation to hot conditions, it is recommended that their full clothing and equipment be introduced slowly so that, for example, they do not wear body armour in the first few days of joining.

### 7.3.3 Environmental conditions

The efficiency of the body to thermoregulate and cool itself is also determined by external environmental conditions, such as the ambient temperature, humidity and wind speed. Whenever conducting exercises outdoors, commanders are required to check the weather conditions and plan appropriately. They can do this by obtaining weather data from the Joint Operational Meteorology and Oceanographic Centre (JOMOC) and/or the Met Office. Unexpected changes in the weather should be taken into account when making dynamic risk assessments.

The ambient weather is only part of the equation when dealing with heat illness and so the military use the Wet Bulb Globe Temperature (WGBT) heat stress monitor to assess the risk posed of heat illness to any particular activity. The monitor is a mechanism the size of a radio that should be readily available to commanders, who are trained on how to use it. The WGBT refers to the index that is used in this assessment, which takes into account environmental factors and provides a 'threshold' value (in minutes) for continuous physical activity that can be undertaken at any given temperature. Exceeding these thresholds would increase the risk of heat illness.

Further details on the WGBT measurement are set out in *Annexes C and F to Section 1 in JSP 539 Part 2*. There are some very important things to bear in mind in respect of the use of the WGBT monitor:

- The measurement is only accurate if taken at the time and precise location of the activity being assessed and so long as the mechanism itself has been set up and maintained properly.
- Acclimatisation is an essential factor. The less a service person is acclimatised, the greater the risk of heat illness. *Table 3 of Section 1 in JSP 539 Part 2* provides a summary of the recommended acclimatisation procedure.
- The WGBT index should *not* be used in isolation. It does not negate the need for a full and proper risk assessment.

### 7.3.4 Water intake

It is the duty of commanders to provide sufficient water for the service personnel under their charge. This simple but essential requirement involves more than just providing water but also includes:

- Monitoring the intake of water.
- Ensuring that personnel eat their food (another source of daily water intake).
- Ensuring that personnel have salt either with their meals or in the form of electrolyte drinks to offset the impact of excessive activity and sweating.

*Table 2 of Section 1 in JSP 539 Part 2* provides the minimum requirements of water intake dependent on the intensity of the activity being undertaken.

### 7.3.5 Training and education

All the considerations set out at **6.2.3** above will be relevant here. In summary:

- *JSP 539* is mandatory and must be referenced in training guidelines and written orders.

- Whether or not the right training was delivered to your client and/or whether it would have made any material difference to the outcome of their injury will largely be a question of fact.

- Your client may have contributed to the negligence, or liability may not attach, if it can be proved that they had the knowledge and means to mitigate their injuries.

- Witness evidence may be needed to support any allegations that the training or pre-exercise briefings was not given or inadequate.

### 7.3.6 Clinical negligence

*Section 2 of JSP 539 Part 2* sets out detailed guidance to Medical Officers on the diagnosis and treatment of heat illness. There are some key points to consider:

- The symptoms of heat illness may occur singularly or in combination. Just because some symptoms are absent does not mean that the doctor should exclude the possibility of heat illness.

- Observations should be recorded in the standard way in the medical records. Importantly, an accurate reading of temperature should be taken (rectally). However, just because a reading is higher than normal (i.e. higher than 37 degrees Celsius), this does not necessarily indicate the severity of the condition and should instead be the starting point for immediate steps to cool the patient.

- Initial treatment should involve cooling the patient (by stripping, soaking and fanning).

- Any patient with suspected heat illness who suffers a seizure, loss of consciousness, maintains a regular internal temperature of 40 degrees Celsius or above and/or does not show improved symptoms within 30 minutes of cooling, should be evacuated to a hospital.

- *JSP 539* sets out steps that must be taken to protect and rehabilitate service personnel following heat illness. They may be very weak and also suffer with heat intolerance for an unspecified amount of time (normally several months but this can vary greatly). The steps to be taken in respect of referral for further assessment, their return to work and follow-up will relate to the severity of the heat illness that was suffered.

- Any heat illness beyond 'mild' should be referred to the INM for further tests. Firstly, the patient should be assisted by an Exercise Remedial instructor (ERI), whose aim will be to build up the patient's fitness slowly and without risking thermal stress. This is in preparation for a heat tolerance assessment (HTA). This test will assess the patient's ability to thermoregulate under the stress of exercise.

- All cases of heat illness must be reported using a designated form provided in *JSP 539*.

- Where patients do not improve then the likelihood is that they will be medically discharged or at least permanently medically downgraded.

Where any of the steps above have not been complied with there may be an argument of breach of duty, but weather such steps have helped cause or contributed to the injury will be a far more complicated issue and you will need guidance from your medical expert.

## 7.4 Establishing liability

Your client will have to prove that there was a breach of duty. They will be assisted by (and should directly reference) the obligations under *JSP 539* and you may wish to consider some of the examples of negligence at **7.3** above. As with cold injuries, MoD policy acknowledges that climatic injuries are largely a management issue; they should *not* occur when exercises are managed appropriately. This is the foundation of any claim for climatic injury.

Obtaining weather data in the period running up to and during the exercise will also be helpful (and fairly straightforward using online databases). You must establish the conditions that were likely to result in an increased risk of heat illness occurring. Your medical expert will need to address medical causation of injury having been provided with the medical records, a background of the nature of the exercise and details of the weather conditions.

In respect of factual evidence, like NFCI claims, heat illness claims can occur in clusters and normally when an outdoor exercise has been poorly planned or managed. The considerations set out at 6.3 above in respect of witness evidence and the attitude of service personnel will apply equally here.

As mentioned above, where your client has received training then this may influence your considerations of contributory negligence and increase the risk profile of any case. However, it is suggested that refresher training immediately before the exercise in question would be preferable as well as reminders issued to personnel where the risk of heat illness is high.

## 7.5 Damages

Assessing damages in heat illness claims is not straight forward because the extent and nature of injury will vary greatly and depend on the exposure and person.

Where your client has been medically discharged, they may have a very significant claim for loss of earnings, benefits and pension. Where your client has suffered a heat illness as a result of negligence and recovered, then their special damages will largely depend on any negative impact on their career. They may have missed out on career development and/or promotion, in which case their claim may remain financially significant. In either case, and except in respect of minor injuries, you will probably need an employment consultant with a specialism in military careers to comment on the impact on their careers and any ongoing disadvantage in the employment market.

Your client may have miscellaneous further losses which are related to their heat illness:

- Aids and appliances – fans, air conditioners or other methods of cooling at home.
- Additional clothing – for example, light or hot weather clothing which they may prefer to the sensation of wearing heavy or impervious clothing.
- Medication – depending on any conditions (e.g. organ damage) following injury and during recovery. There might be a large range here.
- Treatment – where there career has ended, they may require ongoing medical treatment on a private basis in respect of any ongoing psychical impairments. They may have also suffered psychiatric injury and require therapy.

- Care – during their recovery or if left with any permanent injury your client may require loved ones or family to assist with tasks around the home. Alternatively, your client may choose to pay privately for services.

For more on damages see **Chapter 13**.

## 7.6 Points for practice

- Heat illness is caused when the body's temperature rises excessively. Most people recover from heat illness, but in serious cases it can be fatal. It is a mistake to assume that heat illness cannot be caused outside of high temperature environments and there are many factors that might contribute to the condition.

- *JSP 539* provides guidance on all issues regarding climatic injuries, including the steps that commanders have to take to minimize the risk. Let it lead your enquiries and form the basis of your pleadings.

- Early statements from those 'on the ground' will be crucial to help establish liability. Try to ascertain the precise nature of the activities that your client was required to undertake on a day by day basis, their access to water, shade and rest, and particularly any appropriate measures taken to help acclimatise them to the conditions. Your client may not recall the late stages of their heat illness because of their condition, and may not necessarily be the most reliable witness because of their confused state at the time. Meteorological evidence will also be necessary.

- Make sure to inspect the medical records for potential avenues of clinical negligence. Medical Officers should be very aware of the risk of heat illness and the symptoms.

- Most people recover from heat illness, depending on the severity. But just because your client's military career has not ended does not mean that their claim will be uneconomical. Consider the impact that their recovery may have had on career prospects or promotion.

# CHAPTER EIGHT
# HEARING LOSS

## Introduction

Your hearing, unfortunately and like most of the rest of your body, can (and probably will) get worse with age. It can also get worse if regularly exposed to excessive noise. If the exposure is loud enough, then the hearing loss may be significant, abrupt and life-changing.

Service personnel are by the nature of their work often exposed to loud, hazardous and persistently noisy environments that can be damaging to their hearing. Whether it is on the firing range, dealing with explosives, piloting aircraft, operating heavy machinery or playing in a brass band; there will be many circumstances where noise exposure can become harmful. They can also suffer hearing loss after head injuries or serious accidents. It is no wonder that the MoD has faced a growing problem of hearing loss claims.

Hearing loss claims are best assessed by specialists. There are books on industrial disease which are devoted to this subject and it would be beyond the scope of this book to cover that level of detail. In this chapter, we will explore some of the basic elements of hearing loss claims and consider the practical points to bear in mind in the context of armed forces personnel.

## 8.1 Hearing loss and associated conditions

We measure the intensity of sound (sound pressure) in units of measurement called decibels (dB). For service personnel, the sounds they experience during their activities and working environments will often test and exceed the boundaries of what is safe. For example, most weapon firing will exceed 140 dB. Travelling in an armoured vehicle or in an aircraft will expose them to consistent noise in excess of 100 dB. By comparison, a full symphony orchestra might typically generate 110 dB, whilst the sound generated in a typical office workspace would be approximately 40dB.

There are a number of conditions that may result from exposure to excessive sound. The main conditions that arise in military claims are explained below. It is not uncommon for clients to present having been diagnosed with a combination of these conditions. Bear in mind:

- Hearing loss can be permanent and degenerative in nature.
- Those having suffered hearing loss may become susceptible to further harm and so must be protected from further exposure promptly.
- Hearing loss may only be part of the problem and there are a number of associated (often psychiatric) conditions which may arise.

### 8.1.1 Noise-induced hearing loss

NIHL (alternatively referred to as "industrial deafness") is a condition caused by the harmful exposure to noise, as opposed to the gradual loss of hearing that might occur naturally.

There are two main ways that noise-induced hearing loss can occur. The first is when person is exposed to sound of approximately 140 dB or more. Exposure to extremely loud noise over a short space of time is dangerous and is typical of percussive noise, such as that encountered with explosions or when firing a weapon. When this happens, the delicate structures in the ear are stretched beyond their natural limits and physical damage is caused. This can lead to immediate and permanent hearing loss.

The second method of hearing loss involves a more protracted exposure to persistent noise levels (of over 75 – 85 dB), which results in biochemical changes in the ear and eventual damage to certain tissues.

NIHL can be partial or total, and can be temporary or permanent. It is quite common, for example in the Army, for hearing loss to occur in the right ear. This is because most service personnel are right handed and will hold their rifle against their right shoulder. This exposes their right ear to the most noise.

### 8.1.2 Acoustic shock

Acoustic shock is the term used to describe a number of symptoms that may manifest following harmful exposure to high pitched noise, either through a headset or speaker, and usually involving high pitched frequencies (for example, an alarm on a vessel). A person who has suffered in this way may experience pain, discomfort, nausea, dizziness and hypersensitivity. Acoustic shock is often but not always followed by hearing loss, depending on the nature and extent of the exposure.

### 8.1.3 Tinnitus

Tinnitus is a somewhat unpredictable symptom of hearing loss (although it can be a symptom of other underlying conditions). Sufferers experience sound when there is no sound, which is normally described as a humming, ringing or buzzing. This sound can come and go, and can be very distracting. In serious cases, it can become chronic and debilitating. The condition can wreak havoc on sleep and mental health. It can occur without associated hearing loss.

People tend to experience tinnitus in different ways. Sometimes they experience it in one ear, or both, or have the sensation that the sound is inside their head. It has been closely linked to stress and can be exacerbated by low mood and poor mental health. Unfortunately, this sometimes creates a cycle whereby a person struggling with tinnitus will become stressed and depressed, and consequently their symptoms will become exacerbated.

### 8.1.4 Hearing sensitivity

Following harmful exposure to noise your client may develop sensitivity to sounds in a number of ways:

- *Hyperacusis* – everyday sounds are perceived louder than they actually are.
- *Misophonia* – where certain sounds make the sufferer angry.
- *Phonophobia* – where certain sounds make the sufferer anxious.
- *Diplacusis* – where the same sound is perceived differently in each ear.
- *Recruitment* – where the sufferer has difficulty adjusting between loud and quiet noises.

## 8.2 Treatments

There are a variety of available treatments:

- Hearing aids – available on the NHS or privately.
- Hearing implants – these hearing aids are surgically implanted either deep inside the ear or attached to the skull.
- Sound therapy – particularly for tinnitus, this treatment aims to retrain the brain by tuning out the offending noise, often by introducing ambient noise. Sometimes the use of a 'sound pillow' at night will aid sleep.
- Cognitive Behavioural Therapy (CBT) and/or counselling – to help reduce anxiety and come to terms with the condition.

- Different ways of communicating – your client may need to learn new ways of communication, such as sign language. Depending on whether the hearing loss is total or not, your client may need the help of specialist speech and language therapists.

## 8.3 How negligence can arise

The MoD is required like any other employer to provide a safe system of work and, whenever possible, reduce the risks of injury to ALARP. The Health and Safety Executive provides advice to employers about their duties in accordance with the Health and Safety at Work etc Act 1974 and its associated Regulations, which can be summarised as follows:

- Control the noise exposure by making adjustments or engineering solutions.

- Change the work pattern or the layout of the workplace (i.e. not just rely on hearing protection).

- Provide the quietest machinery that will do the job (manufacturers also have a duty to limit noise of machinery to acceptable levels under the Supply of Machinery (Safety) Regulations 2008).

- Issue adequate hearing protection.

- Send workers for regular hearing checks.

- Provide health and safety training and information.

- Risk assess.

The Control of Noise at Work Regulations 2005 require employers to prevent or reduce the risks of noise exposure at work, so far as is reasonably practicable. This includes taking action when the average noise levels or any maximum noise level ('peak sound pressure') exceeds acceptable limits. The exposure limit values are currently 87 dB (calculated on an average daily or weekly basis) and/or a peak sound pressure of 140 dB. The length of exposure will also be highly relevant when assessing safety limits, because this contributes to the 'noise dose' that your client may have been exposed to and will be highly relevant for expert assessment.

When assessing whether a safe system of work is in place at a base or other facility, in addition to considering whether the above duties have been discharged, you might pay particular attention to whether:

- Certain working zones are designated as hazardous.
- Appropriate reminders and warnings are in place for personnel (i.e. to wear protection).
- Loud noises are caused successively or in unison, or in such circumstances where the noise may be amplified (e.g. underground or in a confined space).

Negligence may arise in a number of ways for your client and below are a few examples:

- They may have been tasked with duties that resulted in an exposure to harmful levels of noise which were not properly risk assessed.
- They may have not been provided with adequate training and/or PPE to protect their hearing.
- They may have already been medically downgraded for damage to their hearing but then negligently ordered by their chain of command to carry out duties which resulted in further, harmful

noise exposure (and therefore suffered an exacerbation of their injury).

- They may have been referred to a Medical Officer by their chain of command, or having presented to the medical centre themselves, but their symptoms may have been missed or ignored. Alternatively they may have been treated inadequately and not followed-up or referred for specialist assessment.

- Their hearing may not have been monitored regularly enough and/or hearing test results may have been ignored by medical staff, so they may have continued with tasks and/or deployments that potentially exacerbated their condition. Bear in mind that once a condition is diagnosed it may be appropriate to increase the regularity of follow-up assessments.

- They may have suffered harm as a result of exposure to harmful noise in circumstances where the noise was unexpected (e.g. an explosion), but which may have resulted from some negligent act or omission.

Some of the factors which may influence these scenarios are explored below.

### 8.3.1 Risk assessments

Risk assessments must be made in accordance with *JSP 375* and written down (see **Chapter 5**). Generic risk assessments should be treated with caution and should be checked against the particular circumstances of your client's noise exposure. For example, the risk of hearing injury in an open firing range will not necessarily be the same as that in a covered range or in a confined space where sound may be magnified.

In respect of the risks of hearing loss and injury, assessments should:

- Identify where there may be a risk from noise and who is likely to be affected.

- Contain a reliable estimate of the noise exposure.

- Identify what noise-control measures are needed and whether hearing protection is needed and, if so, where and what type.

- Identify personnel who are at particular risk and whether they should be regularly screened.

### 8.3.2 Personal protective equipment

The typical PPE used to help reduce noise exposure are:

- Ear defenders (or muffs) – These headsets provide a cup which covers the outer ear and are sound reducing.

- Ear plugs – These normally consist of foam or other substance in the form of a plug, which is either moulded (reusable) or expands when inserted into the inner ear (disposable). Special ear plugs were introduced during the Afghanistan War which permitted service personnel to maintain radio contact during operations whilst providing some protection.

- 'Double protection' – When both ear plugs and ear defenders are used to limit noise exposure.

Obviously, where sound is going to be excessive and PPE might not be sufficient then the safety to staff must be reassessed dynamically and in accordance with *JSP 375*. This may include avoiding the task all together or redeploying staff to a safe distance from the offending noise. You will also need to check whether the PPE provided to your client worked and/or fitted properly.

### 8.3.3 Training and education

Health and safety training for all personnel is provided annually and specific training should be provided to those personnel at high risk of hearing loss. In conjunction with any warnings about the risk of hearing loss and symptoms, this must include clear advice on how and when to use ear protection.

Whether or not the right training was delivered for your client and/or whether it would have made any material difference to the outcome of their injury will largely be a question of fact. You will need to obtain and scrutinise all training records that are disclosed. You may also need witness evidence to corroborate any allegations that the training was not given or inadequate.

Of course training without protection is meaningless and so whether your client was given the right hearing protection or any protection at all may be determinative. Equally, the Noise at Work Regulations 2005 impose duties on employees (i.e. which will apply to your client):

- To work in a way that is in accordance with their employer's instructions.
- To wear hearing protection in accordance with their employer's instructions.
- To take care of hearing protectors and noise-control equipment.
- To report faults and difficulties in using noise-control equipment.
- To attend occupational health appointments.

Where your client has not complied reasonably with requests and/or training then this may influence your appreciation of any litigation risk and/or risk of a finding of contributory negligence.

### 8.3.4 Clinical negligence

The MoD have been required to carry out regular hearing tests on personnel since 1976, but the regularity of these tests may depend on the risk posed to the particular service person and this in turn may depend on your client's trade and duties. Currently, hearing tests should also be carried out on new recruits. Hearing tests are normally carried out:

- At pre-entry to the service.
- Annually.
- Within six months prior to or after operational deployment.

A hearing test normally consists of placing the service person in a sound-proof room and exposing them to intermittent noises at different frequencies. The service person is asked to indicate when they can hear any specific noise by pressing a button. The results of these tests are plotted on an audiogram and assessed by an appropriate medical expert, who should be able to say whether the hearing loss is constitutional (i.e. part of the natural ageing process), or more likely noise-induced. The rule of thumb is that loss of hearing in the lower frequencies is more likely constitutional in nature, whereas loss of hearing in the higher frequencies may indicate noise-induced hearing loss.

Your client may have presented to their Medical Officer during their service, finding it difficult to hear high frequency noises, such as whistles, phones or buzzers, or find that they are straining to hear friends and family and often asking them to speak up, or in fact starting to rely more heavily on reading lips when communicating with others. In such circumstances they should be referred for assessment.

There are standards found in *JSP 950* in respect of when to assess personnel for hearing and what medical grading should apply (see **Chapter 4**). There is also guidance found in single-Service publications, which may be specific to service personnel in high risk roles, such as aircrew. You should request disclosure of any regulations for the assessment of personnel which may exist for their service and/or trade. A few things to bear in mind when considering your client's medical records:

- Hearing for service personnel is graded as follows:

  H1 – good hearing
  H2 – acceptable hearing
  H3 – impaired hearing
  H4 – poor hearing

  Any change in the H degree (except a drop from 1 to 2) will mandate a referral to a Consultant ENT surgeon for assessment.

- Those with a grading of H2 will be marked as a potential risk and this may influence their duties and employability.

- Those graded H3 or H4 will be graded either MLD (Medically Limited Deployable) or MND (Medically Non-Deployable). Realistically, most in the former category and all in the latter category will be medically discharged.

Clinical negligence can arise in a number of ways:

- Failing to carry out regular screening/hearing tests, or referring when one is indicated.

- Failing to treat hearing loss once it has been diagnosed (normally a referral to a specialist is mandated).

- Failing to medically downgrade or restrict duties (to avoid further exposure).

- Failing to properly inform the patient about the hearing loss and methods of mitigating that loss.

Anyone suspected of having suffered hearing loss should also be advised to avoid further exposure at home.

In respect of return to work, this should be carefully managed and a 'hearing conservation programme' put in place. This is most often done by providing a sick chit limiting the service person's duties until a full assessment is carried out, following which a temporary or permanent downgrade of their medical category may be appropriate. The chain of command should be made aware of any medical limitations as they will have access to your client's medical grading and employability standard.

## 8.4 Establishing liability

You will need to prove:

- The nature of the noise exposure i.e. that it in fact occurred in the way your client described it and was of a level that was capable of causing harm.
- That there was a breach of duty i.e. the exposure was negligent because of an unsafe system of work or clinical negligence (failure to medically downgrade).
- That the exposure caused your client injury and loss i.e. that your client's hearing loss was noise-induced, rather than caused by age or for some other reason.

Your client may have a relatively straightforward claim where they present with a medical history of good hearing but where injury or deterioration can be identified in the medical records following a specific negligent exposure to noise. But more often than not, they will present with a complex history of noise exposure; potentially many exposures from many sources over many years of service.

For some clients, their hearing loss may also have worsened as a result of age, which is often when the 'penny drops' for them and they are induced into asking questions about their condition and its cause. Others will have struggled with symptoms for many years, but either as a result of ignorance or fear that they would endanger their career had decided not to speak to a doctor. Such clients may face significant hurdles in respect of limitation, depending on their 'date of knowledge', so it will be important for you to ascertain not just how and when they were potentially exposed to harmful noise but also when they first noticed that they had symptoms of hearing loss.

You will need to instruct a medical expert, normally a Consultant ENT surgeon, Audiologist or similar expert. You will be led by them in respect of which exposures caused what damage, but the expert will need to be led by you in respect of the history, timing and factual circumstances of each exposure. They will need an understanding of the noise exposure, both in respect of the level of sound and the period of time for which your client was exposed. More often than not they will make an educated guess about these factors when dealing with a case involving gun fire, for example. But as a case develops there may be a need for further expert input to help your medical expert reach firmer conclusions (see below).

In addition to taking a detailed history from your client, you may be assisted where they have had regular hearing tests throughout their career. After obtaining your client's medical records, you should collate and tabulate any hearing test results and any comments provided by treating doctors, as well as review their medical profile. You will need to check these details against your client's instructions to highlight any inconstancies. You can fall into a trap of assuming that your client's condition is a result of exposure to noise in combat or in firing ranges, only to discover that their hearing was damaged well before any operational deployment but not properly investigated. Equally, where there may be some doubt about the specific exposure that caused your client's loss, the MoD may seek to argue that they probably suffered the injury during combat and thereby attract combat immunity (see **3.3**).

In respect of the nature of the noise exposure itself and the alleged breach of duty, you will need to obtain factual evidence and statements to corroborate when and how the exposure occurred. Bear in mind that where your client has suffered multiple exposures, then many different witnesses may be needed to progress a claim, and this will become labour intensive and costly.

Assuming that your medical expert has indicated that your client's hearing is probably noise induced (as opposed to constitutional), you may then need further guidance from other experts to help clarify and buttress this suggestion. Normally this means obtaining a report from an engineer and health and safety specialist, to assess the likely level of noise exposure and any inadequacies in providing a safe system of work. They may also need to comment on the attenuation (i.e. protection) against noise exposure provided by PPE and whether it was adequate in the circumstances. Such expert evidence is often left to the later stages of litigation. This is in part because of the expense, which may be avoided if an admission of breach of duty is forthcoming, but also because disclosure will need to be completed and statements made available to the expert before a fully reasoned opinion can be given. Obtaining a screening report at an early stage may assist in limiting litigation risk and inform your enquiries. In addition to your client's medical and training records, you may need to request specific disclosure of:

- Regulations specific to your client's Service or trade which deal with protecting against hearing loss.

- The manuals and/or specifications for any weaponry, machinery or devices that may have caused – Such disclosure may be limited because of the interests of national security but can often be redacted to allow disclosure of information relevant to noise exposure and safety precautions. You might also be able to obtain disclosure from the manufacturer directly.

- All risk assessments and any guidance to commanders in respect of hearing risks to personnel.

- Sound level monitoring records for the base, establishment or ship where your client was stationed.

- MoD studies and/or manuals for the use of hearing related PPE.

In respect of liability for clinical negligence, the majority of breaches in the context of military claims will be those made by an occupational health doctor/GP (i.e. the Medical Officer) and an expert with a similar specialty should be instructed to report.

## 8.5 Damages

A suitable medical expert should be instructed to report on your client's condition and prognosis (normally an ENT surgeon). Sometimes your client's prognosis will be complicated by the fact that their hearing is likely to worsen with age. In other cases, prognosis will be guarded and very much dependent on whether your client is protected from further exposures and/or is able to engage with therapy. The other aspect that should not be underestimated is the psychological harm that might be caused as a result of the hearing condition and the impact on your client's career.

You may need a number of other experts from different fields:

- A Consultant Psychiatrist – to comment on any psychiatric condition and prognosis.

- A GP or Occupational Health expert with a military background – to comment on medical downgrade issues i.e. continued employability within the forces and/or in respect of clinical negligence.

- An employment consultant with a specialism in military careers – to comment on employability, loss of career and any ongoing disadvantage in the employment market.

Your client may have miscellaneous further losses:

- Aids and appliances – hearing aids or implants and any treatment or replacement costs.
- Medical expenses – the cost of therapy and/or medication for any psychiatric condition.
- Care – your client may require loved ones or family to assist with a variety of tasks, for example, in avoiding crowds or noisy places. Alternatively, your client may need to pay privately for services.

Where your client's military career has ended, they may have a very significant claim for loss of earnings, benefits and pension. In ***Inglis v Ministry of Defence [2019] EWHC 1153 (QB)*** a former Royal Marine was awarded £545,766 for his NIHL, to include £25,000 in respect of PSLA. The case is considered in more detail in **Chapter 13**.

## 8.6 Points for practice

- Noise-induced hearing loss is a preventable disease. It can be caused by an acute exposure to excessive sound (140 dB or more), or by a long-term exposure to loud noises (levels higher than 75–85 dB).
- Service personnel are at risk of hearing loss and associated conditions. The MoD has a duty of care to minimise these risks to ALARP. This includes providing a safe system of work, risk assessing, providing PPE, providing adequate training and occupational health screenings.
- Causation will be your main focus in these claims and this will involve a thorough review of the medical records, audiograms and history. Most clients will present with a lengthy history of

noise exposure, and so these case require a great deal of 'front loading' to investigate and assess every potential noise exposure.

- Because of the stoic nature of service personnel, some will "soldier on" despite worsening symptoms in their hearing. If this was the case with your client then you may face significant hurdles in respect of contributory negligence and/or limitation.

- Bear in mind that your client may come to you for one type of claim, unrelated to their hearing, but may also have an unexplored hearing loss claim. Where this hearing loss is not actionable, for whatever reason, then this may impact on the viability of any other civil claim, because it might be argued that they would have lost their military career as a result of the hearing loss in any event.

- The generic disclosure provided by the MoD in hearing loss claims is voluminous. Consider your approach to such generic disclosure, the need to clarify what documents are specifically relevant in your client's case and the cost of considering the disclosure (which should also be reflected in your client's costs budget).

- In addition to a duty of care to protect the hearing of personnel, the MoD have a statutory obligation to protect the public from excessive noise. Their regulatory document *JSP 418* ("*Management of Environmental Protection in Defence*") and the associated leaflet 04-1 ("*Environmental Noise*") sets out its policy in respect of protecting and compensating the public.

# CHAPTER NINE
# WELFARE, PTSD AND STRESS AT WORK

## Introduction

Service personnel sometimes live and work in dangerous environments. They may encounter traumatic events, particularly in combat. Experience and training can build resilience to these events, but there is no foolproof defence to the potential impact on their mental health and wellbeing. Of course it is not just traumatic events that can contribute mental illness and, like any other vocation, work can be stressful for its own sake and when excessive, harmful.

In this chapter we will consider the psychiatric harm that might be caused to service personnel as a result of stress at work, combat and/or other traumatic events. It is important to appreciate that post-traumatic stress disorder (PTSD) and stress at work are entirely different things, but in the military context they can arise together and interrelate in important ways, not least in respect of the systems that are in place to identify those at risk and help alleviate their suffering. It is these occupational welfare systems that we must consider first.

## 9.1 Occupational support

There are a number of systems and processes in place in the military working environment to enable the management of the wellbeing of service personnel. These are largely in place to ensure operational effectiveness, but also to satisfy health and safety obligations under domestic law.

Whether occupational support was not provided and/or welfare policy was not followed may be very relevant to considerations of the issue of breach of duty in respect of a civil claim and particularly in relation to stress at work and PTSD (mentioned below).

### 9.1.1 Welfare

The MoD's welfare policy can be found in *JSP 770: Tri-Service Operational and Non-Operational Welfare Policy*. The following extract from the 'welfare charter' provides a succinct introduction to this system:

> *"Service personnel are not merely civilians in uniform; there are few groups in our society who are required by the nature of their duties to risk potential emotional or physical injury or expressly sacrifice their lives for the nation. Thus they form a distinctive group within UK society with support needs that greatly differ from many of those prevailing in civilian life. Welfare is recognised as an important and integral element of operational efficiency and MOD has a duty of care to ensure that welfare measures are in place, within the funding confines, wherever personnel are required to serve. The measures should provide timely and effective assistance necessary to maintain operational effectiveness. Welfare is therefore core Armed Forces business and it will be delivered through a mix of public and Service non-public funds and charitable sources."*

In practice, the military welfare system involves layers of support for service personnel and their families, both at home and when deployed abroad, particularly but not exclusively when they are wounded, injured or sick (WIS) and to those leaving service. *JSP 770* is supported by a number of single-Service regulations and together they set out:

- Who is entitled to welfare services.
- Who is responsible for these services.
- How to deliver, monitor and record the services provided.

The responsibility of welfare is spread across the Services, starting with the responsibility for each service person to take care of their own welfare. However, this responsibility is focused on the chain of command and, in particular, the Commanding Officer.

For our purposes, welfare services will be relevant when dealing with WIS personnel. Details of how WIS personnel are to be managed are first found in *Chapter 5 of JSP 770: the Tri-Service Recovery Policy*, which introduces the Defence Recoverability Capability (DRC), an initiative between the MoD and various charities to provide coordinated support and management of WIS personnel. When a service person is eligible for support, a number of things may happen depending on their circumstances and the relevant 'recovery pathway' (a generic term used to describe the route through which actions are taken for or by WIS personnel). This may include:

- Assignment to a Personnel Recovery Unit (PRU) or Centre (PRC) – WIS personnel who require specialist rehabilitation beyond their unit's capabilities will either be assigned to a PRU or a PRC. PRCs are run in conjunction with Service charities and are often residential.

- The appointment of a Personnel Recovery Officer (PRO) – they act as a case manager and primary contact for the WIS person.

- An Individual Recovery Plan (IRP) – An IRP should be tailored to the specific circumstances of the WIS person and incorporate all aspects of their recovery according to the acronym HARD-FACTS: Health; Accommodation; Relocation; Drugs, Alcohol and Stress; Finance and Benefits; Attitude, Thinking, Behaviour and Welfare; Children and Family; Training, Education and Employment; Supporting Agencies.

In addition, all actions and decisions should be recorded electronically on the welfare management system. The Army and RAF use WISMIS (Wounded, Injured and Sick Management Information System). The Royal Navy may also use FECA ('Flotilla Employment Capability Application'). Both are platforms on which relevant welfare records should be kept and allow commanders to view the current location, condition and recovery plan for any WIS personnel.

### 9.1.2 Unit health committees

The Commanding Officer of any unit has sole responsibility for all the service personnel in that unit. Unit Health Committees (UHCs) are held to review and manage the physical, mental and spiritual health of the unit. Single-Service regulations will provide commanders with guidance on:

- the purpose of UHCs;
- how frequently to hold them; and
- how they should be constituted.

Various stakeholders should normally be involved in UHCs, to include the CO, senior officers, the Senior Medical Officer, the Padre and other senior staff within the chain of command. UHCs aim to help ensure that units are at all times fit and ready to deploy or, as an establishment, that the establishment is efficient and able to deliver whatever services are required.

Another aspect of these meetings is to manage individual service personnel through discussions with medical staff, and this is where they may become very relevant to practitioners. For example, all service personnel who are not medically fully deployable must be managed through unit health committees. Where appropriate, the CO will discuss how to restrict their duties with their direct line manager and this may include agreeing a Gradual Return to Work (GRoW) programme. These are workplace-based support programmes that are normally appropriate where a WIS service person is rehabilitating and in the hope of returning them to full duties. A GRoW programme must be considered, documented and reviewed. The responsibility of a GRoW programme is jointly held by the CO and medical staff.

All commanders should have access to employability standard (JMES) for their service personnel, but specific medical conditions cannot normally be discussed between medical staff and commanders without the consent of the individual service person. Consent is normally waived when they provide their commanders with a sick chit, which will normally allow the commander to discuss their condition in unit health committee meetings. This may be important when assessing whether or not your client's chain of command was aware of the nature of their medical condition and/or limitations.

### 9.1.3 Stress management training

All personnel are given health and safety training which is aimed at increasing their awareness of mental health issues and stress management. *Chapter 17 of JSP 375* deals exclusively with stress management and provides a helpful introduction to the objectives of such training. The following is a summary of the key points:

- Stress management training is mandatory and should form part of annual health and safety training

- Service personnel are taught to recognise stress in themselves and in others, and to report to their chain of command when appropriate.

- Managers are taught to identify stress in those they manage, including the obligation to proactively look for signs of stress. A list of symptoms of stress is provided as well as guidance on the emotional signs that stressed personnel may exhibit. Importantly, changes in behaviour

- In addition to stress management training, *JSP 375* requires commanders to carry out risk assessments on all manner of tasks and to include stress as a factor in their assessments. This is especially the case when units are undergoing organisational changes and/or where service personnel may not have received sufficient training or support for their duties.

### 9.1.4 Trauma risk management

Trauma Risk Management (TRiM) is a system designed to identify and record those who may have witnessed or been involved in traumatic events, and who might benefit from increased support from their chain of command, whether through simple monitoring, counselling, pastoral care and/or referral to primary healthcare.

The current Tri-Service policy can be found at *Chapter 2 of Part 2 JSP 770*, which was originally developed by the Royal Marines but successfully rolled out to all the Services. Each Service has its own policy, but the provisions and objectives remain largely the same:

- Royal Navy – *BR 3 Chapter 34, Annex H*
- British Army – *LFSO 3217*
- RAF – *AP 9012, Chapter 10*

TRiM is not exclusively used in relation to operations and can cover any traumatic incident that may have occurred to a service person, including in their home and family life. All TRiM interventions should be recorded on JPA and it remains a responsibility of the chain of command to provide training and implement its proactive use.

### 9.1.5 Suicide vulnerability risk management

The purpose of a Suicide Vulnerability Risk Management (SVRM) policy is to help identify those who may be at risk of suicide, and give structure to subsequent support and monitoring. Each Service has its own policy, which all focuses on:

- engagement with the individual;
- identifying risk factors;
- the development of a care assessment plan;
- liaising with medical staff; and
- regular review.

As with TRiM interventions, all actions and decisions should be carefully documented on the JPA system. Where a service person has been identified as at risk, then failures to adhere to SVRM policy may result in a claim where a lack of support and appropriate management has led to self-harm or death.

### 9.1.6 Operations

There should be a number of processes in place to help service personnel manage the challenges of operational deployment and combat.

- **Training**

Preoperational, operational and post operational briefings should be provided to include training on the risks of operational stress and PTSD.

- **The 'Harmony Guidelines'**

These are different for each Service and should stipulate the length of time that any unit should be deployed on operational tour. The Army, for example, normally requires that each tour of duty should not last for more than six months and that they should be followed by a 24-month break. However, in reality this may not happen and you should ascertain the actual amount of time that your client may have spent on operational tour.

- **Decompression**

This is a period of time during which service personnel are meant to rest, relax and reflect following operational tour. This does not always happen and you should check what breaks from service your client was afforded. Failing to provide decompression is a possible breach of duty and may increase the stress and risk of mental health issues occurring or becoming exacerbated.

### 9.1.7 Implications for civil claims

The military welfare system is comprehensive and well documented. It cannot be underestimated as a tool for exploring and potentially buttressing civil claims:

- The MoD acknowledge their duties to service personnel; welfare is a core part of the human resource structure in the military.
- Detailed records are kept (or should be kept) electronically which will set out your client's condition, needs, employability and any recovery plan. This information should be available to their managers.
- Failures to follow these processes, whether to monitor, train or refer, may lead to a breach of duty.
- These systems often have input from primary healthcare, so you may come across actions or failures which may amount to a breach of clinical duty of care.
- In addition to the joint and single-Service provisions, you may find that your client's unit has its own policies and guidance material which supplement the management of WIS personnel.

## 9.2 PTSD claims

Post-Traumatic Stress Disorder (PTSD) is a condition that has become somewhat synonymous with combat and service personnel, but can in fact affect anyone from any walk of life. It is nevertheless a very serious condition, often long-term, disabling and a recognised risk to service personnel. It is also an underreported condition. A study by King's College London of nearly 9,000 service personnel was published in 2018 in the British Journal of Psychiatry and showed that among veterans deployed in a combat role to Iraq or Afghanistan, 17% reported symptoms suggesting probable PTSD, compared to 6% deployed in support roles such as doctors and aircrew. This indicated that service personnel deployed in combat were far more likely to develop the condition.

### 9.2.1 What is PTSD and how is it caused?

PTSD is a reactionary anxiety disorder normally caused by a traumatic event or multiple traumatic events. Some examples of traumatic events might be:

- Being in danger and/or helpless.
- Seeing others in danger and being helpless to assist.
- Seeing distressing events, such as death or serious injury.
- Being responsible or believing that you are responsible for death or injury to others.
- Being assaulted, raped or the victim of sustained bullying.
- Women can also suffer PTSD following a difficult birth.

There is still some uncertainty about why some people suffer PTSD after traumatic events and others do not. Your client may be pre-disposed to PTSD because of their genetics, their pre-existing mental health issues or a combination of these factors. The crucial element, the spark, is the traumatic event. Sufferers may present with a number of symptoms:

- Flashbacks
- Nightmares
- Insomnia
- Distraction and lacking focus
- Irritability
- Hyper-arousal (and hyper-vigilance) – being constantly on guard and/or fearing attack
- Suicidal ideation
- Nausea, headaches, dizziness, chest pains and stomach aches

They may also have feelings of:

- Losing control
- Guilt
- Shame
- Anger
- Distrust

PTSD is an insidious disease, which can surface immediately after a traumatic incident or, in some cases, take many weeks, months or even years to manifest. This is sometimes referred to as '*delayed-onset PTSD*', although not a separate condition in itself. Sometimes this delayed onset is triggered by another traumatic event, for example a car accident, or in conjunction with another psychiatric condition. In such cases we might say that the PTSD has been exacerbated (made worse) and/or accelerated (brought forward).

For those who may have experienced repeated traumatic events, PTSD can become more complex and persistent; referred to as '*complex PTSD*' or CPTSD. This tends to take place in individuals who have suffered trauma in childhood or at the hands of someone who was in a position of trust, and is quite typical in circumstances involving historic abuse, for example.

From the perspective of service personnel, most you encounter with PTSD would have developed the condition as a result of exposure in combat to stressful and life-threatening events. Typically, they will relive these traumatic incidents through nightmares and flashbacks. They may also experience an onset of symptoms by 'triggers' in their everyday life. A trigger is an event which sparks a flashback and precipitates an onset of symptoms. Triggers can vary entirely between sufferers and are specific to the person. These episodes can be upsetting, exhausting and in serious cases disabling for the individual. They can also be traumatic to their loved ones and acquaintances. Sufferers with PTSD will often engage in behavior which is indicative of their condition. Below are a few examples:

- They may be destructive. For example, they may have difficulty maintaining relationships and/or may turn to self-harm. In other cases, a sufferer may contemplate or attempt suicide. Some will succeed.

- Research suggests that men and women suffer PTSD in different ways and it is thought that women may tend to be more self-destructive whilst men will tend to be outwardly destructive. This is somewhat of a generalisation and the experience of PTSD can still vary greatly between people and the sexes.

- They may become more disposed to risk taking behaviour. On operational tour, for example, this may manifest in behaviour which goes beyond heroic and becomes reckless.

- They may turn to alcohol and/or other drugs to help manage their symptoms. Your client may be an alcoholic or a drug addict and these may indicate an underlying PTSD problem. Drugs are strictly forbidden and screened for regularly in the military.

- Avoidance is another category of behaviour that sufferers might engage in. They will do what they can to avoid triggering symptoms these and this may mean stepping away from their commitments, loved ones and career, as well as missing appointments for treatment and therapy. In the military context you may come across a client who has been disciplined for going absent without leave (AWOL). This is sometimes an indicator that they are suffering with mental health issues, possibly PTSD.

- In very serious cases of PTSD where treatment has not helped or been provided, a patient may dissociate completely from reality and develop *psychosis*. Although this is rare, in such circumstances you must put in place steps to consider your client's capacity and this will necessarily involve assessment by a Psychiatrist.

From the perspective of a military claims lawyer, you will have to be aware of these behavioural issues when reviewing your client's records and particularly when asking whether or not these behaviours may have indicated to their chain of command and/or doctors that your client had a mental health issue.

### 9.2.2 Condition and prognosis

The condition and prognosis for PTSD sufferers varies too greatly to be able to give any clear indication here. Some patients take months to recover, others years. Most medical experts will agree that early intervention and treatment will result in a better prognosis. Where patients have made no improvement in their first year, despite treatment, then their prognosis is usually poor. For very serious cases there may be very little likelihood of total recovery, but treatment may help alleviate symptoms and develop coping strategies. Your client's long-term prognosis may depend on a number of factors, such as:

- The severity of and regularity of the trauma (and if it is ongoing).
- Their physical condition (any ongoing injury or pain).
- Support at home.
- Any pre-existing and/or ongoing mental health issues (80% of PTSD patients will suffer with other mental health disorders).
- The availability and/or lack of treatment to date.
- Alcohol and/or other drug misuse.

You will need to instruct a Consultant Psychiatrist to assess your client and prepare a report. Ideally they will have an interest or specialty in treating PTSD. They do not necessarily need a military background or have experience of treating service personnel, though this sometimes helps with other issues in the case. They may need to comment on:

- Your client's condition and any functional impairment.
- The cause of their PTSD, including any contribution to their condition that may be due to pre-existing conditions or factors unrelated to the claim.
- Their likely prognosis.
- Treatment options and cost.
- Any pre-existing conditions and/or susceptibility to psychiatric injury.

In respect of treatment, there are several types that are recommended, including:

- Watchful waiting – Some who suffer PTSD symptoms improve within a short space of time, sometimes be referred to as '*partial PTSD*'. For these early phases of the condition, a period of observing symptoms to see if they improve or get worse is recommended. A follow-up session should normally be arranged within the first month of onset.
- Antidepressants – approximately 60-70% of patients with PTSD respond well to anti-depressants. Patients describe an improvement in their sleep and hyper-arousal in particular.
- Trauma-focused cognitive behavioral therapy (TF CBT) – this modifies traditional CBT techniques but may include confronting the offending trauma.

- Eye-Movement Desensitisation Reprocessing (EMDR) – a relatively new treatment that involves using eye-movement, finger tapping or sound to alter how a patient perceives the trauma.

- Group therapy – some patients have described an improvement in their symptoms having been able to discuss them openly with others, including other sufferers of the condition.

In practice, a combination of treatments may be used and depending on how the patient may react to each, a treatment plan can be varied accordingly. The stress of litigation and the inevitable challenge of having to face the issues surrounding the trauma time and again will often mean that treatment is unlikely to be successful until after the litigation is concluded. So you may expect your medical expert to provide a prognosis and treatment plan on the basis that the litigation first concludes.

### 9.2.3 How negligence can arise

Below are a few examples of circumstances in the military context where negligence may have caused and/or exacerbated PTSD in your client:

- They may have suffered serious injury during training or deployment, which has resulted in PTSD.

- They may have been bullied or harassed at work (for PTSD sufferers this is likely to have taken the form of a prolonged campaign of harassment).

- They may have been the victim of threats and/or violence (see **Chapter 10**).

- They may have had their symptoms ignored by their chain of command, who failed to take action to refer them or otherwise manage them appropriately.

- They may have had their symptoms ignored by their Medical Officer, who may have failed to diagnose, refer for specialist treatment, medically downgrade and/or arrange a follow-up appointment.

- They may have been diagnosed with PTSD and/or identified as a risk to themselves, but then not followed up through the non-clinical welfare system (see **9.1**).

The National Institute for Health and Care Excellence ('NICE') publishes online guidance on best treatment for PTSD (NICE guideline NG116). The guidelines are very helpful and can be used as a point of reference when assessing your client's treatment history and instructing medical experts.

### 9.2.4 Establishing liability

Your expert psychiatrist should be able to comment on:

- The principle cause of the PTSD.

- Whether there was any exacerbation or acceleration of the condition as a result of either a clinical failure or by non-clinical management (i.e. your client's chain of command).

In respect of the principle cause of the PTSD, you will need to provide factual evidence (or at least a description) in your instructions to the expert so that they may assess whether any particular incident was sufficiently traumatic so as to cause PTSD.

Bear in mind that:

- If the traumatic incident was caused as a result of negligence, then your client may be able to claim for the onset of PTSD in its entirety. Alternatively, their underlying PTSD may have been exacerbated by some other, negligent act or omission.

- A breach may lay in a failure to identify, diagnose and/or treat the condition after onset. In such a case your client will have a claim for an acceleration and/or exacerbation of the condition. Such a claim can remain financially significant, depending on the underlying nature of the PTSD and whether and when it might have otherwise manifested and impacted on their military career.

- Where your client has a pre-existing mental health issue and/or has suffered a series of traumas or stresses in their life (none of which may be related to the claim), then there will probably be complex arguments about causation and loss.

- Where your client has suffered PTSD as a result of combat, they may be precluded from bringing a civil claim because of the doctrine of combat immunity (see **3.3**), but this would not affect an ability to bring a claim for a subsequent (non-combat related) breach of duty, which may have exacerbated the condition.

Where the claim involves alleged clinical negligence, your expert psychiatrist should also be able to comment on the impact of any:

- Delay in diagnosis.
- Misdiagnosis.
- Delay in treatment.
- Appropriateness of any treatment.

Many medical experts will agree that the prognosis for PTSD sufferers is almost always better where there has been early intervention and treatment, but the effectiveness of treatment remains arguable. Sometimes the condition can be so severe that medical experts will conclude that earlier intervention may not have improved the patient's prognosis in any significant way. This is appoint often argued by defendants and, if successful, may significantly impact on the value of the claim.

In respect of the standard of care:

- If the negligent act or omission was that of a psychiatrist, then in addition to assessing condition and prognosis your psychiatric expert may also be willing to comment on breach of duty.

- If the breach of duty was the responsibility of a Medical Officer, then you will need a GP or occupational health physician, ideally with military experience, to comment on the standard of care. Medical Officers should be well versed in recognising the symptoms PTSD, but they would normally refer the patient to the nearest DCMH for assessment and diagnosis by a psychiatrist. Negligence claims against Medical Officers in this context will tend to focus on failures to refer.

- Your client may have been treated negligently by a Community Psychiatric Nurses (CPN), but given that these individuals are not doctors, the bar for fault is set quite high and you may struggle to prove negligence except in the most serious of failures. More often than not, the referral for treatment by a CPN would have been made by a Medical Officer or Consultant Psychiatrist, and the CPN might be expected to rely on the diagnosis made by such clinicians and not to second guess them.

- You should also scrutinise the treatment your client received after their military career ended and they transferred their care to a civilian GP practice. Civilian GPs are not necessarily best suited to deal with service personnel and/or PTSD. They may miss the symptoms or over diagnose the condition; assuming that PTSD comes part and parcel with military service when in fact your client has a different condition altogether.

Clinical failures are regrettable but also very challenging from a claimant's perspective. Your client may wish to argue that they presented to their doctor with classic signs of PTSD, but some experts will argue that presentation is rarely 'typical' and it is a highly personalised condition. Diagnosing PTSD is sometimes challenging for doctors because the condition has symptoms that overlap with a number of other psychiatric conditions, such as other anxiety or adjustment disorders. As such, an expert psychiatrist may be forced to accept that an alternative diagnosis was not necessarily negligent. Patients may also suffer with multiple conditions. For example, it is perhaps unsurprising that a service person who has developed PTSD and lost their military career goes on to develop depression.

Much will depend on the contemporaneous medical records. A judge is more likely to be swayed by these records rather than the account given by your client many years after the event. Your client's condition may also be so severe that it may cause a judge to doubt the reliability of their evidence; often PTSD sufferers will have trouble concentrating and with their memory, especially under stress.

Given the variety of potential breaches and standards of care that may apply to a case, it will be essential for you to:

- Obtain and review all the medical records.
- Prepare a chronology.
- Identify which appointments are relevant to your client's claim, who the clinician involved was and their specialty (for the purposes of assessing the standard of care).
- Check the chronology with your client.

You will also need to review your client's pre-military medical history, and this may involve tracing their civilian GP records to several practices. Where your client has a pre-existing condition or susceptibility, for example, where they have had a troubled past or been the victim of abuse, your medical expert will need to be aware of those facts and address what may have contributed to your client's current condition.

As mentioned above, sufferers of PTSD may wish to avoid treatment because they find confronting the trauma that caused their condition difficult, or because they fear their symptoms will be triggered. They may also be concerned about the impact that a diagnosis will have on their military career. As such, they may have missed medical appointments, and this might fuel any argument that they have not mitigated their loss. Just as frequently service personnel may 'soldier on' despite worsening symptoms. If this was the case with your client then they may face hurdles in respect of both contributory negligence and/or limitation.

Your client's claim may relate to a failure by their chain of command to recognise their symptoms and intervene (either by referring them to a Medical Officer or taking steps to engage with them and adjust their work). In such circumstances you may be able to argue that managers should have had training to help them identify the symptoms of PTSD and act accordingly (see **9.1**). Normally, your client would have to show that they engaged in extreme and/or uncharacteristic behaviour to establish that (i) reasonable steps could have been taken and (ii) any harm was foreseeable. Here your client's personnel file and welfare records might assist, especially where they have a consistent record of good behaviour and appraisals, or where they may have already been identified 'at risk' and requiring additional support. In either case, whether any earlier intervention or failure to support would have made any material difference to your client's condition or prognosis will be a question for the medical expert.

## 9.3 Stress at work claims

Stress is a vastly underestimated problem. In the financial year 2017/18 alone there was estimated to have been 595,000 workers in the UK suffering from work-related stress, depression and/or anxiety, accounting for 15.4 million lost working days that year. However, we also must appreciate the benefits of stress. It can hone our concentration and push us to succeed and achieve things in our daily lives. This is something that the courts recognise too. So the question is one of balance. Where the balance has gone wrong, this can lead to harm.

For the vast majority of their service, service personnel will not be deployed or on operational tour, but based at home, undertaking day-to-day duties and 'defence business', often involving complex planning, logistical exercises and administrative tasks. They are also regularly appraised and under the scrutiny of promotional courses and boards. This can lead to stress and so workloads need to be managed appropriately.

### 9.3.1 How negligence can arise

A stress at work claim will normally involve circumstances where an employee has suffered from a recognisable psychiatric condition as a result of some act or omission (a failure to take reasonable steps) by their employer. Below are a few examples of circumstances:

- They may be 'overworked' and tasked with too many duties and/or with little support.
- They may not be overworked as such but are struggling for other reasons, for example because of underlying mental health issues or problems at home.
- They may have been deployed or having returned from operational tour, with little or no rest, decompression, supervision and/or support.
- They may have complained about or presented with symptoms of stress to their Medical Officer, who may have failed to diagnose, refer for treatment, medically downgrade and/or arrange a follow-up appointment.

### 9.3.2 Establishing liability

You will need to establish that your client:

- has suffered a psychiatric condition;

- that was caused by an act and/or omission by their line manager and/or chain of command; and
- that the harm was foreseeable.

The case of ***Hatton v Sutherland [2002] EWCA Civ 76*** provided the most comprehensive guidance for stress at work claims, in which Lady Hale laid down 16 guiding principles:

1. *There are no special control mechanisms applying to claims for psychiatric (or physical) illness or injury arising from the stress of doing the work the employee is required to do. The ordinary principles of employer's liability apply.*

2. *The threshold question is whether this kind of harm to this particular employee was reasonably foreseeable: this has two components (a) an injury to health (as distinct from occupational stress) which (b) is attributable to stress at work (as distinct from other factors).*

3. *Foreseeability depends upon what the employer knows (or ought reasonably to know) about the individual employee. Because of the nature of mental disorder, it is harder to foresee than physical injury, but may be easier to foresee in a known individual than in the population at large. An employer is usually entitled to assume that the employee can withstand the normal pressures of the job unless he knows of some particular problem or vulnerability.*

4. *The test is the same whatever the employment: there are no occupations which should be regarded as intrinsically dangerous to mental health.*

5. *Factors likely to be relevant in answering the threshold question include:*

a. *The nature and extent of the work done by the employee. Is the workload much more than is normal for the particular job? Is the work particularly intellectually or emotionally demanding for this employee? Are demands being made of this employee unreasonable when compared with the demands made of others in the same or comparable jobs? Or are there signs that others doing this job are suffering harmful levels of stress. Is there an abnormal level of sickness or absenteeism in the same job or the same department?*

b. *Signs from the employee of impending harm to health. Has he a particular problem or vulnerability? Has he already suffered from illness attributable to stress at work? Have there recently been frequent or prolonged absences which are uncharacteristic of him? Is there reason to think that these are attributable to stress at work, for example because of complaints or warnings from him or others?*

6. *The employer is generally entitled to take what he is told by his employee at face value, unless he has good reason to think to the contrary. He does not generally have to make searching enquiries of the employee or seek permission to make further enquiries of his medical advisers.*

7. *To trigger a duty to take steps, the indications of impending harm to health arising from stress at work must be plain enough for any reasonable employer to realise that he should do something about it.*

8. *The employer is only in breach of duty if he has failed to take the steps which are reasonable in the circumstances, bearing in mind the magnitude of the risk of harm occurring, the gravity of the harm which may occur, the costs and practicability of preventing it, and the justifications for running the risk.*

9. *The size and scope of the employer's operation, its resources and the demands it faces are relevant in deciding what is reasonable;*

*these include the interests of other employees and the need to treat them fairly, for example, in any redistribution of duties.*

10. *An employer can only reasonably be expected to take steps which are likely to do some good: the court is likely to need expert evidence on this.*

11. *An employer who offers a confidential advice service, with referral to appropriate counselling or treatment services, is unlikely to be found in breach of duty.*

12. *If the only reasonable and effective step would have been to dismiss or demote the employee, the employer will not be in breach of duty in allowing a willing employee to continue in the job.*

13. *In all cases, therefore, it is necessary to identify the steps which the employer both could and should have taken before finding him in breach of his duty of care.*

14. *The claimant must show that that breach of duty has caused or materially contributed to the harm suffered. It is not enough to show that occupational stress has caused the harm.*

15. *Where the harm suffered has more than one cause, the employer should only pay for that proportion of the harm suffered which is attributable to his wrongdoing, unless the harm is truly indivisible. It is for the defendant to raise the question of apportionment.*

16. *The assessment of damages will take account of any pre-existing disorder or vulnerability and of the chance that the claimant would have succumbed to a stress related disorder in any event.*

There have been a number of cases which have followed ***Hatton*** which have sought to expand on these principles. It is beyond the scope of this book to consider all of these authorities. For now, ***Hatton*** remains authoritative and its principles should be the starting point for your analysis of any particular claim. Whilst the principles are intended to apply equally to all forms of employment, these cases will be very fact specific and depend on the nature of the work and working environment. There are some points specific to military claims which may help or hinder your client's case:

- *Occupational health* – Defendants to stress at work claims will seek refuge in the provision of occupational health services, but this is not a panacea. Arguably, the military system for monitoring occupational health is far more stringent and in-depth than in the civilian sector. So it might be argued that with such a comprehensive occupational health system in place, there is little else that a defendant could do to identify vulnerable personnel and reduce the risk of harm. However, this cuts both ways because the system involves strict measures which regulate and inform management about stress at work, including mandatory monitoring processes, discussions between medical staff and managers, return to work programmes and readily accessible information relating to employability. These facts may help you argue that reasonable steps should have been taken to adjust duties and reduce the risk of harm.

- *Training* – Stress management training in the military is comprehensive. This encourages service personnel to recognise the symptoms of stress in themselves and in others. Commanders have a significant responsibility to monitor and maintain the health of their personnel, in fact their effectiveness as commanders is often gauged by how healthy their units are and whether they are operationally deployable. So you can argue that managing stress is intrinsic to what they do. Equally, where your client has not received appropriate training, this may amount to a breach of duty.

- *Orders* – Your client will be under orders to complete their tasks and duties. The military is a hierarchical system and refusing to comply with orders, inefficiency at work and failing to complete tasks can all result in reprimands and discipline. In these ways, service personnel will feel significant pressure to carry out their work and the dynamic between them and their commander can be very different to that between an employee and a manager in the civilian sector. Again this may be an important factor when assessing the obligation on service personnel to report their symptoms. They may argue that they have little or no choice but to continue with their work.

- *Culture and stigma* – Service personnel are generally reluctant to complain about illness and even less so about stress or psychological issues. This may be because it is the culture to "soldier on", and you may find service personnel will carry out their work with little regard to their own health. Alternatively, this may be because of the fear that such admissions will have on their careers and promotion prospects. Such concerns are very real for personnel who plan on serving long careers and/or whose families rely entirely on their income. These issues are acknowledged in the MoD welfare and associated policies, but a failure to raise concerns with their chain of command may be fatal to a stress at work claim (and often is).

- *Workload* – Service personnel will tend to have versatile job descriptions. Their duties and responsibilities can vary greatly and may encompass a mixture of physical and sedentary tasks. This can create problems in finding an appropriate comparator in cases involving alleged 'overwork'. Ideally, these will take the form of witness statements from colleagues in similar roles, who may be able to corroborate that your client (at the same rank and with the same duties) was tasked with too many duties.

- *Bullying and harassment* – Bullying at work is also a recognised factor for stress. Whilst this can happen in both civilian roles and in the military, the service complaints process (the military's grievance process) can be protracted and hugely exhausting for complainants. Were it has been managed poorly, this may also impact on stress at work and buttress a claim. We explore this process in **Chapter 11**.

These are all aspects of military service which may not be immediately apparent to a judge and which should be explored in detail when preparing your client's evidence.

## 9.4 Damages

Your client may have suffered a psychiatric injury, or a combination of psychiatric injuries, either as a result of exposure to trauma or following stress in the workplace. In respect of PSLA, Chapter 4 of the Judicial Studies Board guidelines provides direction on the factors that will influence your client's damages. The 14th edition of the guidelines provides the following spectrum of awards (which reflect a 10% uplift courtesy of ***Simmons v Castle [2013] 1 All ER 334***):

| Severity | Psychiatric damage generally | PTSD |
|---|---|---|
| Less severe | £1,350 to £5,130 | £3,460 to £7,170 |
| Moderate | £5,130 to £16,720 | £7,170 to £20,290 |
| Moderately severe | £16,720 to £48,080 | £20,290 to £52,490 |
| Severe | £48,080 to £101,470 | £52,490 to £88,270 |

Most claimants will present with conditions that are likely to last for more than a year, and who may arguably be 'disabled' in law (see **Chapter 13**). You will need to ask your medical expert to comment on the level of disability and/or functional impairment.

Where your client has been medically discharged, you will normally need to instruct an employment expert to comment on these career losses. Your client's current and future earning capacity might be greatly curtailed, and so a claim may remain financially significant even where your client is unable to argue that they have lost their military career as a result of any negligence. However, and in addition, you may need to instruct a GP or occupational health expert with a military background to comment on medical downgrade issues and causation i.e. the prospect of your client's continued employability within the forces in the circumstances and *but for* the negligence. In this respect, having a psychiatric disorder is not a bar to service of itself, but this will depend on the severity of the condition, your client's prognosis, role and duties. For example, a pilot will be more at risk of medical discharge because they will normally be "grounded" following a psychiatric injury and unable to carry out flying duties. They may also find difficulty in securing an alternative civilian career given their specialist skill set and medical history.

Your client may have miscellaneous further losses which are related to their psychiatric condition. Some examples are:

- Medical expenses – the cost of therapy and/or medication.
- Care – they may require loved ones or family to assist with a variety of tasks, for example, in avoiding crowds or noisy places. Alternatively, your client may need to pay privately for services.
- Driving – PTSD and other serious psychiatric conditions may invalidate them from holding a license. They may then incur significant travel expenses and/or be disadvantaged in the workplace.

## 9.5 Points for practice

- The military's welfare system and process are comprehensive and largely mandatory. They guide commanders in how to manage the risks of stress and psychiatric harm to service personnel. These systems are largely in place to ensure operational effectiveness and satisfy statutory health and safety obligations. The records will often be crucial to your assessment of any breach of duty.

- PTSD is an anxiety condition caused by a traumatic experience or experiences, which is exacerbated by stress and certain triggers. The condition is most often long-term and career limiting. Where the primary cause of PTSD has been exposure to traumatic events in combat, your client may be precluded from bringing a claim because of combat immunity. But they may still have a claim for an exacerbation or acceleration of the injury as a result of some other negligence.

- Client's suffering with PTSD can be fragile, volatile and difficult to manage. From an evidential perspective, they can be distracted and find it hard to focus on the issues in their case, or they may avoid doing so because of a fear of triggering their symptoms. Developing trust with your client at an early stage will be crucial to managing them and the litigation. You will also need to be careful when questioning any client who suffers with PTSD. Experts recommend that questions about the trauma itself are best avoided and should be reserved to medical professionals.

- Stress at work claims are complex and wrought with challenges in respect of causation and foreseeability. ***Hatton v Sutherland*** provides us with helpful guidance on the principles that you should apply, but they cannot be applied in a vacuum and there are a number of factors that are typical of military working environments which may help or hinder your client's case, not least the obligation on service personnel to follow orders.

- It seems to be a feature in military claims that some service personnel will repress or ignore their symptoms until their condition becomes unmanageable. This may be due to their stoic nature, or as a result of the stigma that still attaches to mental health issues. This may feed into arguments that they did not mitigate their loss, or indeed that they never engaged the defendant's duty of care in the first place because they failed to report symptoms.

- Litigation is a stressful and lengthy process. Consider the impact of the timetable on your client, who may still be suffering with their psychiatric condition. You will need to invest additional time in taking their statement and liaising with them about the case, which may be traumatic for them. Let these considerations be reflected in the court timetable and your client's costs budget.

- Where your client is a suicide risk, consider obtaining advice from a suitable medical expert about how to help manage them as well as review your professional obligations if and when your client reports to you in a time of crisis.

# CHAPTER TEN
# INTENTIONAL TORTS, CRIME AND PUNISHMENT

## Introduction

In this chapter we will touch on various forms of intentional harm that might befall your client during their service and which might give rise to a civil claim, either as against the individual perpetrators of the harm or the MoD vicariously. We will also consider the criminal and disciplinary military systems here briefly, because whether a tortfeasor has been convicted or disciplined in respect of an act against your client may assist their pursuit of a civil claim.

## 10.1 Trespass to the person

The tort of trespass to the person can take four forms (or a combination of these forms);

1. assault;

2. battery;

3. false imprisonment; and/or

4. intentional infliction of harm (also referred to as the principle in ***Wilkinson v Downton***).

Some will argue that the fourth form of the tort, the principle in ***Wilkinson v Downton***, has nothing to do with tort of trespass to the person and is a new tort of its own right. In either case, the principle is a helpful tool in pursuing claims involving intentional harm, and so will be explored here.

These torts can be established if an act has been done intentionally or negligently. The difference being that in respect of intentional acts your client would not need to prove foreseeability of loss and damage. Practically speaking, the loss suffered following an act which is meant to harm is usually but not always foreseeable, and so this does not constitute a significant hurdle when proceeding on the basis of a negligent act only. In any event, and because of the approach taken by the courts, practitioners are encouraged to prepare their cases on the assumption that they will have to prove the foreseeability of loss and damage. What follows is a very brief summary of these aspects of the tort of trespass to the person and some of the developments in this area of law.

### 10.1.1 Battery

Battery is any unwanted physical contact, regardless of any apprehension of harm and/or actual harm. The contact must be deliberate, but the consequences do not necessarily have to be intended. Obviously, where no harm is caused then this may render a civil claim low in value, but will not affect a claimant's ability to bring that claim or indeed a potential criminal prosecution. It can also constitute battery if the perpetrator does not personally make physical contact with the victim, for example, by throwing and striking them with an object, spitting at them or turning over their chair (whilst they were sitting on it).

Battery will not be established if the person on whom the trespass is being committed consented to it, nor if the conduct was part of the "*ordinary conduct of everyday life*" (***F v West Berkshire HA UKHL 1***). For example, the contact that is made without intent on public transport or in a crowd would not constitute battery. The question posed in ***F v West Berkshire*** was whether it was lawful to carry out an operation (sterilisation) on the appellant, who was a mentally incapable woman and so unable to consent to the procedure. Would such an operation constitute battery? The answer was that despite lacking consent, the procedure was in the interests of the appellant's health and so permissible, and her appeal was dismissed. Aside from the strict parameters explored in this case, the principle that a person's body is inviolate is one that is rigorously upheld by the courts.

In ***Livingstone v MoD [1984] NILR 356*** British soldiers in Northern Ireland fired 'baton rounds' into a group of rioters. Batton rounds are a form of non-lethal projectile used to suppress crowds. The claimant brought a claim against the MoD after being struck by one of these rounds and alleged he had been the victim of battery and assault (see below). The MoD argued that the soldier responsible for this act had not intended to hit the claimant, but had in fact been aiming at another person in the crowd. At first instance the claim in negligence was dismissed by the trial judge. The claimant successfully appealed to the Northern Ireland Court of Appeal. Hutton J, providing the leading judgment, rejected the MoD's arguments that there had been no battery:

> *"In my judgment when a soldier deliberately fires at one rioter intending to strike him and he misses him and hits another rioter nearby, the soldier has "intentionally" applied force to the rioter who has been struck. Similarly if a soldier fires a rifle bullet at a rioter intending to strike him and the bullet strikes that rioter and passes through his body and wounds another rioter directly behind the first rioter, whom the soldier had not seen, both rioters have been "intentionally" struck by the soldier and, assuming that the force used was not justified, the soldier has committed a battery against both."*

In this way the doctrine of transferred malice was seemingly applied to a civil tort; the act of firing at one person with intent was sufficient to establish the tort of trespass against another.

### 10.1.2 Assault

It is quite common today to use the term 'assault' when one actually means 'battery', but in law they are very different. An assault constitutes an act directed at a victim who then *apprehends* immediate harm to themselves i.e. they are afraid for themselves without actual physical contact being made (which is the essential element of battery). Of course, there will be cases which may involve both assault and battery.

Typically an assault will involve threatening conduct. The person being threatened must not only have apprehended immediate harm to themselves, but the person threatening them must have had the immediate means to cause them harm. So no matter how vile the threats or language may be, if the perpetrator is physically unable to cause immediate harm to the victim, then their behavior will not normally constitute an assault.

Obstructing someone so as to cause them to believe that their advancing any further would lead to them suffering physical harm can also constitute an assault. It might also, depending on the circumstances, amount to false imprisonment (see below).

Words alone will probably not be enough to establish an assault in tort. Often you will need to show that there was some form of intimidation, for example by way of body language or other circumstances created by the perpetrator of the assault.

### 10.1.3 False imprisonment

Any unlawful constraint placed on someone's freedom to move may constitute false imprisonment. The constraint must normally be gauged by reference to a particular space so, for example, where someone is locked in a room and unable to leave it, they may be able to establish that they have been falsely imprisoned. This will equally apply where the victim is not physically constrained, but believes that for them to leave a particular space might result in them suffering harm. You will need to show that the perpetrator intended to detain the victim and also had the means to do it. This tort can often be seen in actions against the Police. In a military context, it can similarly appear where service personnel who have been detained unlawfully.

In ***Murray v Ministry of Defence (Northern Ireland) [1988] UKHL 13***, Mrs Murray was arrested by the Royal Military Police (RMP) and searched on suspicion of aiding the IRA. She claimed trespass against the person in that she had been unlawfully detained at her home for 30 minutes before her formal arrest, during which time she and her family had been asked to remain in the living room of her home whilst the RMP carried out a search of the premises. Mrs Murray's case, having failed at first instance and the Court of Appeal, reached the House of Lords, by which point she had accepted that there were reasonable ground for her arrest. The question remained whether the failure to tell her that she was being arrested until the RMP were about to leave the house rendered the arrest unlawful. The House found that it was lawful (per Lord Griffiths):

> *"That very short period of restraint when they* [the Appellant and her family] *were asked to assemble in the living room was a proper and necessary part of the procedure for effecting the peaceable arrest of the plaintiff. It was a temporary restraint of very short duration imposed not only for the benefit of those effecting the arrest but also for the protection of the occupants of the house and would be wholly insufficient to found an action for unlawful imprisonment."*

### 10.1.4 Intentional infliction of harm

In the case of ***Wilkinson v Downton*** *[1897] 2 QBD7 s3 57* the claimant, Mrs Wilkinson, was caused serious distress when she was told falsely that her husband had come to harm, as summarised in the opening paragraph of Wright Js judgment in the case:

> *"In this case the defendant, in the execution of what he seems to have regarded as a practical joke, represented to the plaintiff that he was charged by her husband with a message to her to the effect that her husband was smashed up in an accident, and was lying at The Elms at Leytonstone with both legs broken, and that she was to go at once in a cab with two pillows to fetch him home. All this was false. The effect of the statement on the plaintiff was a violent shock to her nervous system, producing vomiting and other more serious and permanent physical consequences at one time threatening her reason, and entailing weeks of suffering and incapacity to her as well as expense to her husband for medical attendance."*

Mrs Wilkinson subsequently succeeded in bringing a case against the defendant for trespass against the person. The distinction here, as opposed to cases involving battery and assault, is that there was neither physical contact with the claimant by the defendant, nor did she immediately apprehend harm to herself. Her loss was caused purely out of the distress caused by the defendant's statement, but was recoverable nonetheless. Wright J again:

> *"It is difficult to imagine that such a statement, made suddenly and with apparent seriousness, could fail to produce grave effects under the circumstances upon any but an exceptionally indifferent person, and therefore an intention to produce such an effect must be imputed, and it is no answer in law to say that more harm was done than was anticipated, for that is commonly the case with all wrongs."*

The judgment has since been approved and expanded upon. ***Janvier v Sweeney [1919] 2 KB 31*** concerned a French woman engaged to a German man who was interned in the Isle of Man during the First World War. She succeeded in bringing a claim under the principles of ***Wilkinson v Downton*** after a private detective and his assistant sought to deceive her into helping an investigation by pretending that she was suspected of corresponding with a spy. She succeeded in winning damages for the nervous shock and illness she suffered as a result.

In ***Rhodes v OPO (by his litigation friend BHM) and another [2015] UKSC 32*** provides us with some more guidance. Mr Rhodes, a prominent musician and film maker, had written an autobiography which included graphic descriptions of sexual abuse he had suffered as a child and the impact that this had on his mental state and wellbeing. His son brought a claim (by his uncle and litigation friend) seeking an injunction to stop publication of the book on the basis that this would cause him harm; he sought to redact significant sections of the book which dealt with this sensitive material. The claim was rejected at first instance but successful at the Court of Appeal, where it was determined that whilst no cause of action lay in negligence an interim injunction should be granted to restrict publication on the basis of the principle in ***Wilkinson v Downton***. Mr Rhodes appealed to the Supreme Court, and was successful. It held that there were three elements to the principle in ***Wilkinson v Downton***:

- A conduct element – this required words or conduct to be directed towards the claimant, for which there was no justification.

- A mental element – the defendant intended to cause severe distress (note that there is no need to show that the defendant intended to cause the psychological harm that in fact resulted and recklessness is not enough, there must be intent)

- A consequence element – physical harm or psychiatric illness was suffered as a direct consequence of the offensive act.

None of these elements were satisfied. The publication of the book was not directed at Mr Rhodes' son. Mr Rhodes had not intended to cause his son any harm by publishing the book. The third element was also not relevant because the son had suffered no harm, albeit evidence was submitted to show that such harm was likely to occur if his son read the book. ***Rhodes*** is instructive because it sets out the elements of the principle in ***Wilkinson v Downton***, although more exploration of these elements will need to be elicited in future cases. Note that the case also involved public policy considerations, given that Mr Rhodes was also arguing that his freedom of speech was being curtailed.

***Wilkinson v Downton*** and the cases which have followed it have created an important principle; that an unwarranted act that was intended to cause distress is actionable in tort regardless of the fact that no battery or assault may have occurred. The development of this tort has in some ways been superseded by the tort created by the Protection from Harassment Act 1997, but they are distinct causes of action. It is suggested that one distinction (and potential great benefit) is that a claimant would not need to prove a 'course of conduct' under ***Wilkinson v Downton*** (i.e. as opposed to the requirement of two or more acts under the Protection from Harassment Act, discussed below); a single act might suffice to establish liability albeit the act complained of would probably have to be "*extreme and outrageous*" in nature.

## 10.2 Harassment

The Protection from Harassment Act 1997 (PHA) was created primarily to deal with stalkers. It also provided a cause of action for the recovery of damages where an individual had been harassed:

*(1) A person must not pursue a course of conduct –*

*(a) which amounts to harassment of another, and*

*(b) which he knows or ought to know amounts to harassment of the other.*

*(1A) A person must not pursue a course of conduct –*

*(a) which involves harassment of two or more persons, and*

*(b) which he knows or ought to know involves harassment of those persons, and*

*(c) by which he intends to persuade any person (whether or not one of those mentioned above) –*

*(i) not to do something that he is entitled or required to do, or*

*(ii) to do something that he is not under any obligation to do.*

Section 2 and 2A of the Act create the criminal offences of harassment and stalking respectively.

Section 3 of the Act introduces the civil remedy under which your client may proceed with a claim for damages, but also the opportunity to apply for an injunction under the Act (typically for a restraining order against the harasser).

As such, any person who harasses another (on at least two occasions) or intimidates two or more persons (into doing or not doing something that they are obliged to do) may be subject to civil proceedings and/or criminal prosecution.

Section 6 of the Act disapplies the relevant section of the Limitation Act that would ordinarily apply to common law claims for personal injury, which means that a claim under the act will have a longer limitation period of six years from the date of the first incident of harassment. But be aware, a claim must be brought for at least two incidents of harassment and these incidents must be connected to show a course of conduct. There will be scope for argument about whether or not each incident that your client complains about is connected. There may also be instances of lengthy campaigns of harassment involving different individuals which either cannot be connected or which may face limitation issues. Early analysis and the preparation of a chronology is strongly recommended.

In the context of military claims, the Act will most often be of use to you in cases involving bullying in the workplace. But the Act does not provide a definition of harassment. We can look to the common law for some guidance here, but whether behaviour in fact amounts to harassment under the Act will be fact sensitive.

The case of ***Majrowski v Guys St Thomas' Trust Ltd [2006] UKHL 34*** involved the alleged harassment of a hospital worker by his manager. Mr Majrowski was employed by the Trust as a clinical audit co-ordinator. He alleged that he was bullied, intimidated and harassed by his manager, Mrs Freeman. He alleged, inter alia, that she was (i) excessively critical of his time-keeping, (ii) isolated him by refusing to talk to him, (iii) treated him less favourably to other staff (iv) was rude and abusive to him in front of others and (v) she imposed unrealistic targets for his performance, and (vi) threatened him unjustifiably with disciplinary action. Interestingly, Mr Majrowski only pursued his claim under the PHA and not in negligence or contract as against Mrs Freeman's employer, the NHS Trust and there is some indication that this may have been because of concerns over limitation and/or foreseeability. The case is useful to us in many ways. Having reached the House of Lords on the issue of whether the defendant NHS Trust could be held liable for the behaviour of its employee; their Lordships found that it could. They also provided some guidance on where behaviour might not amount to harassment, Per Lord Nicholls:

> *"Where....the quality of the conduct said to constitute harassment is being examined, courts will have in mind that irritations, annoyances, even a measure of upsets, arise at times in everybody's day to day dealings with other people. Courts are well able to recognise the boundary between conduct which is unattractive, even unreasonable and conduct which is oppressive and unacceptable."*

Or as Baroness Hale observed in that same judgment:

> *"A great deal is left to the wisdom of the courts to draw sensible lines between the ordinary banter and badinage of life and genuinely offensive and unacceptable behaviour."*

Incidentally but helpfully in ***Majrowski***, the House of Lords confirmed the position in respect of vicarious liability (discussed in detail below), which it found would attach to the employer regardless of the suggestion that vicarious liability could only attach to common law wrongs and so not the civil remedy provided by statute (i.e. the PHA).

In ***Rayment v MoD [2010] EWHC 218 (QB***), Ms Rayment was a former member of the Territorial Army (now the Reserves), who subsequently joined the Honorable Artillery Company as a civilian employee. She brought a claim both in negligence and under the PHA in respect of a number of allegations of harassment. Davies J adopted criteria for the assessment of behaviour that could amount to harassment, which had first been promulgated by Owen J in ***Green v DB Group Services [2006] EWHC 1899 (QB)*** and later utilised in ***Hammond v International Network Services [2007] EWHC 2604 (QB)***, namely, that in order to establish harassment under the PHA, there must be conduct:

i. which occurs on at least two occasions;

ii. which is targeted at the claimant;

iii. which is calculated in an objective sense to cause alarm or distress; and

iv. which is objectively judged to be oppressive and unreasonable.

Davies J found that there were three incidents which did satisfy the above criteria, having first considered all the claimant's allegations and discounted those which would not:

> *"In this judgment I have identified a number of individual incidents which are relied upon to support a claim under the 1997 Act. Many more are alleged, examples include the state of the female lavatory..., the refusal...to provide the claimant with transport in order to attend a medical appointment, an alleged refusal by a military clerk to assist the claimant with a computer program. I do not seek to minimise the other incidents but having read or listened to the relevant evidence, I am satisfied that none would satisfy the test enunciated by Maurice Kay LJ in* ***Veakins*** *[**Veakins v Kier Islington Ltd** [2009] EWCA CIV1288] namely that the conduct was "oppressive and unacceptable". There were faults on both sides. The claimant was a challenging employee, those who worked with her were increasingly frustrated by her attitude and conduct and on occasions, this showed...the claimant presented as a woman well able to challenge that which she did not accept and accustomed to military establishments where robust language could be used."*

However, Davies J also rejected Ms Rayment's claims in common law negligence in respect of those same incidents because she had not satisfied the test of foreseeability. She awarded Ms Rayment £5,500 in damages. The judgment in ***Rayment*** is helpful in highlighting the interplay and overlap between claims in common law negligence and those brought under the PHA. It also identifies the complex issues of causation that can arise in such cases, Ms Rayment having been identified by the medical expert as having a pre-existing susceptibility to psychiatric injury.

We were provided with further guidance in the case of ***Dowson v CC Northumbria** [2010] EWHC 2612 (QB)*. This involved claims under the PHA brought by several police officers in relation to the behaviour of their superior, a Detective Chief Inspector, who they alleged was a bully, behaved aggressively and required them to act in unprofessional and potentially unlawful ways. Simon J found against all the claimants, despite accepting that the Detective Chief Inspector had been *"insensitive, belittling and overbearing"*. In dismissing Mr Dowson's case, Simon J stressed how the nature of the working environment influenced his judgment:

> *"The question is whether this conduct constituted harassment. I have concluded that it did not. This was a stressful working environment in which case-hardened officers were dealing with career-hardened criminals. Although this was more than simply a clash of personalities, it was not conduct which was calculated to cause distress and, although it was unacceptable, it was not oppressive in the sense described in the cases. It was not a tormenting by constant interference or intimidation. Rather it was a curt and dismissive attitude which was likely to have the effect, even if unintended, of undermining both Mr Dowson's own self-confidence and the esteem in which he was held by others…In the light of the above and, while keeping in mind that for conduct to amount to the civil tort of harassment it must be of an order which would sustain criminal liability, I have concluded that Mr Dowson's claim fails by a considerable margin."*

The working environment that Simon J found to exist in ***Dowson*** may be comparable to that in a military context and so you should consider whether this may 'lower the bar' in respect of the appropriate level of conduct where your client is found to be in similar circumstances. But one cannot assume that simply because a case involves the military, police or other stressful environs, that unreasonable conduct is to be tolerated. In fact, given the strict disciplinary requirements and moral standards which the armed forces must live by and the potentially hazardous working environment, it might just as easily be argued that such work demands a higher level of conduct. Practitioners should also be warned against arguments from defendants that seek to disguise oppressive and unreasonable behaviour as 'banter' in the workplace, which the MoD specifically warns against in its own guidance material (see Annex A to *JSP 763*). Ultimately such considerations will be fact specific, but what is clear is that any assessment should go beyond the specific incidents of alleged harassment and take into account all the circumstances. In reaching his judgment, Simon J offered helpful criteria against which to assess conduct that would amount to harassment:

1. *There must be conduct which occurs on at least two occasions,*
2. *which is targeted at the claimant,*
3. *which is calculated in an objective sense to cause alarm or distress, and*
4. *which is objectively judged to be oppressive and unacceptable.*
5. *What is oppressive and unacceptable may depend on the social or working context in which the conduct occurs.*
6. *A line is to be drawn between conduct which is unattractive and unreasonable, and conduct which has been described in various ways: 'torment' of the victim, 'of an order which would sustain criminal liability'.*

Note that in the subsequent case of ***Levi v Bates [2015] EWCA Civ 206*** the court of appeal made clear that the decision in ***Dowson*** had taken too far the concept that the conduct must target the claimant, which was not a pre-requisite of the statutory test. The claimant must be a victim of the conduct, but the conduct need not directly target them.

The criteria applied in ***Rayment*** and later developed in ***Dowson*** are to be assessed objectively. The intention of the perpetrator is irrelevant, though evidence of intent, if proven, may go a long way to satisfying the other tests. There are some distinct advantages to proceeding under the PHA for your client (as opposed to solely a common law claim in negligence):

- They would not have to show foreseeability.
- They would not have to prove that they have suffered a diagnosed psychiatric condition. They would be entitled to claim damages on the basis of the anxiety/distress they have suffered alone. Practically speaking, they may have difficulty causally connecting any significant losses without establishing a diagnosable psychiatric condition.
- Unlike discrimination (see **11.7.1**), the harassment does not have to be related to a protected characteristic.
- The PHA has a limitation period of six years, which is a considerable advantage to claimants whose common law claims may have expired.

Ideally, where the facts allow, your client would proceed to make a claim under the PHA in addition to a claim in negligence, to maximize their chances of success.

## 10.3 How intentional torts can arise

The circumstances in which intentional harm can arise are varied. In a military context, these cases will tend to arise when your client has been the victim of:

- an assault and/or battery (including rape and/or sexual assault); and/or
- bullying on the workplace.

There will be those cases which are isolated in nature, usually involving an altercation on a night out or at a formal function. Often, but not always, alcohol will be involved. Drinking culture in the military is a recognised problem.

In other cases your client may present with a far more comprehensive history, perhaps they were the victim of a campaign of harassment which was prolonged and culminated in a physical altercation or threatening behaviour.

Whatever the circumstances of your client's case, be aware that there may be a number of causes of action for you to investigate and prove.

## 10.4 Establishing liability

As claimant, it will be your client's obligation to satisfy the legal requirements under either the torts of trespass or the PHA discussed above, including the facts relied on: that the act(s) complained of occurred and that the defendant intended to carry out the offensive act(s). In addition, in accordance with the principles of negligence, you will need to establish causation of injury and loss. Bear in mind:

- There are a number of defences to the tort of trespass, such as consent, self-defence (of the person or property), or acts taken in the investigation or prevention of a crime.
- There are no specific torts for harm which is aggravated for reasons of a protected characteristic, for example, sexual assault, rape or racial abuse. Whilst the criminal law may deal with these offences differently, as torts they will normally be classified as an assault or battery etc.
- Section 11 of the Civil Evidence Act 1968 will allow your client to rely on the facts of any conviction in bringing a civil claim. Equally, any disciplinary action that has been taken against the tortfeasor will also buttress your client's civil claim.

Whether or not your client has strong evidence in support of their claim does not mean that vicarious liability will necessarily attach to the tortfeasor's employer. You will therefore need to make a number of tactical decisions on how to proceed in any given case:

- It will almost always be more advantageous for your client to bring their claim as against the tortfeasor's employer (i.e. the MoD for service personnel). The reason for this is because the defendant who committed the intentional harm is more often than not unable to satisfy any judgment for damages awarded by the court.

- Your client may wish to pursue both the MoD and the perpetrator of the harm, to maximise the chances of recovering damages as against at least one of these defendants. Where the perpetrator of the harm is an officer, this may also add an 'embarrassment' factor and influence the MoD to seek a prompt, amicable (and often confidential) resolution.

- In cases involving very serious harm, your client may not want to allow the tortfeasor an opportunity to influence the proceedings.. This may be on principle, or because they will find dealing with them, stressful and traumatic. Whilst pursuing the MoD alone may avoid the eccentricities of pursuing a tortfeasor who may not have legal representation, cause mischief and delay, your client may also bear the risk that if vicarious liability is not established against the MoD then they may be left without a remedy.

Before you make your recommendation on how to proceed and against whom, you may need to:

- Instruct an enquiry agent to investigate the financial solvency of any potential defendant (to establish if they could potentially satisfy any judgment debt).

- Consider the prospects of whether the MoD (or any other employer) will be found to be vicariously liable.

In respect of vicarious liability, there has been established jurisprudence over many years to say that an employer should be liable for the wrongs of its servant, employee and/or agent, and below we explore a few key cases. Generally, there are a number of factors which the courts have taken into account, including:

- The control that the employer had over the tortfeasor.

- Any relationship between the claimant, the tortfeasor and their employer.

- The circumstances of the act and whether it occurred during the course of the tortfeasor's employment.

- An abuse of power or authority.

- Whether it is fair, just and reasonable to impose vicarious liability.

- Public policy.

In ***Copeland v Ministry of Defence and Clarke [1999] NIQB 12***, Mr Copeland was attending the funeral of a paramilitary member of the IRA. The deceased had been killed by a bomb of his own making, which had also killed a number of other people. Whilst waiting outside the deceased's home, Mr Copeland was shot twice by the second Defendant, Mr Clarke, who was a soldier serving in the Army at the time. Mr Copeland survived the attack but was very seriously injured. Mr Clarke was subsequently convicted of attempted murder. Mr Copeland brought a claim for damages against both Mr Clarke and the MoD. The MoD argued that Mr Clarke was at all material times acting outside the course and scope of his employment.

Sheil J found as a matter of fact that Mr Clarke had warned his colleagues and a superior immediately before committing the crime of his intentions, but that they had assumed he was joking, and found no liability in negligence against the MoD. Having found that the act was intentional and not negligent, he then went on to determine whether the MoD could be held vicariously liable for trespass to the person in respect of the battery and assault that Mr Copeland had suffered:

> *"In deciding whether or not the Ministry of Defence is vicariously liable in the present case for trespass to the person, I do not consider that anything is to be gained by setting out examples of the many cases which are referred to in the text books as falling on one or other side of the dividing line of what is and what is not "in the course of employment"... I hold that the Ministry of Defence has not shown that the shooting was one for which they were not responsible in law... Further, I consider that, as a matter of public policy, when the State sends out a soldier or police officer armed with a lethal weapon which he is authorised to use in certain circumstances and that soldier or police officer, while on duty, intentionally or otherwise fires that weapon injuring a third party in circumstances which are not authorised and in which, as in the present case, there is no justification or defence for so doing, the State should be liable in damages at common law for any injury, loss or damage sustained by that third party."*

The decision was steered primarily by public policy. It is interesting to us because of the military context, and informative because of the challenges faced (as expressed by the Judge) in applying principles of vicarious liability to what can be very unusual facts in military cases (the test at the time of ***Copeland*** being one of whether or not the tort committed was "*in the course of employment*"). The jurisprudence has developed considerably since ***Copeland***, but assessing vicarious liability remains a challenging exercise.

To make a thorough assessment in your client's case, you will need to apply the modern test of vicarious liability, which is set out in ***Lister and others v Hesley Hall Ltd [2002] 1 AC 215***. This case involved historic sexual abuse that occurred in a boarding school in Doncaster. The warden of the school carried out abuse on a number of resident children. The claimants, who were all victims of that abuse brought claims against the company that owned the school, Hesley Hall Ltd. The central question in the case was whether the defendant company could be held vicariously liable for the criminal acts of the school warden. The defendant was held vicariously liable, as per Lord Steyn:

> *"The question is whether the warden's torts were so* ***closely connected*** *with his employment that it would be fair and just to hold the employers vicariously liable. On the facts of the case the answer is yes. After all, the sexual abuse was inextricably interwoven with the carrying out by the warden of his duties..."*

In ***Lister***, the fact that the employee, the Warden, had abused his position of authority was highly relevant to the decision to hold the employer liable.

More guidance on the test of '*close connection*' was provided in the case of ***Mohamud v Wm Morrison Supermarkets [2016] AC 667***. In this case, the claimant had stopped at the defendant's petrol station in Birmingham and asked the station attendant whether he could print some documents. The station attendant, Mr Khan, was employed by the defendant. Mr Khan refused Mr Mohamud's request and was verbally and racially abusive to him. To make matters worse, Mr Khan followed Mr Mohamud to his car subjected him to serious assault and battery, demanding that he never return to the station again and causing him serious harm. At first instance, the trial judge found that the defendant could not be held liable for Mr Khan's actions because, whilst he was an employee, he was acting for reasons of his own and entirely outside the scope of his employment and duties. Mr Mohamud unsuccessfully appealed to the Court of Appeal, but was successful at the Supreme Court. Lord Toulson confirmed the proper use of the close connection test:

> *"In the simplest terms, the court has to consider two matters. The first question is what functions or "field of activities" have been entrusted by the employer to the employee, or, in everyday language, what was*

*the nature of his job. As has been emphasised in several cases, this question must be addressed broadly; ...Secondly, the court must decide whether there was sufficient connection between the position in which he was employed and his wrongful conduct to make it right for the employer to be held liable under the principle of social justice..."*

Mr Khan's motive was irrelevant here. The fact that he had left the petrol station was also irrelevant. What convinced their Lordships on the facts was that he had purported to act for his employer by demanding that Mr Mohamud leave and never return to the petrol station.

In ***Bellman v Northampton Recruitment Ltd [2018] EWCA Civ 2214***, Mr Bellman, an employee of the defendant company, was attacked at a company Christmas party by Mr Major, the Managing Director. Most of the employees were present at the party, which at Mr Major's suggestion moved to the bar of a nearby hotel. Mr Bellman and Mr Major had an argument about a work-related issue, and Mr Major punched Mr Bellman twice, the second strike caused him to fall and hit his head on the floor, resulting in a severe brain injury. Mr Bellman sued the defendant company on the basis that it was vicariously liable for Mr Major's actions, but was unsuccessful at first instance on the basis that, in summary, the decision to continue to drink after the work Christmas party had been a *personal* decision and therefore removed the ultimate act from the circumstances of employment which may otherwise have made the defendant vicariously liable. At the Court of Appeal, the test in ***Mohamud*** was applied again, but with an entirely different outcome and the appeal was allowed. Cotter J delivered the leading judgment:

*The judge here* [at first instance] *made no reference to his own "broad assessment of what functions or fields of activity were entrusted ... to Mr Major". His findings that Mr Major had a "wide remit", that he was the company's "directing mind and will" who like to see things were done "his way" and who saw "the maintenance of his managerial authority as a central part of his role", that his role had no "set hours" so that "much of what Mr Major did during the average working day was directly or indirectly connected to" this "round the clock" small company.*

Thus Mr Major was found to be in a position of control; he could assert his authority over the staff who were present and indeed did so throughout that evening. Consequently, vicarious liability was found to apply to his actions. There may be very similar considerations to be applied in the military context, where subordinates are required to do what their superiors want "*round the clock*". But note in particular the words of warning of Irwin LJ in ***Bellman***:

> *"Liability will not arise merely because there is an argument about work matters between colleagues, which leads to an assault, even when one colleague is markedly more senior than another. This case is emphatically not authority for the proposition that employers became insurers for violent or other tortious acts by their employees."*

The more recent case of ***TPKN v MoD [2019] EWHC 1488 (QB)*** provides a broad exploration of the issue of vicarious liability in the context of military claims. The Claimant was a NCO in the Navy and stationed in Gibraltar. Her assailant, TS, was a Private in the British Army who had been temporarily stationed on the island. The Claimant alleged that after a social event in May 2012, TS drugged and raped her. She bore a child subsequent to this assault and was initially afraid to report the incident because she was concerned about how she would be treated by her superiors (in addition to raising a service complaint about the rape she also complained about discrimination in the workplace). In November 2013 she developed PSTD and reported the rape to the civilian police, but no prosecution was pursued. In 2017 the claimant brought a claim against the MoD, alleging that it was vicariously liable for the tort she suffered at the hands of TS and for his misfeasance in public office. The MoD denied liability on the basis that TS had not been acting in the course of his employment and applied to strike out the claim. Master Thornett allowed the application and struck out the claim because the claimant had:

- no real prospect of succeeding in her claim that the MoD was vicariously liable (in part because both claimant and defendant were 'off-duty' at the relevant time); and

- had not disclosed any reasonable grounds for bringing a claim of misfeasance in public office.

The question of what amounts to misfeasance in public office was considered by the House of Lords in ***Three Rivers District Council and Others v Bank of England (No 3) [2003]***:

- the conduct must be that of a public officer, exercising power in that capacity;

- the officer must either intend to injure the claimant or knowingly/recklessly act beyond his or her powers, causing damage; and

- in circumstances where they knew or were recklessly indifferent as to whether the act would probably cause such damage.

The claimant appealed. She argued inter alia that her assailant could not be held as truly having been 'off-duty' because he:

- was required to be at the base;

- was in receipt of pay;

- would be liable to the service authorities and service law for any unlawful acts or omissions whilst on base; and

- remained under the direction and control of his chain of command.

The appeal was successful, Sweeney J finding that the Master had erred in:

- concluding that the Claimant had no real prospects of arguing vicarious liability; and

- applying the test in ***Three Rivers*** (an act of misfeasance in public office *can* include a criminal act).

No substantive decision has been made in respect of the merits of the claimant's claim that the MoD should be held vicariously liable, only an acknowledgment that her arguments have a chance of success and should be tried. The judgment has allowed her to pursue her claim for compensation and it will be interesting to see whether or not the case returns to court. It is nevertheless an instructive judgment that deserves study, setting out a number of factual considerations, arguments and the legal framework for these types of cases.

It is suggested that ***TPKN*** can support a claim where harm occurs to your client 'off-duty'. When living and working in a hierarchical system, such as the military, the concept of being on 'active duty' is more often in reference to being tasked with something to do. There are some good reasons why the issue of being on or off duty may be a red herring:

- Even if a service person is off-duty, they would still be required to comply with their superior's commands.

- Service personnel are at all times subject to service law and discipline for acts they commit (i.e. arguably they are never in a real sense 'off duty').

- Many social functions (and there are many) in the military are in reality mandated and service personnel may face scrutiny, criticism and, in serious cases, bullying for not taking part.

Whether the parties were 'on' or 'off' duty is by no means determinative in these cases, which will be fact sensitive. In assessing vicarious liability, you will need to apply the modern test of 'close connection' in ***Lister***, as developed in ***Mohamud*** and confirmed in ***Bellman***, whilst being aware that there can be great variance in judicial approach to the test.

## 10.5 Damages

Your client's losses will depend on their injury and any impact that this may have had on their military career (see **Chapter 13**).

An award for PSLA will depend on the injuries sustained. Where these injuries are minor, perhaps lacerations or bruising, these might be assessed by an expert GP. More serious injuries may require specialist assessment, depending on the injury and condition of your client. The psychological harm that your client may suffer should not be underestimated and often becomes the most long-term factor.

You may also need a number of other experts from different fields:

- A Consultant Psychiatrist – to comment on any psychiatric condition
- A GP or Occupational Health expert with a military background – to comment on medical downgrade issues i.e. continued employability within the forces and/or in respect of clinical negligence.
- An employment consultant with a specialism in military careers – to comment on employability, loss of military career and any ongoing disadvantage in the employment market.

Your client may have miscellaneous further losses which are related to their injuries. Here are some examples:

- Medical expenses – pain killers and/or the cost of therapy and/or medication for any psychiatric condition.
- Care – your client may require loved ones or family to assist with a variety of tasks. Alternatively, your client may need to pay privately for services.

## 10.6 Statutory compensation schemes

Your client may be able to claim compensation through government run schemes. They may apply under the Criminal Injuries Compensation Scheme (CICA) if they were a victim of a violent crime, including where:

- They were injured.
- A close relative died.
- They witnessed the crime or its aftermath.
- They paid for funeral expenses of someone who died.
- They took a 'justified and exceptional' risk trying to stop a crime.

The time limit to make a claim is normally two years from the incident, which must have been reported to the police before an application is made. Any compensation would have to be credited in the event of a settlement in any civil claim against the same perpetrator. As such, it is sometimes common to stay a claim under the scheme subject to the outcome of related civil proceedings.

They may also be entitled to a lump sum award under the Criminal Injuries Compensation (Overseas) Scheme (CIC(O) Scheme), managed by the MoD. This operates in a similar way to CICA, but also provides awards to dependents of service personnel who may be injured or killed as a result of crime abroad.

Your client may also be entitled to an award under the Armed Forces Compensation Scheme (AFCS). This is a no-fault scheme (i.e. your client would not have to prove that they were injured as a result of someone's negligence, only that they were injury was related to their service). The scheme is explored in more detail at **13.5** below.

## 10.7 Crime and punishment

The intentional torts explored above can also amount to criminal acts and, where a conviction has been secured, your client may be entitled to adduce this evidence to bolster their civil claims (by virtue of Section 11 of the Civil Evidence Act 1968). In some cases, the tortfeasor may not have been convicted but may have been subject to disciplinary and/or administrative action under service law, which again may be supportive.

All service personnel are subject to UK criminal law and, when serving in the UK, are treated in precisely the same way as a civilian if they commit an offence. They are also subject to the jurisdiction of the Court Martial, which extends anywhere in the world (including in the UK). Where a crime has allegedly been committed in the UK, the civilian police would normally decide whether to refer the matter to the Crown Prosecution Service or rely on the Service to refer the matter to the Service Prosecuting Authority. Where a crime has taken place on defence property and involves only service personnel, it is more likely to be investigated by the Service Police and prosecuted by that Service Prosecuting Authority.

In some special circumstances service law can also apply to civilians, for example:

- Those living with a service person at a military base or facility.
- Those travelling on-board a military aircraft or ship.
- Certain contractors for the MoD.

### 10.7.1 Disciplinary and administrative action

Discipline in the military is kept to maintain the order, function, values and standards of the Services. The Armed Forces Act 2006 replaced three separate Service Discipline Acts (the Army Act 1955, the Air

Force Act 1955 and the Naval Discipline Act 1957), harmonising service law and codifying its unique disciplinary offences.

Commanding Officers are an integral part of the disciplinary system and have recourse to a range of statutory powers. They are provided with written guidance on disciplinary procedure (*JSP 830: Manual of Service Law*).

Where a service person has misbehaved or breached service law, their Commanding Officer must normally decide whether to take administrative or disciplinary action; the former is meant to adjust behavior; the latter to punish. Administrative action should only be taken when there is insufficient evidence to suggest criminal intent and/or it is not necessary, proportionate or desirable to pursue formal disciplinary action.

Generally, administrative action can be either 'minor' or 'major', depending on the seriousness of the offence. These may relate to issues such as inefficiency, tardiness and misbehaviour. Where an offence is not categorised as minor, the Commanding Officer must then consider whether to take major administrative action. Sanctions will range depending on the conduct. For minor administrative action these sanctions might involve additional duties, for example. For major administrative action sanctions might include censure (a mark on the personnel record which, depending on the punishment, may be shown to a career board and hinder promotion), demotion or termination from service, amongst others.

Disciplinary action, as opposed to administrative action, involves the Service Criminal Justice process. Service personnel can be charged for any criminal offence committed under service law as well as any criminal offence under civilian criminal law. Sanctions following any conviction will vary and in serious cases will include imprisonment. Depending on the offence, the Commanding Officer may in the first instance elect to charge the accused through 'summary dealing'. This is a relatively informal hearing held in private. The purpose of this summary process is to provide swift resolution to minor offences. The accused will be charged and given an opportunity to admit or deny the allegations. They will have access to an Assisting Officer and a right to appeal to a Summary Appeal Court, which is conducted by a Judge Advocate assisted by two officers. However, service personnel have a right to elect trial by the Court Martial instead of a summary dealing (see below).

Commanding Officers are entitled to pursue administrative action in addition to formal disciplinary action, but would normally wait for the conclusion of the disciplinary proceedings before taking action. This is not normally allowed where both the formal disciplinary action and administrative action relate to the same, minor misdemeanor. They must also as a matter of law report all alleged sexual offences which are listed in Schedule 2 of the Armed Forces Act 2006 to the Service Police for investigation. There are a number of sexual offences which are not listed in Schedule 2 of the Act but cannot be dealt with summarily (including sexual assault, voyeurism and exposure).

### 10.7.2 The Service Police

Where formal disciplinary action must be taken, or where a crime has been reported, this will first have to be investigated by the military police (MP). Each service has its own military police force, often referred to as the 'service police':

- The Royal Military Police (RMP) – for the Army
- The Royal Navy Police (RNP)
- Royal Air Force Police (RAFP)

Each of these forces also has a Special Investigation Branch (SIB), which is the detective branch of the police force. SIB detectives often operate in plain clothes and are tasked with investigating more serious criminal offences.

The role of the service police is to police their respective service personnel in accordance with service law and uphold values and standards. Often they will liaise closely with Commanding Officers. A few general points:

- They are empowered to arrest and charge any service person or civilian who is subject to service law. The Armed Forces Act 2006 sets out a number of circumstances in which civilians would be held accountable under service law, including amongst others those who are travelling on board a military ship or aircraft.

- They do not ordinarily have the power to arrest civilians (who are not subject to service law), but they are able to make arrests of civilians under the Police Criminal Evidence Act 1984 s.24 (A), where a constable is not available to make the arrest.

- All service police interviews must be conducted in accordance with the Police and Criminal Evidence Act (PACE), in the same way that the civilian police conduct their interviews.

- Once an investigation has concluded, the service police will report to the Service Prosecuting Authority (mentioned below), who decide whether or not to make a recommendation for a prosecution.

The MoD also operate a number of civilian police forces who are tasked with policing the 'defence estate' (i.e. MoD property), these may include the Ministry of Defence Police, the Sovereign Base Areas Police and the Gibraltar Defence Police.

Unlike the civilian police, the service police have no equivalent of the Independent Office for Police Conduct (IOPC), and so no independent oversight. This has attracted criticism in the press and from lawyers who are skeptical of the transparency and fairness of the system.

### 10.7.3 The Service Prosecuting Authority

The Service Prosecuting Authority ("SPA") provides for the military the same role that the Criminal Prosecution Authority does for civilian police, that is to review criminal cases referred to it by the service police (or in some instances the chain of command) and to prosecute these where appropriate in the Court Martial.

The SPAs headquarters are based in RAF Northolt. The head of the authority is Mr Andrew Cayley CMG QC who fills the post of Director Service Prosecutions (DSP).

Following an investigation by the service police, the SPA will review the available evidence in any particular case and make a recommendation to the relevant Commanding Officer. The SPA will also make a recommendation of any punishment they are seeking. It is the Commanding Officer who technically decides whether or not the accused should be charged, but practically speaking they will take action whenever the SPA recommends it.

Where a defendant to a civil claim was prosecuted and/or convicted, then records may be held by the SPA. More problematic will be those cases where a prospective defendant has not been successfully prosecuted and you may wish to explore why before embarking on a civil claim. The SPA, being closely linked but independent of the MoD, will be a third party to the claim and so requesting and/or applying for disclosure will be less straightforward.

### 10.7.4 The Court Martial

The Armed Forces Act also provides for the jurisdiction of the Court Martial, which is empowered to try any service offence under the Act. There are some unique features to bear in mind:

- The Court Marital is a 'standing court' and can sit and dispense justice anywhere in the world.

- The Judge in the Court Martial is called the 'Judge Advocate'. Judges are not paid by the MoD, nor answerable to it. They are all civilians, normally barristers or solicitors that are appointed in the same way as circuit-judges. They are supported by the Office of the Judge Advocate General (OJAG).

- The jury is called the 'Board', and consists of anything between three and seven officers and Warrant Officers, normally depending on the complexity and severity of the alleged crime.

- A defendant can be represented by a solicitor or barrister, and will also have access to an Assisting Officer. Court Martial procedure is governed by the Armed Forces (Court Martial) Rules 2009. Practitioners can ask the Judge Advocate for guidance on protocol and procedure.

- The Judge Advocate will sum up the case and the Board will then determine whether the accused is guilty or innocent.

- The Court Martial has the same sentencing powers as a Crown Court, including life imprisonment. Where a defendant is convicted, the Board will retire with the Judge Advocate to determine the sentence. The Judge Advocate will advise the Board on sentencing guidelines. The Board advises the Judge Advocate of any service considerations, such as the impact that any sentence will have on the defendant's career. They will then determine sentence, each member of the Board and the Judge Advocate holding a vote. The Judge Advocate will hold the casting vote if this proves necessary.

- Appeals from a decision of the Court Martial is to the Court Martial Appeal Court.

- The procedure will change if the accused is a civilian subject to service law. For example, civilians may be tried for minor offences by the Service Civilian Court (consisting of a Judge Advocate sitting alone). For more serious offences they will be tried in the Court Martial.

- Both service personnel and civilians subject to service law may be eligible for legal aid by application to the Armed Forces Criminal Legal Aid Authority (AFCLAA).

## 10.8 Points for practice

- Battery is unwanted, deliberate physical contact.

- An assault is an act which causes someone to apprehend harm to themselves.

- False imprisonment in the unlawful restriction of someone's liberty to move.

- ***Wilkinson v Downton*** allows claimants to pursue defendants in tort who have intentionally caused them harm by way of a single, unwarranted statement or act.

- The Protection from Harassment Act creates a distinct cause of action with a limitation period of six years. There is no definition of harassment under the Act, but the case law suggest that your client will have to prove a course of conduct (i.e. at least two incidents) which was oppressive and unreasonable. They will not have to prove foreseeability, or that they have suffered a recognised psychiatric disorder or that the harassment was connected to a protected characteristic.

- When pursuing a claim against a service person/tortfeasor for any intentional harm, it will almost always be more advantageous to proceed against the MoD vicariously. This is not straightforward. The modern test requires you to show that the act complained of was 'closely connected' with the tortfeasor's employment. Vicarious liability can still attach to the MoD in cases where the parties were 'off-duty' at the relevant time, but ultimately this issue will turn on the specific facts of any case.

- The Armed Forces Act unified and codified military disciplinary rules and processes. It also provided for the jurisdiction of the Court Martial. The Service Police and/or the Service Prosecuting Authority may play an integral part in helping you establish a claim for your client. You may wish to seek their cooperation and/or disclosure.

- When representing a client who has suffered an intentional tort, you will have to decide how to use evidence gathered in any related criminal or disciplinary proceedings. You may also choose to wait for the conclusion of those proceedings, in the hope of a conviction, before progressing the civil claim. In some cases, claimants will come to you having not raised a complaint and you may have to encourage them to contact the Service Police (or civilian police) and/or raise a service complaint.

- If your own client has a criminal conviction and/or disciplinary history, this may affect their prospects of promotion and impact on the value of their civil claim where they are claiming loss of a military career.

# CHAPTER ELEVEN
# SERVICE COMPLAINTS

## Introduction

In this chapter we explore some of the work-related grievances and claims that service personnel can bring. Before doing so, we must familiarise ourselves with the military's internal grievance process: the service complaint system.

Most employees think twice before raising a complaint with their employers because they fear negative repercussions from them and/or their colleagues. This is magnified for service personnel, perhaps because of the cultural stigma attached to 'complainants', but also because of what is at stake in respect of their careers. In fact, as an example, the Armed Forces Continuous Attitude Survey of 2019 found that only 7% of service personnel who experiencing bullying, harassment or discrimination raised a formal complaint. The data gathered indicated overwhelmingly that service personnel did not trust the formal grievance process and were concerned about reprisals.

## 11.2 The system

The formal grievances of service personnel are governed by *JSP 831 Redress of Individual Grievances: Service Complaints*. This sets out the means by which complaints can be raised under the powers of sections 334 to 339 of the Armed Forces Act (which deal with redress of individual grievances) and its associated statutory regulations.

The purpose of the service complaints system is: *"to provide service personnel with a process that is fair, effective and efficient through which they can have valid grievances on matters relating to their service in the Armed Forces addressed and can seek redress."*

*JSP 831* is divided into two parts; the first part is the Directive and sets out the policy, rules and procedures. The second part is the Guidance, and provides commentary to service personnel and decision makers on how to comply with the provisions.

Civilian employees of the MoD have a separate Civilian Grievance Policy. If a grievance relates to bullying and/or harassment there is further guidance on how that complaint should be processed in *JSP 763: the MoD Bullying and Harassment Complaints Procedures* (this will govern such complaints whether brought by a service person or a civilian employee).

The military operates what is in essence a three-tier system of complaints:

- Service complaint
- Service complaint appeal
- Application to the Service Complaint Ombudsman

## 11.3 Terminology

There is some important terminology which may help you traverse the rules and guidance:

| Term | Definition |
|---|---|
| Complainant | A person who has raised a service complaint. |
| Respondent | A person who is the subject of a service complaint. |

| | |
|---|---|
| Defence Business Services | The human resources department for civilian employees of the MoD. |
| The Defence Council | The body that is constitutionally responsible for the decisions and appointments made in the service complaints system. In practice it will delegate the majority of its functions to individuals (called 'delegates'). |
| The Secretariat | The service complaints system is administered by both a joint and single service secretariat. |
| Specified Officer (SO) | The person to whom a formal service complaint is first submitted. This is usually the complainant's Commanding Officer. |
| Commanding Officer (CO) | An officer in Command of a ship, unit or military establishment. |
| Assisting Officer (AO) | A person assigned to assist either a complainant or a respondent during the service complaints process. |
| Investigating Officer (IO) | A person assigned to investigate a service complaint. |
| Harassment Investigating Officer (HIO) | A person specifically assigned to investigate a service complaint that involves allegations of harassment. |

| | |
|---|---|
| Decision Body (DB) or Appeal Body (AB) | An individual or group of individuals assigned by the Secretariat to investigate and make a decision on a complaint. An officer charged with deciding a complaint may sometimes be referred to as the 'Deciding Officer' or 'DO' (see, for example, *JSP 763*). An appeal body must include at least one independent (non-military/non civil service) member in certain cases, for example, where complaints involve discrimination, harassment or dishonest behaviour. |
| The Service Complaints Ombudsman (previously SCO but now SCOAF) | The Ombudsman provides independent oversight of the service complaints system and has a number of powers to help her achieve an efficient, effective and fair complaints system. The position has recently been rebranded to the "Service Complaints Ombudsman for the Armed Forces". |
| Equality and Diversity Advisor (EDA) | A person who has received training so that they may provide impartial advice about equality and diversity issues in their unit. |
| Redress | The remedy sought by the complainant, or that determined by the decision or appeal body to be an appropriate remedy in answer to a Service complaint which has been upheld or partially upheld. A decision or appeal body is obliged to consider appropriate redress which may differ from the redress requested by a complainant. |
| Special-to-type matters (STT) | Certain matters such as healthcare, housing, pay and allowances, must go through their own complaints process before a service complaint can be raised. |

The official Glossary and further terms can be found at *Annex A of JSP 831*.

## 11.4 The process

*JSP 831* provides step-by-step guidance on what should happen when a service person has a grievance, as well as charts to help illustrate the process. The key steps and rules are summarised in short form below (but be aware that these do not comprise all the steps in the process):

- Informal resolution of any complaints is encouraged first and, where possible, line managers are to seek advice from Equality and Diversity Advisers and/or their service legal departments, and to offer mediation where appropriate.
- If informal resolution is not possible or satisfactory, a service person may raise a formal service complaint by completed the necessary form (the "Annex F") and submitting it to their Specified Officer. Usually their immediate line manager/superior in their chain of command. If that individual is implicated in the complaint, then the complaint will move up the chain of command.
- An alternative method of raising a service compliant is to contact the SCOAF for a referral, mentioned further below.
- The Annex F form must be submitted **within three months of the act** which is the subject of the complaint. Where the complaint relates to a series of acts, the time limit will run from the last act which they are complaining about. The Specified Officer must then make a decision about whether the complaint has been validly raised and is in time. If a complaint is out of time, the complainant must give reasons. The Specified Officer can accept complaints out of time where it is just and equitable to do so.

- If the Specified Officer determines that the complaint is inadmissible, the complainant may appeal directly to the Service Complaints Ombudsman and must do so within four weeks of receiving the decision.

- If a complaint is raised in time or accepted out of time, the complainant will not then be able to add any further allegations to it. Any new allegations would have to be subject to the same test of admissibility.

- Any admissible complaint is then referred to the Defence Council, which appoints a Decision Body. The Decision Body can appoint an Investigating Officer (or Harassment Investigating Officer in cases involving harassment). They will then investigate the complaints, interview the complainant, respondents and any witnesses, gather any relevant evidence and then report to the Decision Body.

- The Decision Body will then make a decision on the service complaint. It will have to set out the basis for that decision in writing to the complainant and also advise on their right to appeal. The standard of proof for any decision made during a service complaint is based on the 'balance of probabilities' i.e. that a wrong probably occurred.

- The process for a service complaint appeal mimics that for the service complaints at first instance. If a complainant decides to appeal, they will normally have **six weeks** to submit this in writing. If they are out of time they will have to explain why. The Defence Council delegate will have to decide whether the appeal can proceed. They can accept complaints out of time where it is just and equitable to do so.

- An Appeal Body is appointed and that body may appoint an investigator. An appeal decision with reasons must be set out in writing to the complainant. Appeals can be determined on the evidence alone, or the appeal body may consider it right to hold an appeal hearing.

- If the complainant is still unsatisfied with the decision following the appeal, or has complaints about how the appeal was handled, then they will have the option of applying to the Service Complaints Ombudsman (mentioned below).

## 11.5 Redress

When raising a service complaint, the complainant is required to specify what remedy they are seeking. There is no restriction on what they may request. Below are a few examples:

- Financial compensation.
- Administrative action against the respondents.
- Amending records, such as annual reports.
- Reinstatement or promotion.
- Compulsory education to personnel.
- An apology.
- Consolatory compensation for injury to feelings.

Any decision or appeal body is obliged to consider providing the complainant with a remedy if they are successful, even if they have not stipulated it in their complaint. Financial compensation is sometimes awarded but the discretion is wide and the awards rarely satisfy. These tend to range from a few hundred pounds to a few thousand pounds.

The Defence Council can decide to reconsider a service complaint (or aspects of that complaint) where the SCOAF's recommendations indicate this. However, recommendations made by the SCOAF are not binding on the Defence Council (or the MoD). What this means is that technically a service person may have had the decision of their service complaint reversed in their favour by the SCOAF, only to be left without an appropriate redress.

## 11.5 The Service Complaints Ombudsman for the Armed Forces

The Office of the SCOAF opened on 1st January 2016, replacing the Office of the Service Complaints Commissioner which ran from 2008-2015. The SCOAF has powers to:

- Make referrals of any service person's complaints to a Specified Officer (i.e. get the complaints process started by nominating someone to consider whether it is valid and in time).
- Investigate complaints that have been finally determined for reasons of maladministration (e.g. undue delay) or in relation to the substance of any decision (i.e. whether it was right or not).
- Make recommendations to the Defence Council.

The main role of the SCOAF is to scrutinise decisions and/or maladministration in the service complaints process. The general process is as follows:

- A complainant who has had their service complaint finally determined (i.e. at appeal level), and who wishes to complain about maladministration or the substance of that decision, must make an application to the Ombudsman within six weeks of the final decision.

- The application to the Ombudsman must be in writing. There is a specified form available on the Ombudsman's website that should be used.

- The Ombudsman will consider whether any complaints of maladministration, delay or failings in the substance of a decision are well founded and to set out her decision in a report with any recommendations. It is fairly normal practice for the Ombudsman to share the contents of a draft report with the parties and invite comment in the first instance.

The SCOAF has the same authority as the High Court in being able to require witnesses to attend and give evidence and/or in respect of the production of documents. If necessary, the SCOAF can apply to the High Court and initiate contempt proceedings against any individual who does not lawfully comply with such a request.

The SCOAF has more freedom in the way that complaints are investigated, including whether:

- To investigate at all.

- To investigate only parts of any allegations made in the original service complaint.

- To hold an oral hearing, privately or in public.

- Anyone involved is permitted legal representation.

A decision of the SCOAF can be judicially reviewed, but strict time limits will apply (normally these must be made promptly and in any event no later than three months from the date of any decision).

## 11.6 Implications for civil claims

You may be approached by a client who has raised or is contemplating raising a service complaint. Within their complaint might lay a number of civil claims that they will want to progress either in tandem with the service complaint or after that process has concluded. A few examples of service complaints which may result in civil claims are those involving:

- Bullying and harassment – can result in a claim under the Protection from Harassment Act and/or in negligence.
- Discrimination – either in respect of harassment that relates to a protected characteristic (see above) or some other act that has resulted in the complainant being treated differently (which they can also pursue in the employment tribunal).
- Personal injury – where a service person has suffered harm that was the fault of their commanders or peers.
- Mismanagement – can potentially result in a claim in negligence for stress at work where there is a recognisable psychiatric injury.

All service complaints are meant to be concluded within 24 weeks, but this remains more an aspiration than a reality. It is generally a far slower process than civilian grievance processes. There is also the possibility of an appeal and, if that decision is unhelpful an application to the SCOAF. By the time the process is concluded and a final decision is made, your client may have been waiting for over a year (in fact, complex complaints can take several years to conclude).

You must therefore have a clear strategy from the outset, otherwise claims involving service complaints can become risky and uneconomical for many reasons. Generally, you will have little or no control over the process, which will introduce many unknowns and risks. There are also a number of specific points that you should bear in mind:

- Your client may approach you having been disappointed with the outcome of their service complaint. By the time they have exhausted the complaints system, and depending on what stage they may have reached, many months may have passed since the original offending act(s) or behaviour. They may have limitation issues in respect of any or all of the claims that you identify, and they will have to decide tactically when to issue their claims and/or notify the MoD of a perspective claim (i.e. by a letter of claim).

- One of the benefits of the service complaint process can be that a thorough investigation is carried out and statements taken from those involved. Such evidence might be difficult or impossible for you to obtain at that stage, primarily because all those involved in service complaints are ordered not to discuss the complaint with anyone. Whereas they are in fact compelled by service law to assist in the investigations into a service complaint.

- Not all complaints are investigated thoroughly or fairly, however. A lot may depend on the Investigating Officer and the Decision Body. Many complainants are left disappointed by the process, and this may mean that they have waited for nothing.

- Your client and other witnesses will be interviewed and may approve statements that they do not check properly. The quality of the statements sometimes may leave a lot to be desired. You will not see this evidence until the Investigating Officer (or HIO) has submitted their report and a service complaint bundle provided to your client, sometimes months later.

- When the service complaint bundle is received, your client will be given a very limited window in which to consider the documents and provide comments, sometimes a few days. For you, this could become a very work intensive period where you will have to familiarise yourself with an entire bundle of evidence, statements, correspondence and reports, so that you can advise your client on any discrepancies that they should be raising. It is often sensible to suggest that your client request more time if needed, which is normally granted to enable advice to be taken.

- A complaint that is rejected may highlight acts or omissions on the part of your client, which may bolster the defence to any civil claim and/or any arguments to contributory negligence.

- Your client's complaints may relate to individuals in their chain of command (i.e. their superiors) and/or colleagues. Not all the actions of these respondents might be relevant to your client's potential civil claims. Equally, not all of their actions might attract vicarious liability as against the MoD. This will mean you will have to advise your client on whether to bring civil claims against one or more of the respondents and/or the MoD. In addition to these tactical considerations, you will need to make enquiries into whether the respondents are solvent and able to satisfy any judgment. This will add a level of complexity and risk to the proceedings.

- Where a complainant alleges behaviour that may be criminal in nature, for example, an allegation of harassment, then the respondent(s) may be subject to investigation and prosecution. The normal procedure will be for any criminal element of the complaint to first be investigated by the RMP. It may be necessary to wait for the conclusion of that investigation and/or prosecution before pursuing a civil claim. This may be advantageous where this leads to a conviction against a respondent, a fact which you might use to bolster your client's civil claim. However, this will add further delay because the service complaints process will not resume until after the criminal element has been determined. In such circumstances it is not uncommon for some service complaints to take years to conclude.

- As a lawyer, you are not normally permitted to become formally involved in the service compliant process, although complainants can request a legal representative to be present at hearings. Hearings are normally only held in appeals, but this will depend on the circumstances of the case, for example, where there is complexity or where a lot may hinge on witness evidence and the appeal body wishes to ear directly from those witnesses. The decision or appeal body will determine whether or not to allow for a hearing and/or legal representation. This means that you will have very limited influence on the service complaint proceedings.

- Any decision made during the service complaints process will not prohibit the MoD from disputing liability to a civil claim that relates to the same facts, although where a decision has already been made in your client's favour this can be used to bolster their civil claim. Equally, any decision by the SCOAF will not bind the MoD in respect of whether or not to accept liability for a civil claim. This means that your client may wait for a decision, appeal and then a review by the SCOAF, only to become embroiled in a defended civil claim on the same facts raised in the complaint. It will be a lengthy and stressful process for them.

- Any decision of the SCOAF can be challenged further by way of judicial review. A claim for judicial review must be made "promptly" and in any event within three months of the date of the decision that is being appealed. Judicial review is a highly specialised process, sometimes risky and often expensive. In some cases it may be your client's last resort.

- Just because your client is pursuing a service complaint does not mean that the right tactical decision is to wait for the conclusion of those proceedings before proceeding with a civil claim. In fact, you might decide to issue proceedings in order to apply pressure or because, for example, you are confident that there is sufficient evidence to succeed. These tactical considerations are delicate and require careful planning.

## 11.7 Claims in the employment tribunal

This book does not cover employment law in any great depth, but you will need to have a general understanding of your client's rights in the employment tribunal, particularly where they may overlap with common law claims for any injury or loss that they have suffered. Some key elements of employment rights for service personnel are explored below. For a better understanding, readers are encouraged to refer to employment law textbooks and familiarise themselves with the legal framework:

- Employment Rights Act 1996
- Equality Act 2010
- Employment Tribunal Rules of Procedure 2013 (as amended)

### 11.7.1 Discrimination and other claims

Service personnel enter into service agreements with the State, as opposed to a contract of employment. They are not 'employees' in law, but are often treated in the same way. As servants of the Crown they have a very unique status, but they also lose many rights that civilians would take for granted. For example, they are not entitled to bring certain claims in the employment tribunal for:

- Wage protection
- Whistleblowing
- Rights on redundancy
- Wrongful dismissal (i.e. breach of contract)
- Constructive dismissal
- Most forms of unfair dismissal

If your client is an employee of the MoD, as opposed to a service person, then they will enjoy greater freedom of employment law rights, including the right to bring a claim for breach of contract.

Service personnel can bring a claim for discrimination, which is a claim intended to prohibit unlawful behavior in respect of certain 'protected characteristics' (S. 4 Equality Act 2010), which are:

- Age
- Disability
- Gender reassignment
- Marriage and civil partnership
- Pregnancy and maternity
- Race
- Religion or belief
- Sex
- Sexual orientation

The Crown owes duties to service personnel as if they were 'employees' (s.83(3)(a) Equality Act 2010). Though there are some exceptions, in fact:

- The age and disability discrimination provisions do not apply to the MoD at all.

- The MoD is able to restrict decisions about recruitment, promotion, transfer, training and promotion to men and/or people who are not transsexuals (i.e. ignoring those who are in the process of gender reassignment). This would only be permitted where it could be shown that this ensures combat effectiveness.

This means practically that the MoD can act in ways that discriminate against these protected characteristics and a claimant may have no cause of action.

To succeed in a claim of discrimination, a claimant would have to show that they have been discriminated against in the following ways (reference is made to the relevant sections of the Equality Act 2010 and readers are encouraged to consider the precise wording of the statute):

- Direct discrimination – where they are treated less favourably because of their protected characteristic (s.13).
- Indirect discrimination – where a provision, criterion or practice at work puts them at a disadvantage and there is no legitimate reason for it (s.19).
- Harassment – where they suffer unwanted conduct related to a protected characteristic and which violates their dignity or creates an intimidating, hostile, degrading, humiliating or offensive environment or engages in unwanted conduct of a sexual nature with the same effect (s.26).
- Victimisation – where they are subjected to a detriment for doing a protected act, such as bringing proceedings in the employment tribunal or giving evidence in such proceedings (s.27).

Once a claimant has shown facts from which the employment tribunal could conclude that there has been an act of unlawful discrimination, the burden shifts to the employer defending the claim (termed the 'Respondent'), who will have to show that there was no discrimination and, if it fails to satisfy this burden, the complaint of discrimination must be upheld (s.136 Equality Act 2010).

A claim for discrimination can also be brought against the perpetrator of the act of discrimination (s.110 Equality Act 2010), although you would invariably be recommending that a claim be brought against the MoD vicariously. Although the principles considered in respect of vicarious liability in tort will be similar here, helpfully the employment tribunal has a much broader discretion to interpret what is and what is not "closely connected" to employment, particularly in cases involving sexual or racial harassment (the most prevalent types of discrimination claim brought by service personnel).

### 11.7.2 Procedure

Claims in the employment tribunal attract tight deadlines; they normally have to be issued within three months of the date of the last act complained of (though readers should please note that the procedure and impact of ACAS conciliation on time limits is complex and beyond the scope of this book).

The process for bringing a claim is largely done online. A claimant will need to complete a claim form (ET1), setting out the types of claims that they are making and the grounds for their complaint. Where there are many connected incidents over a period of time, then the three months will normally be taken to run from the date of the last incident (s.123(3) Equality Act 2010), but there may be arguments about interpretation and your client may have to prove that the incidents complained of were sufficiently connected.

Once a claim has been accepted, the Respondent will have to file a response in the form 'ET3' within 28 days of receiving the ET1. The case will then be managed by the tribunal through to a final hearing.

The situation for service personnel is different courtesy of sections 121 and 123(2) of the Equality Act 2010. In summary, this will extend the time for bringing a claim in the employment tribunal to six months (from the date of the last act complained of), so long as:

- the service person has raised a service complaint (in time);
- the complaint has not been withdrawn.

Practically this allows time for service complaints to conclude before service personnel raise a claim in the employment tribunal, but realistically this means that claims in the employment tribunal will normally be stayed pending the conclusion of the service complaint process (because that process is rarely resolved quickly enough). This can create a slow and unsatisfactory situation for a client who is seeking a remedy for any immediate issue in their workplace. This also creates a risk when advising prospective clients because, if they withdraw their service complaint, they may be precluded from bringing a claim in the employment tribunal.

The employment tribunal does have a discretion to extend time where it is just and equitable to do so and sometimes it is possible to argue that, even though a claim is out of time, it should be allowed to proceed where there has been a lengthy service complaint and on the basis that there is no prejudice to the respondent (i.e. the MoD, who would have carried out its own investigation).

Employment tribunals were intended to be less formal than the county or high court, but proceedings will mimic those in civil claims (the Employment Tribunal Rules of Procedure are similar in many ways to the Civil Procedure Rules). There will normally be an early hearing (a Case Management Discussion) to agree issues and set a timetable, when directions will be made for disclosure, exchange of witness and expert evidence and a final hearing date set. The panel will consist of one legally qualified Employment Judge and two lay members, from commercial and union backgrounds respectively. Their final decisions are akin to judgments and must be reasoned. Decisions can be appealed to the Employment Appeal Tribunal and, thereafter, to the Court of Appeal and Supreme Court. Deadlines for appealing a decision of the employment tribunal can vary, but this will normally be 42 days from the date of receiving the decision. Tribunal fees are not currently payable.

### 11.7.3 Remedies

The employment tribunal is able to make an award for *injury to feelings*, which cannot be recovered in the civil courts. An award for injury to feelings does not require a diagnosed psychiatric condition, but this will of course buttress a claim as well as other factors like the nature and extent of the harassment will be relevant. The range of awards were originally clarified in ***Vento v Chief Constable of West Yorks Police (No 2) [2002] EWCA Civ 1871***, but have since been stipulated by the President of the Employment Tribunals as case law has developed and in line with inflation. The guidance is updated periodically and currently provides for the following range of awards (often referred to as the '*Vento bands*'):

- Lower band (less serious cases/isolated incidents) – £900 to £8,800
- Middle band (moderate cases) – £8,800 to £26,300
- Upper band (cases involving campaigns of harassment on discriminatory grounds) – £26,300 to £44,000
- Exceptional cases (the most serious/rare cases) – over £44,000

An employment tribunal is entitled to make an award to a claimant for PSLA *in addition* to an award for injury to feelings, but it will need to be conscious of the potential for double recovery. Awards can also be made for aggravated and/or exemplary damages in the most serious cases. In respect of the former, where malice and/or discriminatory conduct has been flagrant. In respect of the latter, where there has been a serious abuse of trust and/or unconstitutional conduct by servants of the Crown.

In respect of special damages/pecuniary loss, an employment tribunal will approach these and particularly future losses in the same way that a civil court would i.e. by applying a multiplicand/multiplier method with reference to the Ogden tables where appropriate. However, some practitioners would argue that civil judges are normally more experienced with these assessments as they will encounter them more often and the key precedents that deal with how to approach the quantification of these awards is largely generated through the civil courts.

The employment tribunal is also able to make recommendations to Respondents to improve working environments and reduce the impact of discriminatory behaviour. Where recommendations are ignored, this may result in an increase in compensation awarded.

### 11.7.4 Choice of venue

Where your client has potential claims in the civil courts and the employment tribunal that stem from the same set of facts, they may not be entitled to bring these claims in both venues because this may amount to an abuse of process (*res judicata*). This will depend on the facts, causes of action and available remedies. A decision will have to be made about which venue is best in the circumstances of their case. Given that the time limits in the employment tribunal are short, that decision may have to be made very quickly.

The table below sets out some pros and cons of proceeding in the employment tribunal as opposed to the county or high court. It is predicated on the basis that your client is considering bringing a claim for discrimination in the employment tribunal vs a common law or statutory (PHA) claim in the county court. These suggestions should be considered in the context of the facts of any case, available funding, your client's circumstances and their objectives.

| Employment Tribunal | County/High Court |
|---|---|
| No fees payable. | Fees payable (and can be significant). |
| Generally shorter timetable but will normally have to conclude service complaint process first. | Generally longer timetable but are not obliged to wait for the conclusion of the service complaints process. |

| | |
|---|---|
| An award for injury to feelings available in addition to any award for PSLA. | Other non-financial remedies may be available, for example an injunction in respect of claims brought under the Protection from Harassment Act 1997. |
| An award for injury to feelings does not require a claimant to have suffered a diagnosable psychiatric injury and there is no need to establish that such injury was reasonably foreseeable). | All injuries must be substantiated with appropriate (normally expert) evidence, which can be expensive. |
| Once the claimant has proved facts from which discrimination may be concluded, the burden of proof shifts to the respondent. | The burden is on the claimant, who will need to establish breach of duty, causation and loss. |
| No need to comply with pre-action protocols, to provide expert evidence when raising a complaint or quantify the claim. | Early stages of a claim can be expensive and time consuming. |
| Costs are not awarded save in special circumstances. | Adverse costs possible in certain circumstances under QOCS and claimant will recover costs where successful. |
| Arguably a much wider discretion in respect of vicarious liability. | The common law test of vicarious liability will have to be applied and is generally more stringent. |

| | |
|---|---|
| The tribunal may not be familiar with service personnel and issues. | Civil judges are more likely to be familiar with military claims but not necessarily so. |
| The tribunal is arguably less well equipped to assess the complex financial losses claimed by service personnel. | Common law and specialist PI judges are arguably better equipped to assess complex claims for future loss that may arise in military claims. |
| Three stages of appeal – Employment Appeal Tribunal, Court of Appeal then Supreme Court. | Two stages of appeal – Court of Appeal then Supreme Court. |

## 11.8 Points for practice

- Service personnel can raise a formal service complaint if they feel they have been wronged on any matter that relates to their service. Complaints can cover a broad spectrum of issues, such as bullying, harassment, discrimination, dishonest behaviour and pay issues.

- The service complaints process may become important for your work. It can be a useful tool for redress for your client and assist in gathering evidence, but it can also cause significant delays and become a hindrance.

- Service complaints must be submitted within three months of any act complained of. Most service personnel will be daunted by the thought of raising a service complaint, and concerned about the potential impact on their careers.

- The SCOAF scrutinises decisions and/or maladministration in the service complaints process. Decisions of the SCOAF will not bind the MoD in respect of civil proceedings.

- Service personnel have limited rights in the employment tribunal, but can bring claims for discrimination where they can show that they have been treated less favourably because of certain protected characteristics.

- When considering whether and how to proceed, your client will need advice on the advantages and disadvantages of their different claims and their best choice of venue. This is not a straightforward exercise and yet may have to be carried out promptly given the short deadlines in the employment tribunal.

# CHAPTER TWELVE
# PROCEDURE

## Introduction

In this chapter, we will look at some fundamentals of proceeding against the MoD and readers are encouraged to review the comments made in **Chapter 1** in respect of this particular defendant.

## 12.1 Jurisdiction and applicable law

Given that service personnel often operate abroad, whether on military exercises or in combat, some torts will be suffered in other jurisdictions. This means that you will have to consider:

- Whether the English courts can hear the case.
- Which law would apply.
- Which venue or law is more advantageous to your client.
- Available funding, interim applications and remedies.
- The costs bearing in mind the location of witnesses, evidence, sites of accidents.

The legal principles behind determining jurisdiction and applicable law go well beyond this book and involve the interaction of common law, European Law (principally EC Regulation 864/2007, known as "Rome II") and international agreements. As such, readers are encouraged to consider specialist texts. There are a few general principles which may help:

- The defendant's domicile normally determines jurisdiction. It has been long established in the common law that the State can be sued in its own jurisdiction for acts and omissions that occur overseas. So whether the tort has occurred at a base abroad (and this includes Scotland and Northern Ireland), or on board a vessel travelling in international waters, then the MoD can normally be sued in this jurisdiction.

- The applicable law would normally be *"the law of the country in which the damage occurred..."* (Article 4(1) Rome II).

- The applicable law can be displaced where both claimant and defendant are habitually resident in the same country when the damage occurs (Article 4(2) Rome II). In such circumstances it may be open to argue that law of the country in which they share residence should apply. Such arguments are not straight forward – see ***Winrow v Hemphill [2014] EWHC 3164 (QB).***

- Alternatively, it may be open to you to argue that English law should apply where the "*tort is manifestly more closely connected with the United Kingdom*" (Article 4(3) Rome II). This argument may succeed in cases involving contractual agreements or other special relationships between the parties.

The position becomes complicated when your client is pursuing additional defendants, for example a negligent company, hospital and/or doctor who may have no connection to the MoD. In such cases, you might consider seeking to agree jurisdiction and applicable law with the defendants, to save costs and time. Alternatively, where your client is proceeding on the basis that the MoD is vicariously liable for the actions of defendants who are domiciled outside of the jurisdiction, you may make the tactical and economic decision to proceed against the MoD only.

Defendant solicitors will invariably seek to select the option that is most advantageous to their client (as would a claimant's solicitor for that matter). In ***Jikhabanadur Rai v Ministry of Defence 2016 WL 02641890*** the Claimant, Mr Rai, was a soldier in the British Army who had been stationed in Canada and was undertaking training with horses when he suffered serious injury. The training had been arranged by the MoD but delivered by a private company, 'Lazy H Trail', which was incorporated in Alberta, Canada. Mr Rai brought a claim against the MoD in England. The MoD disputed the claim and denied any breach of duty. It averred that the law applicable to the claim was that of Alberta. The question posed to the High Court was whether Canadian or English law applied.

In the first instance the court had to discern whether European or domestic law guided its decision on applicable law, namely, whether the claim fell within the definition of "*civil and commercial matters*" under Article 1(1) of Rome II, or alternatively whether it was excluded because it related to "*liability of the State for acts and omissions in the exercise of State authority*". The MoD argued that the claim fell under the latter category, in which case:

- Rome II would not apply (virtue of Art1(1) of the same Regulation);
- the issue would have to be determined according to common law principles, which would mean that;
- the applicable law would be that of Alberta (which was more favourable to the MoD because the law on limitations in Alberta would preclude the claimant from pursuing his claim).

Gargan J rejected this argument and found that the claim was a *"civil and commercial matter"* under Rome II because, inter alia:

- The injury did not arise out of some positive exercise or projection of State power.
- The MoD was using facilities in Canada and not exercising its sovereign rights. It had arranged training in the same way that a private employer would have done for its employees.
- Mr Rai could not properly be regarded as undertaking any military operation on behalf of the State.

Having found that Rome II determined jurisdiction, the law applicable to the issues in the case would be English because both parties were habitually resident in England (courtesy of Article 4(2) of those Regulations).

The MoD then sought to disapply English law in favour of the law of Alberta by arguing that the injury was "*manifestly more closely connected with*" Canada (under Article 4(3) of Rome II). Gargan J rejected this argument also and held that English law remained the correct and applicable law:

> *"I accept that the tort occurred in Alberta and that the immediate injury was sustained in Alberta. Further, I accept the Defendant's argument that examination of breach of duty will principally involve consideration of events which occurred in Alberta and that Lazy H Trail was providing its services under a contract which was subject to the law of Alberta. However, I must balance against this a number of other factors:*
>
> 1. *The parties involved were both habitually resident in England;*
> 2. *The relationship between the parties was governed by a contract of service made in England and subject to English law;*
> 3. *The claim is based on the non-delegable duty of care which arises out of the contract of service. This will involve the examination of the conduct of members of the British Army resident in England who were responsible for risk assessments;*
> 4. *The Defendant had agreed that it would, so far as reasonably practicable, adopt English standards for decisions relating to health and safety. (I accept that this is not an agreement to apply English law but it is nevertheless a factor which shows a connection with England and tends to rebut a manifestly closer connection to Alberta);*
> 5. *The medium and long term consequences of the injury sustained will be suffered in England and the Defendant must have*

> *known that this was likely to be the result of any injury to one of its soldiers carrying out his duties in Canada;*
>
> *Taking all those factors into consideration it seems to me that the closer connection was to England rather than Alberta and in any event the Defendant falls some way short of establishing a manifestly closer connection to Alberta."*

Interestingly, Gargan J also stated obiter that had the Rome II Regulation not applied (i.e. on the basis that the claim involved the exercise of sovereign power) then it would still have been appropriate to find the applicable law to be English because of the operation of section 12 of the Private International Law (Miscellaneous Provisions) Act 1995 (PILA) i.e. the Claimant had shown that it was substantially more appropriate for English law to apply to his claim.

***Rai*** is a helpful case and can be used as good authority for the proposition that any claim brought by a service person in relation to training abroad is likely to still be governed by English law. It also helps illustrate the complicated nature and potential risk of jurisdictional issues in these cases.

## 12.2 Limitation

Many service personnel will come to you out of time to bring their claims. Some will say that they were informed by colleagues and/or superiors that they would have to wait until the end of their service to bring a claim. This may be because of some confusion with claims under the Armed Forces Compensation Scheme (although they would be wrong on both counts – see **13.5**). Other clients may simply have waited until their service terminated, fearing the consequences that a civil claim would bring on their career. Whatever the reason, late claims are a regular theme in dealing with military clients.

For most civil claims in respect of personal injury these will have to be issued at court within three years of the date of the injury (Limitation Act 1980 s.11 (4)). More time is allowed where the 'date of knowledge' of the injury comes later, for example, where an injury has a late onset. A claimant's date of knowledge is taken from when they first had knowledge of the following facts (Limitation Act 1980 s.14 (1)):

(a) that the injury in question was significant; and

(b) that the injury was attributable in whole or in part to the act or omission which is alleged to constitute negligence, nuisance or breach of duty; and

(c) the identity of the defendant; and

(d) if it is alleged that the act or omission was that of a person other than the defendant, the identity of that person and the additional facts supporting the bringing of an action against the defendant;

As an example, date of knowledge arguments will sometimes arise in NFCI claims, when a service person is told following a cold exposure that they may have an NFCI, but they may still have no real understanding that such a condition is potentially significant and/or long-term. This realisation may happen months if not years later, when they are first told of the prospect of their medical discharge. Such situations are sometimes compounded by well-meaning Medical Officers who, in an attempt to reassure and encourage the service person, fail to advise on the potential implications of their injury.

Another issue, and again a common feature, is that service personnel will be stoic and not complain of symptoms when seeing their Medical Officer. Bearing this in mind, readers are encouraged to go beyond the medical records and explore directly with their clients when symptoms were first experienced, which may trigger the limitation period for the purposes of 'date of knowledge' and push a claim out of time. You may also find that what your client is saying to their Medical Officer is different to what they might be reporting to their line manager. One needs to temper these situations with some compassion and insight:

- A visit to the Medical Officer is sometimes daunting for other ranks. The Medical Officer is normally a superior and part of their chain of command. The service person will be aware that discussions occur between medical staff and their career managers. Therefore there is a dynamic of deference between service personnel and Medical Officers which is unlike the circumstances of a civilian attending a civilian GP.

- Visits to the Medical Officer may be pre-scheduled checkups and/or vaccinations and are not instigated by the service person, who may not deem it necessary or appropriate to raise concerns about other issues.

- The service person will be concerned not to appear to be a 'whinger' and/or that any complaints they make may lead to medical investigations that may impact on their medical category and/or career.

Of course the law takes a very strict view of time limits and a claimant would normally have to satisfy the test under section 33 of the Limitation Act to bring their claim out of time. This section provides the court with a discretion to disapply the relevant limitation period where it is just to do so. This exercise is done with reference to to *all the circumstances* of the case and in particular to (Limitation Act 1980 s.33(3)):

(a) the length of, and the reasons for, the delay on the part of the plaintiff;

(b) the extent to which, having regard to the delay, the evidence adduced or likely to be adduced by the plaintiff or the defendant is or is likely to be less cogent than if the action had been brought within the time allowed by section 11;

(c) the conduct of the defendant after the cause of action arose, including the extent (if any) to which he responded to requests reasonably made by the plaintiff for information or inspection for the purpose of ascertaining facts which were or might be relevant to the plaintiff's cause of action against the defendant;

(d) the duration of any disability of the plaintiff arising after the date of the accrual of the cause of action;

(e) the extent to which the plaintiff acted promptly and reasonably once he knew whether or not the act or omission of the defendant, to which the injury was attributable, might be capable at that time of giving rise to an action for damages; and

(f) the steps, if any, taken by the plaintiff to obtain medical, legal or other expert advice and the nature of any such advice he may have received.

The discretion under the Act is wide but its application is rare. The courts must strike a balance between allowing a claimant access to justice and, on the other, prejudicing defendants with late claims. Where you find your client in need of such arguments, you will need to take a detailed statement dealing with the reasons for their delay and addressing the specific factors above. You may also have to take immediate steps to issue their claim form and forward a letter of claim, to limit any ongoing delay and/or prejudice. The courts may sympathise with a service person where:

- They have been misinformed by their superiors about the time limits in bring a claim.
- They have been deployed abroad or on operations and therefore physically unable to take advice or action in respect of any negligence.
- Records are readily available; the MoD has a lengthy retention policy for documents and, more often than not, these will be

stored electronically and easily accessed, so you may be able to argue against suggestions of prejudice.

- They have suffered with serious PTSD and have found addressing the issues of the alleged negligence difficult and/or traumatic.

- They have raised a service complaint in the hope that this would result in justice only to suffer delays in that process and disappointment with the decision. Arguably where a service complaint has concluded recently the MoD will face little or no prejudice because they have had control of the investigation and evidence.

None of these arguments of themselves would necessarily result in a successful application under Section 33, but they may well contribute to one. Such applications are invariably fact specific. An excellent demonstration of these principles and the court's approach is provided in ***Smith v MoD [2005] EWHC 682 (QB)***.

There are a few other specific limitation periods to be aware of:

- Where a claimant is under the age of 18 the normal three-year limitation period will run from the date they reach majority.

- For claims by dependents and/or the Estate of a deceased person these must be issued within three years of the death or three years of the date of knowledge of the personal representative, whichever is later (Limitation Act 1980 s.11 (4)). Note however that a claim under the Fatal Accidents Act 1976 cannot be brought beyond 3 years after the death; section 33 will not extend to such claims.

- Claims under the Protection from Harassment Act must be brought within six years of the date of the first incident of harassment (see **10.2**).

- Claims under the Human Rights Act must be brought within one year. The Act provides a discretion to the court to extend the time limit to "*such longer period as the court or tribunal considers equitable having regard to all the circumstances*" (HRA Section 7(5)(b)).

## 12.3 Pre-action

Before you issue proceedings, assuming that limitation allows, you should first engage with the defendant by following the necessary pre-action protocol. Generally speaking there are two routes for notification, set out below.

For all personal injury claims you should first contact the MoD's claims handlers:

Topmark Claims Management Ltd
160 Bath Street
Glasgow
G2 4TB

For all clinical negligence claims you should first contact:

Common Law Claims & Policy Division
Ministry of Defence
Main Building Floor 3 Zone I
Whitehall
London
SW1A 2HB

The MoD's Common Law Claims & Policy Division (CLC&P) is responsible for processing common-law, non-contractual compensation claims on behalf of the MoD. The CLC&P has a broader remit than this alone and is involved in a number of other official capacities, including providing policy advice, dealing with Parliamentary Questions and ministerial correspondence, handling third party claims against foreign forces based in the UK, issuing indemnities for training operations and handling requests under the Freedom of Information Act, to name a few.

You might find that those claims that are complex or sensitive would be retained by the CLC&P, for example, claims relating to historic allegations in Northern Ireland, civilian claims following operations in Iraq and Afghanistan and claims involving combat immunity issues. Reader's must check online and periodically for changes for claims policy. Wherever there is any doubt, the CLC&P must be the first port of call and can direct you to which office should be handling the claim.

Your client's claim may be governed by one or more different pre-action protocols and you will need to be familiar with the obligations imposed by the Civil Procedure Rules on both parties before embarking on litigation. Depending on the nature of your client's claim, readers are encouraged to familiarise themselves with the following:

- The practice direction to pre-action conduct and protocols
- The pre-action protocol for personal injury claims
- The pre-action protocol for the resolution of clinical disputes
- The pre-action protocol for disease and illness claims

The protocols are not mandatory, but failure to comply with them can result in consequences, including costs. In particular, they provide for time limits on replying to letter of claim and requests for disclosure (which are extended in cases involving injury abroad). They are a crucial tool and can provide many tactical advantages if you get the process right. Where there may be an overlap of these protocols, it is helpful to consider the principle objectives of the protocols, as set out in paragraph 3 of the above practice direction:

> *Before commencing proceedings, the court will expect the parties to have exchanged sufficient information to –*

*(a) understand each other's position;*

*(b) make decisions about how to proceed;*

*(c) try to settle the issues without proceedings;*

*(d) consider a form of Alternative Dispute Resolution (ADR) to assist with settlement;*

*(e) support the efficient management of those proceedings; and*

*(f) reduce the costs of resolving the dispute.*

Once you have notified either the CLC&P or Topmark that your client's claim form has been issued, they will normally transfer the case to the Government Legal Department (i.e. the Treasury Solicitor) or to a firm on the MoD's panel of solicitors.

## 12.4 Applying for disclosure

Another theme of military claims which is stressed throughout this book is the sheer amount of investigation and particularly early expert evidence that will be needed to help assess and steer a claim. You will need early disclosure and make your request clear in your client's letter of notification and/or claim. It helps to provide your client with a list of postings at an early stage and ask them to complete this. This will help both parties in their search for records.

Your client is entitled to access their military occupational health and service records and the process for this requires them to complete a Subject Access Request (SAR) on a requisite form. The process differs depending on which service your client is in and/or whether they are still serving. Details for the process and the forms can be found online.

Where you have notified the MoD of a claim, be aware that it is notoriously slow at providing disclosure. At times, when the disclosure is unit specific it may be able to rely on operational reasons for the delays, for example, specific individuals in your client's chain of command may be deployed and uncontactable. However, more often than not, delays are not explained save with reference to a 'back-log' of claims. Whilst some judges will sympathise with a government department during an era where resources are stretched, most will (and should) treat the MoD like any other defendant. In ***Eaglesham v MoD [2016] EWHC 3011 (QB)*** Mrs Justice Andrews struck out the MoD's defence to a claim involving 'Q fever' and judgment was entered against it for consistently failing to adhere to orders for disclosure. Your recourse therefore when there are delays is to apply for disclosure. You can issue:

- An application for pre-action disclosure (CPR r.31.16).
- An application for specific disclosure after proceedings have been issued (CPR r.31.12).

The principles behind both applications are virtually identical and should be studied. They must be supported by evidence, normally consisting of a witness statement and an exhibit of correspondence. You may be able to argue that:

- Where proceedings are not yet issued, that the defendant is in breach of the relevant pre-action protocol under CPR.
- You are not able to fully prepare your client's pleadings without the requested disclosure (and an order may avoid the prospect of amending pleadings at a later date).
- The documents are readily available (often in electronic format) and any delay is disproportionate.
- The disclosure may help avoid litigation entirely and/or dispose of the proceedings fairly (or avoid proceedings all together).
- Your client is disadvantaged in the litigation.

- Your client is in need of rehabilitation and/or medical assessment and requires access to their records.
- An order will save costs and time.

You should approach disclosure with clarity. Judges do not like 'fishing exercises' and generic requests will be treated with derision. Be clear about what documents should exist by providing a schedule of documents (or classes of documents) that are outstanding. Costs are regularly recovered when the MoD does not sensibly engage in such requests and, helpfully, they are often compelled to provide an early disclosure statement setting out the parameters of any search that has been conducted (this should be checked carefully against any subsequent disclosure in the proceedings).

The following list provides some key documents that you may wish to request at the outset of a claim, but this is not exhaustive and there will be other documents mentioned in this book or which are specific to your client's case that you may wish to request also:

- Any relevant JSP.
- Any relevant single-Service publication.
- Unit, ship or establishment Standing Orders.
- Written orders (for an operation or training exercise) – this will include kit list and training requirements.
- Training records.
- Guidance for Medical Officers – including any policy material or directives from the Surgeon General's Department.
- Risk assessments.

- Personnel file – to include a print of your client's JPA records.
- Unit file – similar to your client's personnel file but often more up-to-date where your client is still serving, as this is held and updated by their unit.
- Welfare records – including all WISMIS records.
- FMed 4 – the physical folder of your client's primary healthcare records, normally held by their MO.
- DMICP – electronically stored primary healthcare records.
- FMed 23 – Medical Board records.
- FMed 9 – military treatment records, for example, DCMH (mental health) or INM records.
- Service complaint bundle.
- Veterans UK file – to include Armed Forces Compensation and/or Pension Scheme (AFCS and AFPS) documents.
- Career, pay and pension forecast.
- Wage slips and pay scales.

## 12.5 Service of proceedings against the MoD

Proceedings against the Crown are governed by the Crown Proceedings Act 1947 as amended and the provisions of Civil Procedure Rules Part 66.

All proceedings against the Crown must be served in accordance with rule 6.10 (b) of the CPR, which stipulates that service on a government department must be effected on the solicitor acting for that Department.

The Practice Direction to Part 66 of CPR directs us to the list of the solicitors acting for the different government departments on whom service is to be effected, published under section 17 of the Crown Proceedings Act 1947. Currently, service of proceedings must be effected on the Government Legal Department (GLD), whose address for service is currently:

> The Treasury Solicitor
> Government Legal Department
> 102 Petty France
> Westminster
> London
> SW1H 9GL

Rule 6.23(7) of CPR extends this rule for service to *all* documents in proceedings, not just the claim form. Note that the GLD does not accept service by email unless expressly agreed in advance.

Depending on the nature of the claim, the GLD will on receipt of claim form (or sometimes sooner) nominate another firm to act. So whilst service of proceedings should normally be effected on the GLD as above, do not be surprised if the next thing you receive is a notice of change of solicitor.

## 12.6 Service of proceedings against service personnel

Your client may be pursuing a claim against a number of service personnel (either in isolation or in tandem with a claim against the MoD vicariously).

The addresses of service personnel are normally kept confidential for security reasons. Where they are stationed in a military establishment, base or other facility, you will not normally be permitted access to make enquiries (nor will any enquiry agent). In such circumstances, the Annex to Practice Direction 6A CPR (service inside the United Kingdom) provides a helpful process to enable Claimants to obtain an address for service of proceedings in this jurisdiction on a service person:

- You will need to know where the potential defendant is serving, their rank and ideally have their service number (this is a unique number given to every service person on entering their service) as well as any information that might help locate the individual, such as their regiment or unit.

- You must then write to a specified officer at the Ministry of Defence setting out the information you have and request their address for service of documents (the Practice Direction provides addresses for the specified officer in each service).

- You will have to provide an undertaking in writing that the address of the service person will be used solely for the purpose of issuing and serving documents in the proceedings and will not be disclosed so far as is possible to any other person within your organisation or to any other person, save only to the court. Normally on receipt of the required information you will be provided with address for service.

If delays are encountered then you will be entitled to apply to the court for an order compelling the MoD to assist you. However, be aware that this process can take time and readers are encouraged to begin their enquiries early on.

## 12.7 Points for practice

- Assessing jurisdiction and applicable law can be very complex and introduce a higher risk profile and expense to a case. For most claims involving negligence by the MoD abroad, your client will be entitled to pursue the MoD here under English law.

But in other cases, where there are multiple tortfeasors, it may serve you to consider the ramifications and benefits of proceeding in a different jurisdiction or under a foreign law, or indeed if you are bound to do so. Early advice from a specialist in jurisdictional issues and/or from foreign lawyers may be necessary.

- Limitation can present a real challenge to military claimants. What procedures do you have in place to test your client's date of knowledge? Where there may be any doubt, issuing a claim to prevent delay and/or prejudice may be the safest option.

- The MoD retain claims handlers to deal with some claims whilst others are dealt with 'in house'. When notifying the MoD and/or their claims handlers of claims and requesting disclosure, you will need to provide them with your client's proof of identity, form of authority, details of their unit and their service number (a unique identity number given to each service person).

- Your client will be entitled to access their records prior to notifying the MoD of their claim. Delays often occur and you should be prepared to issue applications for disclosure where necessary. Be clear with your requests to enhance the chances of success of any application. Diarise the time limits for responses under the relevant pre-action protocol, so that applications can be made without delay.

- Service against the Crown must be effected on the Treasury Solicitor. You will not be entitled to apply for Summary Judgment until the time for filing a Defence has expired (CPR Part 24.4(1A)).

- When serving proceedings against an individual service person, you can follow the procedure under the Annex to Practice Direction 6A CPR to help identify their address for service. You may want to instruct an enquiry agent to carry out an asset report on such defendants to assess the economic viability of pursuing them as a defendant. Where you can strongly argue that the MoD is vicariously liable for their actions, you may make a tactical and economic decision not to pursue them.

- It is worth scouting the government websites for changes to procedure, including claims handler details, requests for records and changes to service addresses. These can change with little notice!

# CHAPTER THIRTEEN
# DAMAGES

## Introduction

Military claims can be high in value. This is largely due to the fact that where a service person has lost their career because of negligence, this will normally result in a significant loss of earnings, benefits and pension. However, recovery of these losses is not straightforward. High value military claims require specialist knowledge, thorough preparation of the evidence and involvement of a variety of experts.

This chapter is predicated on the scenario that your client has lost a military career. Not all claims will involve such loss, but they are likely to remain financially significant where, for example:

- Your client is able to continue to serve regardless of their injury, but their career path or prospects of promotion have been adversely affected.

- They may have left the service for other (non-negligent) reasons, but as a result of their injury and/or ongoing disability, they are left with limited prospects for future civilian employment.

Whilst the key awards are discussed below, these should not be treated as a finite list and readers are encouraged to study specialised texts on the quantification and recovery of damages for a fuller understanding.

## 13.1 General damages

- **Pain, suffering and loss of amenity**

This award will of course depend on the nature of the injuries sustained by your client. Some examples have already been given in other chapters of this book. Guidance can be found in the Judicial College Guidelines of the assessment of general damages in personal injury, currently in its 14th Edition (Sept 2017). Some types of injuries such as NFCI are not covered except within very broad categories and you will need to refer to caselaw for further guidance on general damages.

- **Loss of congenial employment**

This award is meant to compensate those who have lost a career which they particularly enjoyed and valued. Claimants who have lost a lengthy service career are well placed to argue for such an award. Many of the reported awards stem from cases involving public service, such as the police, fire and ambulance services, as well as the military, and that may be because of the vocational aspect to public sector work. They tend to range between £5,000 and £15,000.

In ***Murphy v Ministry of Defence [2016] EWHC 3 (QB)*** a 21 year-old former Sapper in the Royal Parachute Regiment was awarded £10,000 for his loss of congenial employment after an accident at work ended his career.

- **Handicap on the labour market**

This head of loss aims to compensate a claimant for the impact that their injury has had on their capacity to work in the future and is discussed in more detail below in relation to disability and future losses.

## 13.2 Overview of special damages

The majority of your client's losses will stem from their special damages award, which is aimed at compensating them for their expenses and financial losses as a direct result of the negligence. These will comprise both their past losses (as at the date of trial or settlement) plus their future anticipated losses. A few examples are set out below:

- **Salary**

This will largely depend on your client's rank and service. It is sometimes referred to as 'base pay'. Base pay includes an additional element known as the 'X-Factor', which compensates service personnel for the disadvantages that they face as compared to workers in the civilian sector. Defendants will sometimes argue that this additional element should not be compensated when calculating loss of earnings because it is a payment given to compensate for certain hardships in military life; if those hardships are not endured then there is no loss. Practitioners should be aware of this argument but may also want to consider the judicial rejection of it in ***Murphy v MoD [2016] EWHC 3 (QB)***.

Pay scales for your client's particular Service (at the time they were serving) can sometimes be found online or obtained through a disclosure request. These will set out salary by rank and increasing with each promotion.

- **Benefits**

Service personnel can receive a plethora of benefits, set out primarily in *JSP 752: the Tri-Service Regulations for Expenses and Allowances*.

Some benefits are compensatory in nature and remunerate service personnel for tasks undertaken or environmental conditions endured, which are considered to be over and above those recognised within base pay or the 'X-Factor'. Others are contributory in nature and provide financial assistance towards the additional costs involved in service life, such as moving home, but which may involve a degree of personal choice.

Your client's benefits will largely depend on their circumstances, Service and trade. Below are a few noteworthy examples, but ultimately you may need to rely on your client and their payslips to help inform you of these potential losses:

1. Longer Separation Allowance (LSA) – a payment in respect of becoming involuntarily separated from your client's family home for seven days or more.

2. Unpleasant Work Allowance (UWA) – work or a harrowing or unpleasant nature, or involving exposure to a noxious substance will attract additional pay.

3. Operational Allowance (OA) – when deployed to locations which bear higher risk or danger then your client may benefit from this.

4. Fitness and medical benefits – service personnel receive free gym membership, dental and medical care.

5. Subsidised accommodation, food and travel – Service Family Accommodation (SFA) has very low rental and utility charges compared to private rates.

6. Continuation of Education Allowance (CEA) – an allowance to help maintain continuity of education for service children that would otherwise be denied if they were to change schools every time that your client were assigned.

7. Flying pay, submarine pay and other trade specific pay – specialist trades can attract additional pay depending on their duties. This additional pay can be very significant over time.

8. Forces Help To Buy Scheme (FHTB) – service personnel receive advantageous loans to help them purchase a family home.

You may need an employment expert with military expertise to evaluate these benefits according to the projected career path that your client would have had but for their injury. Alternatively, the MoD provide an online benefits calculator.

The MoD may seek to argue that those benefits which are directly related to operational needs should be considered 'perks' rather than 'benefits', and therefore not claimable. This argument may not attach to all your client's benefits.

- **Pension**

You will need to find out what pension scheme applies to your client and bear in mind that the rules may differ for Reservists. Information and rules for all pension schemes can be found online. Your client will most likely benefit from the Armed Forces Pension Scheme 2015 (AFPS 15), unless they have opted out. The scheme provides that the MoD will pay annually 1/47$^{th}$ of your client's pensionable earnings into their pension pot. The other benefits under the scheme include a tax-free lump sum awards and income payable in the event of ill health or early departure, as well as payments to dependents in the event of death in service. A full pension is paid at age 60.

Your client's notional/post injury pension will have to be credited as against their *but for* pension (what they would have received had they continued to serve). This will mean exploring their potential military career and extrapolating the likely pension awarded. Military pensions remain very generous when compared with other pension schemes. Pension losses can often be the most significant single head of loss and can drive much of the litigation. It may be wise and cost effective to arrange for an employment expert or an expert accountant to calculate them. You can also request pension statements and a pension forecast directly from Veterans UK.

- **Travel expenses**

Your client may no longer be able to drive a car because of their condition and/or medication. Alternatively, they may be much more dependent on car travel and less able to walk, cycle or use public transport. In some circumstances their travel expenses will increase significantly. This can result in significant losses over time and they should be encouraged to keep detailed records of these expenses, especially if you are projecting them into the future. Past loss can be a useful guide to future loss here. Your client may also have incurred expenses in travelling for medical, solicitor and expert appointments.

- **Medical expenses**

Your medical expert will need to guide you on the likely cost of medication and treatment now and into the future for your client, to include possible rehabilitation and physiotherapy. Some medication and treatments will be provided by the NHS free of charge and often clients will be entitled to purchase a pre-payment certificate to save money on prescriptions going forward. Where a medical expert recommends timely intervention and/or treatment, then private medical treatment may be warranted and this will be costly. Your client is not obliged to wait for NHS treatment and can claim private fees for medical treatment.

- **Care and assistance**

Depending on the extent of their injuries, your client may now have to rely on family or friends to care for them or to provide help with normal day to day activities such as housework that they would previously have done themselves. This gratuitous care can be claimed and quantified when you can show that it is necessary and proportionate to the injuries sustained. Where your client does not have a close network that they can rely on for care, then they may be forced to pay for professional services for cleaning, support and maintenance.

In complex cases your client may benefit from a report from an expert in care/occupational health.

- **Help with DIY, gardening or car washing**

As with care and assistance your client may now require assistance with DIY, gardening or car washing when they would previously have done these things themselves. If they now pay someone else to do these things as a result of their injuries you can claim these expenses. Alternatively you can claim a suitable gratuitous rate if they are now being done by family members or friends, usually the appropriate commercial rate less 25%.

- **Adaptations**

Your client may need adaptations made to their home, car or other living arrangements, particularly where they have suffered life-changing or disabling injury. Expert evidence (from an architect or engineer) may also be needed where these adaptations are significant and costly.

- **Alternative accommodation**

Where a military career ends abruptly, the process of resettlement can be challenging, particularly for seriously injured clients who may be preoccupied with dealing with either symptoms and/or treatment. They may need to move from Service Family Accommodation into private rented accommodation and there may be a number of costs associated with this. As set out above in relation to loss of benefits, private accommodation is usually significantly more expensive than service accommodation.

- **Retraining and re-education**

The skill set of service personnel can vary greatly and will depend on how long they have served and their Service and/or trade.

Service personnel are provided with access to secondary and higher education during their service. Their ability to progress their skills, education and qualifications during their service is a great boon and often allows them the ability to transition into a well-paid civilian job at the conclusion of their service. During the resettlement process, whether they are leaving their service because their engagement has finished or because of medical discharge, personnel will be afforded enhanced learning credits to help them pay for further education and retraining.

If your client has to pay for retraining or re-education because of the injury (whether career ending or not) this can be included as part of the claim.

The post-military civilian career may be a crucial aspect to your client's claim and needs to be investigated thoroughly, discussed below.

## 13.3 Future loss of earnings and handicap on the labour market

More often than not the most significant head of loss for your client will be their future loss i.e. the military and then civilian career they would have had *but for* their injury. It is important that we consider how the court might approach this particular head of loss. For those readers who are unfamiliar, the following summary of core concepts may assist:

- This assessment requires the court to calculate the claimant's likely career path *but for* the negligence, and deduct from that their notional future earnings i.e. what they will now earn, if anything, until retirement and whilst injured.

- Firstly, the court calculates the annual loss, termed the '*multiplicand*'. This will be deduced from the claimant's likely career path, so if promotions were likely then the multiplicand would have increased over time.

- Secondly, the court will then apply an appropriate '*multiplier*' to the multiplicand, expressed in years. The multiplier normally takes into account a number of factors, including the claimant's age, likely retirement age, accelerated receipt of damages and contingencies i.e. the risks of life that are unrelated to the negligence but which may affect their future earnings regardless, for example, mortality.

- The multiplier used was previously a figure derived by Judges through estimation and reference to precedents. This developed into a more scientific method with the introduction and use in the industry of the 'Ogden tables' in the 1980s. The Ogden tables (currently in their 7th edition) provide an evidence-based framework to assist the court in deriving the correct multiplier. The use of the Ogden tables is beyond the scope of this book, but what is important is to understand when and how the court might deviate from their use (explored below).

- Where a case involves many uncertainties, this may render the use of the Ogden tables inappropriate and the courts will revert to a 'lump-sum' approach in assessing future loss. This is sometimes referred to as a *Blamire award* (following ***Blamire v South Cumbriw Health Authority [1983] PIQR Q1***). Judicial discretion will vary and this makes it difficult to predict what lump-sums might be awarded.

- Another type of award is for *handicap on the labour market*. This award is normally appropriate where a claimant has secured commensurate work but remains disadvantaged in the open labour market; the award aims to compensate them for the risk that they may find it harder to keep their job and/or are limited in what work they can do. The convention is to refer to such awards as a '*Smith v Manchester*' award (referencing the case of ***Smith v Manchester Corporation (1974) 17 KIR***). This exercise should not merely be a rough estimate, and there is good judicial guidance on how to approach such an award (see the judgment of Brown LJ in ***Moeliker v A. Reyrolle & Co. Ltd [1977] 1WLR 132***). Essentially, the court must consider whether there is a substantial risk that the claimant will lose their current employment before the end of their working life. Normally such awards will vary between a few months to a few years' worth of earnings. It is open to the court to use the Ogden tables to calculate an award for handicap on the labour market instead of adopting the lump-sum approach.

- It is possible for a claimant to claim both types of loss over different periods of time, for example, a claimant may have a loss of military career followed by a handicap in the labour market for a civilian (post-military) career.

Where a judge feels that both the Ogden tables and *Smith v Manchester* approaches are unsatisfactory, the court may adjust the multipliers that would apply to the Ogden calculation. There is a lot of debate on how, when and/or whether such adjustments should be made. Helpfully, some of the key cases on quantum involve service personnel.

In ***Billett v MoD [2014] EWHC 3060*** a former Lance Corporal in the Royal Logistics Corps had brought a claim in negligence against the MoD for having sustained a NFCI during a training exercise in Aldershot in 2009. Having been diagnosed with a NFCI and medically downgraded, he was subsequently upgraded as 'medically fully deployable' (MFD), but decided to terminate his military career.

The parties agreed liability, apportioned 75/25 in the claimant's favour. They could not agree quantum, and so an assessment hearing took place before Edis J (then a QC sitting as a High Court judge). Edis J found that the claimant:

- Had suffered a minor NFCI in his feet only and that, whilst he suffered symptoms in his hands, these did not amount to a NFCI.

- Had not recovered from his NFCI, contrary to what the military doctors had determined. He still suffered symptoms and was likely to suffer these in the long term.

- Had left the Army for reasons unrelated to his injury, and that consequently he had no claim for loss of military career or congenial employment.

- Was working as an HGV driver, but if that employment ended then he would face a handicap in the labour market (a contention supported by the employment experts for both parties). Therefore, this aspect of the claimant's future loss also had to be assessed.

The real issue in ***Billett*** was how to assess the handicap on the labour market. Edis J said:

> *"The Court is therefore presented with a problem to which there are three suggested solutions.*
>
> *(i) A traditional award of a lump sum...* [i.e. Smith v Manchester]
>
> *(ii) An award based on Ogden tables A and B without adjustment.*
>
> *(iii) An award using Ogden tables A and B as suggested in paragraph 32 of the Explanatory Notes* [i.e. with adjustment of the reduction factors]"

He went on to conclude that the claimant was disabled, applying the test set out at in the explanatory notes of the Ogden tables (and Section 6 of the Equality Act to which the Ogden tables refer). The explanatory notes state:

> *"A person is classified as being disabled if all three of the following conditions in relation to the ill-health or disability are met:*
>
> *(i) the person has an illness or disability which has lasted or is expected to last for over a year or is a progressive illness,*
>
> *(ii) the person satisfies the Equality Act 2010 definition that the impact of the disability substantially limits the person's ability to carry out normal day to day activities, and*
>
> *(iii) their condition affects either the kind or the amount of paid work they can do."*

In respect of (ii) above, section 212 of the Equality Act provides that 'substantial' means 'more than trivial'.

Edis J found that the case was not one where a lump sum approach would be appropriate because there was *certainty* in what the claimant would have done uninjured (i.e. he would have left the Army and continued to work in logistics/transport as an HGV driver). He distinguished the case from previous cases involving lump-sum awards, which he considered had far more imponderables. But he also struggled with applying the reduction factors in the tables for disabled individuals, which he considered resulted in too high an award. Instead, he adopted a 'midpoint' for these reduction factors, which resulted in an award for loss of earnings of £99,062.04. In the context of an overall judgment for all heads of loss of £127,956.45 this was the largest aspect of loss.

The MoD appealed and argued that both awards for general damages and loss of earnings were were too high. The Court of Appeal upheld the finding of Edis J that Mr Billett was disabled within the Ogden definition, but the MoD were successful on the second point – ***[2015] EWCA Civ 773***. The Court of Appeal found that adjusting the reduction factors in the Ogden tables provided no more scientific a method of assessment than the broad-brush approach of *Smith v Manchester*. Jackson LJ gave the leading Judgment:

> *"I accept that in many instances the use of Tables A-D* [the Ogden tables] *will be a valuable aid to valuing the claimant's loss of earning capacity. But the present is not such a case. I reach this conclusion for three reasons:*
>
> *(i) Disability covers a broad spectrum. The claimant is at the outer fringe of that spectrum.*
>
> *(ii) The claimant's disability affects his ability to pursue his chosen career much less than it affects his activities outside work.*
>
> *(iii) Because of (i) and (ii) in this case there is no rational basis for determining how the reduction factor should be adjusted."*

He went on to award the claimant £45,000 in respect of his handicap on the labour market, which amounted to approximately two years' worth of earnings (less than half of what had been awarded for this head of loss in the court below).

In ***Herring v Ministry of Defence [2003] EWCA Civ 528***, Mr Herring had been a member of the Special Air Service of the Territorial Army (now 'Reserves'). Unfortunately, he suffered multiple injuries in a parachute accident in 1994 that had left him disabled and unable to walk without the aid of a stick. He brought a claim for personal injury against the MoD and was awarded £131,532.34 for his future loss of earnings at first instance, where the judge found as a matter of fact that, following his military career, Mr Herring would have served with the civilian police for seven years and reached the rank of Sergeant. However, he reduced the appropriate multiplier taken from the Ogden tables by 25% for "uncertainty" (a drop from the normal multiplier of 15.54 years to 11.70 years). He also gave no award for loss of earnings beyond police retirement age of 55.

Mr Herring appealed to the Court of Appeal, which found that:

- It was inappropriate to discount the multiplier by 25%, having found with certainty that the claimant would have served with the civilian police and/or would have secured employment financially commensurate with that career.

- A discount of 10% would have been appropriate in the circumstances of the case. Working on a broad-brush basis, the multiplier was reduced from 15.54 to 14 years (rather than 11.7). This had the effect of increasing the judge's award for future earnings loss by £54,300.

- The judge should have made an award for residual loss after the age of 55. A modest award of £5,000 was given in respect of handicap on the labour market (in line with *Smith v Manchester*).

Potter LJ gave the leading judgment:

> *"In any claim for injury to earning capacity based on long-term disability, the task of the court in assessing a fair figure for future earnings loss can only be effected by forming a view as to the most likely future working career ('the career model') of the claimant had he not been injured. Where, at the time of the accident, a claimant is in an established job or field of work in which he was likely to have remained but for the accident, the working assumption is that he would have done so and the conventional multiplier/multiplicand method of calculation is adopted, the court taking into account any reasonable prospects of promotion and/or movement to a higher salary scale or into a better remunerated field of work, by adjusting the multiplicand at an appropriate point along the scale of the multiplier...If such a move or change is unlikely significantly to affect the future level of earnings, it may be ignored in the multiplicand/multiplier exercise, save that it will generally be appropriate to make a (moderate) discount in the multiplier in respect of contingencies or 'the vicissitudes of life'...The cases in which the percentage 'loss of a chance' approach has been adopted appear to me to be those where the chance to be assessed has been the chance that the career of the claimant will take a particular course leading to significantly higher overall earnings than those which it is otherwise reasonable to take as the baseline for calculation...In a case where the career model adopted by the judge has been chosen because it is itself the appropriate baseline and/or is one of a number of alternatives likely to give more or less similar results, then it is neither necessary nor appropriate to adopt the percentage chance approach in respect of the possibility that the particular career identified will not be followed after all. That seems to be me to be the position in this case."*

***Herring*** is helpful authority for the proposition that, where a claimant is able to put forward a reasonable career model for future loss, that career model should be adopted for the purposes of calculating loss as a 'base line' and for appropriate discounts to multipliers to be made thereafter; such discounts should not be made lightly and always with attention to the evidence.

In ***Inglis v Ministry of Defence* [2019] EWHC 1153 (QB)** Mr Inglis, a former Royal Marine, brought a claim for personal injury in relation to his noise-induced hearing loss caused to him during his military service. By the time of trial, liability was split by agreement of the parties 80/20 in favour of Mr Inglis and presumably there was some element of contributory negligence and/or litigation risk which factored into that agreement.

Mr Inglis had entered into an open engagement for 22 years which would have terminated in September 2019. However, he applied for premature voluntary release (PVR) in May 2011, which terminated his career in May 2012. His evidence was that his decision to leave was because he knew by that stage that his hearing had deteriorated and a medical discharge was likely; he wanted instead to leave of his own volition and before a medical discharge could take place, so that he could pursue an opportunity to work in the maritime security industry. This has been a common feature in many military claims.

Mr Peter Marquand (sitting as a High Court Judge) found that:

- Mr Inglis had decided to leave military service voluntarily because to stay would have led to an exacerbation of his NIHL. The judge was convinced by the evidence given by the claimant and his wife.

- Although his NIHL was classified as mild, it was still a significant and long-term condition that affected his day-to-day activities and so he satisfied the definition of 'disability' in law.

- He should be awarded special damages for loss of military earnings, benefits and income, which would have to be calculated in accordance with the principles of the Ogden tables. He was awarded £545,766 in total, to include £25,000 in respect of PSLA.

***Inglis*** is a helpful judgment and explores a number of factors, factual and expert, which can influence the court's view on loss of career. The fulcrum in the case was the determination of the first issue of causation: *"whether the Claimant left the Royal Marines because of his hearing loss or in order to take up more lucrative employment in the maritime security industry. The Claimant must prove on the balance of probabilities, that the hearing loss was his reason for leaving in order to establish a causal link to his claim for any future loss of earnings and any future loss of pension."* The judge's decision fell in favour of the claimant primarily because of his own evidence in chief and that of his wife, although experts in the fields of employment and occupational medicine also helped the court reach its determination by exploring the impact that a medical downgrade would have had on the claimant's military career and prospects. Had the claimant's evidence wavered, the value of the claim would have toppled downwards. Practitioners are urged to bear this in mind when preparing witness statements; ultimately so much can rest on your client's evidence in court.

There are some common threads to be gathered from the case law:

- Where service personnel have lost a career as a result of negligence, they are normally in a much better position than civilian claimants to argue that *Blamire* and *Smith v Manchester* type awards are not appropriate methods of calculating their losses. This is because military careers are lengthy, highly structured and include regular opportunities of promotion and development; so there is generally more certainty on the likely *but for* career path.

- Using the Ogden tables provides a scientifically based method of compensating claimants, and this can avoid under compensating them also.

- Proving that your client is disabled can be determinative. In part this may encourage the court to use the appropriate disability multipliers in the Ogden tables, which will enhance the calculation for losses. However, judges will not be bound to use the Ogden method for calculating future loss just because your client is disabled and retain a wide discretion.

- Where a reasonable career model can be put forward with good prospects, that model must be taken as a 'base line' and appropriate deductions to multipliers made thereafter. Adjustments the reduction factors on the basis of speculation only and there must be tangible reasons (and evidence) to interfere with this 'base line'.

- Claimants must present their cases with as much certainty as possible, both their pleaded injured and uninjured careers should present the court with little doubt about their losses and likely future earnings. This will reduce the chance of the court reverting to a lump sum approach in respect of either loss of career or handicap on the labour market.

- The post-military civilian career is a very important aspect of loss. Service personnel often have the option of entering the civilian sphere as highly skilled and sought-after individuals, but this may depend on their length of service and rank.

## 13.4 Building the case on loss

Your client will have to prove how their military career has been affected (or lost) as a direct result of the negligence. Most clients will have a fairly good idea of where their military career was heading, but a lot may depend on factors which are outside of their knowledge and control. Some clients will have delusions of grandeur, and will have to be brought back down to earth. Others will be modest and underplay their hand. You will have to consider the disclosure, especially pre-injury performance appraisals, and utilise witnesses and experts to build the case on loss.

Career loss is often demonstrated through the medical discharge process, where an injury has invalidated your client from service. This process will involve a referral made to a medical board, whose task it will be to assess your client's condition and determine the correct medical profile before making a recommendation in respect of continued service (see **Chapter** 4). That decision will then be considered by an employability board, which will determine your client's ability to continue to serve. Where this decision results in your client's medical discharge, they will normally not face any difficulty in establishing causation of loss.

Other cases might not be so straight forward and, like in ***Inglis*** above, your client may have decided to circumvent that process by terminating their service. These cases may present problems in proving the reason behind the decision to terminate (see ***Billett***), which are sometimes multifactorial and rarely straightforward.

### 13.4.1 Disclosure

There are a number of documents, most available from your client or the MoD through pre-action disclosure, which will be relevant to your inquiries.

- **Military salary and benefits**

If not immediately available to your client, their payslips will normally be stored electronically by the MoD and should be readily obtainable.

- **Medical Board and personal statement**

The Medical Board record is prepared on a prescribed form (FMed23). In preparation for this, your client will be asked to prepare a personal statement. That statement is meant to be considered by the Medical Board, but will rarely have any bearing on the outcome. It will be disclosable and form part of your client's medical records, so it pays to consider this carefully.

If you are instructed before the Medical Board sits, your client may well ask for your input on the personal statement. Some clients would have spent their time writing a discourse on why their injuries were the fault of others and, having done so in perhaps and angry and irrational state, may have made assertions which might later undermine their civil claim. Others may fail to point out the factual circumstances of their injury and this again may undermine a civil claim at a later stage. Your advice should be to keep this statement short and simple.

The Medical Board decision itself may also be crucial. These will sometimes list a number of other injuries which your client suffers with at the time of the Medical Board and give an indication of which injury is primarily responsible for their current condition. Defendants may use this to undermine any argument that your client's discharge was as a result of the negligent act but, rather, a culmination of other pre-existing conditions. For example, it is very common for service personnel to suffer with musculoskeletal injuries that might be noted as minor at the time of discharge but which defendants will use to muddy the waters of causation, often arguing that these other injuries contributed to your client's discharge or would have curtailed their career at some later stage regardless of the negligence.. The Medical Board record may also include factually inaccurate statements about what your client said during their interview with the Board, and if so then they your client should be encouraged to request that amendments are made to reflect the correct facts.

- **Personnel file**

Your client's personnel file or 'P-file' should include all of their training and occupational records, including a print of your client's Joint Personal Administration (JPA) system records, which is the online human resources programme for the forces. Where your client has been discharged, a copy of their certificate of service should also be included.

Crucially, these records should include your client's annual reports and appraisals, which will enable you and/or an expert to understand your client's likely career progression (see below).

- **Unit file**

This is similar to your client's personnel file but will be physically held by their unit. It may include more up-to-date information on their career, training and status (where your client is still serving).

- **The pay and pension forecast**

The MoD will normally seek to rely on Defence Analytical Services and Advice (DASA) statistics to argue against any claim that your client has lost a potentially lengthy career. DASA was a statistical and economic unit within the MoD, providing and often publishing statistics relevant to a number of key areas of defence business. This included statistics on likely career lengths, prospects of promotion and rates of retention across the services as a whole but also within single services. Since 2013 DASA was rebranded 'Defence Statistics', but undertakes the same work.

You may be served with a career, pay and pension forecast, which in essence a witness statement is prepared by an officer within your client's Service, who will purport to review your client's personnel file and report on their likely career trajectory according to the available statistics. These documents should be treated with great caution and, more often than not, will be unhelpful. You might want to consider whether the career, pay and pension forecast is an attempt to introduce expert evidence without permission.

- **References and letters of commendation**

Service personnel are often commended for their professionalism and hard work, sometimes following operations or when assisting their superiors in training and unit events. These letters can from important evidence to bolster a claim for loss of career and/or congenial employment.

- **Civilian earnings, benefits and pension**

Your client will have to give credit for their current and future earnings. This will include assessing their likely career progression in their current employment. Your client's current employers should hold relevant information, including their contract of employment, payslips, pension plan and a personnel file.

If your client is not currently employed, and depending on their condition and prognosis, you will need to estimate if and when they will re-enter the labour market and in what capacity. You may need an employment expert evidence to help to assess these issues.

### 13.4.2 Appraisals and promotion

Your client should have access to their annual appraisals. Interpreting these is not always straightforward. You may find the rank structure at 2.2.5 helpful here.

Officers have the duty to report on all of those service personnel under their command. From 2001 this process was standardised across the Services for officers and from 2008 for other ranks. Appraisals are completed on a prescribed form known as an Officers' Joint Appraisal Report (OJAR) for officers, and a Service Person's Joint Appraisal Report (SJAR) for other ranks.

The Reporting Officer must indicate whether they are recommending a specific service person for promotion (one rank up) and may also indicate whether they are showing potential for further promotion (a maximum of two ranks up), using the descriptors in the table below:

| Grade | | Promotion 1 Rank up | Promotion 2 Ranks up |
|---|---|---|---|
| Exceptional | Excep | Outstandingly suitable | Exceptional potential |
| High | High | Highly suitable | High potential |
| Yes | Yes | Suitable now | Has potential |
| Developing | Dev | Displays some suitability | Displays some potential |
| No | No | Not suitable | Displays no potential |
| Insufficient Knowledge | IK | Insufficient observation | |
| Not applicable | NA | Not eligible | |

In addition there is a common grading scale for a series of specified individual performance attributes, including amongst others leadership, judgment, communication, reliability and courage. An Overall Performance Grade (OPG) is then given for each attribute according to the following definitions:

| **Grade** | **Definition** |
|---|---|
| A | Performing to the **highest standard** in **all** respects |
| A- | Performing **above the standard** in **all** respects |
| B+ | Performing **above the standard** expected in **most** respects |
| B | Performing **to the standard** in **all** respects |
| B- | Performing **to the standard** expected in **most** respects |
| C | Performing **below the standard** expected in **most** respects |
| D | Performing **below the standard** expected in **all** respects |
| IK | Insufficient Knowledge (not used in OPG) |
| NA | Not Applicable (not used in OPG) |

There are a number of general points about the appraisal and promotion process:

- There are very strict rules about what can and cannot go into an appraisal. For example, no reference should normally be made to a service person's medical condition so that you will not usually find any direct reference to your client's injury, even if it has had a significant impact on their performance. Each service provides guidance on how appraisals should be completed. See *JSP 757: Tri-Service Guidance for Appraisal Writing* but be aware that further single service guidance may be available.

- Service personnel may have up to three Reporting Officers, normally their direct line manager and their superior. Commanding Officers are expected to align reports and address inconsistencies in reporting.

- Appraisals should include a narrative summarising the service person's performance in the past year and potential going forward. It is standard practice for the Reporting Officer to indicate whether your client performs within the bottom third, middle third or top third of the cohort which they manage. A service person who is regularly in the 'top third' will normally indicate excellence and a long career.

- In addition to their overall performance, there will be a number of factors which may contribute to whether your client would have promoted at a particular point in their career, including time served and manning considerations (i.e. if there is a role for them to promote into). They may also be required to complete courses. Details of courses and their pass rates may be obtained through disclosure.

- Promotion boards sit at regular intervals throughout the year and will consider appraisals reports and any recommendations from Commanding Officers for promotion. The wording in reports may be crucial here and can be nuanced; suggestions that your client '*could*' or '*should*' promote will not normally amount to a recommendation.

- Service personnel should also receive a Mid Period Appraisal Report (MPAR), the purpose of which is to give them a steer at the mid-year point on how they are likely to be appraised at the end of the year and allow them time to reflect and rectify any mistakes.

- Where your client has been provided with an unfair appraisal they may decide to raise a service complaint (see **Chapter 11**).

### 13.4.3 Witness evidence

Ideally, all of your client's losses will be supported in the witness evidence and there will be a number of issues to consider:

- Your client's condition and symptoms need to be addressed in detail. Review the expert evidence and medical records with your client. The effect of medication can also be debilitating of itself and this needs to be described carefully. Consider whether a home visit is necessary. You may spot additional issues and needs at their home. Photographs of their circumstances at home may also help you make arguments in respect of the need for certain expenses and/or adaptations.

- Where your client suffers with pre-existing conditions that may have contributed to their medical discharge or limited their career, they may need to address these conditions in detail in their statement.

- Care is a significantly underrated element of loss. Military clients in particular may appear to be stoic but may rely heavily on others at home. Typically, a service person's partner or spouse may have been forced to leave their work in order to provide care at home and undertake tasks which they would not normally have done *but for* your client's injury. Identify what these tasks are and try and estimate the length of time invested on a daily, weekly or monthly basis. Asking carers to keep a diary can help.

Consider how care has changed since your client's medical discharge and how it might change in the future depending on their prognosis.

- In respect of the issue of disability, the court has to focus not on what the Claimant can do but what they *cannot* do as a result of their impairment (***Aderemi v London and South Eastern Railway Ltd [2013] ICR 591 EAT***). Do the same in the statements. What is it that your client no longer is able to do? The Equality Act 2010: '*Guidance on matters to be taken into account in determining questions relating to the definition of disability*' provides significant help here, addressing not only the meaning of 'impairment' but also providing examples with reference to specific conditions. The explanatory notes to the Ogden tables are also a helpful guide and set out a number of factors relevant to disability including mobility, manual dexterity, physical co-ordination etc. They can help you formulate questions for your client, who should provide examples from their day-to-day life where activities may become difficult or simply avoided. Choose those examples that are compelling and easy to relate to.

- Obtaining statements from former colleagues or superiors in support of your client's lost military career may prove difficult, but not impossible. Some witnesses will still be serving and unwilling to assist in the fear that they may endanger their own careers. Where such evidence is not available you may have to rely on the evidence available in the personnel records.

- When addressing your client's military career and where the evidence allows, your role will be to distinguish your client from the 'norm'. Defendants will rely heavily on statistics which may indicate that your client would have left the military voluntarily at a particular point. These statistics often provide a broad and average picture and do not take into account the very many human factors which may convince a judge or an employment expert that your client would have lasted the course of a longer career. You may need guidance from the employment expert on what those factors could be (see below), but they will include things like: having an interest in serving from a young age; coming from a military family, expressing a particular interest or aptitude in a specific military career path. These factors should be addressed in your client's statements and may also be supported by other witnesses apart from your client, such as close family, friends and/or colleagues.

- Equally, defendants may serve statements from your client's chain of command seeking to belittle their career. Treat these with caution and ensure that they tally with your client's personnel file. A commander who is eager to talk down your client's career may find it challenging when cross examined on positive appraisals that they have approved.

- Any civilian career that your client may have engaged in *after* their military service may be a lucrative aspect of their loss (see **13.4.5**).

- You may wish to exhibit evidence of significant expenses to your client's statement, where they may help establish ongoing losses.

### 13.4.4 Instructing the medical expert

You will need an appropriate medical expert (or experts) to opine, depending on the nature of your client's injury(s). Below are a few issues on which you may need their guidance.

1. Your client's current condition and what has caused it.

2. Whether they have any pre-existing conditions or susceptibilities (i.e. prior to injury) and, if so, to what extent they may have contributed to their current condition.

3. What their prognosis is (i.e. how and when might they improve, if at all).

4. Any recommended future treatment and its cost on a private basis.

5. Whether they are limited in their day-to-day activities (i.e. the question of disability).

Some medical experts will be happy to answer the question of whether or not your client is handicapped in the labour market, whereas others may defer to an employment expert. But they should be able to comment on medical limitations and what type of work your client may be suitable for (e.g. sedentary). Ultimately questions of handicap and disability are for the court to determine, but experts can help guide the court in making that determination.

Where there is any doubt as to what may have caused your client's medical discharge, you will probably need to rely on an appropriate medical expert to advise the court on occupational health matters. This may be an expert in occupational health medicine and/or an expert GP with a background in the military. They will need to consider:

- Your client's pre-existing conditions – would these have limited their military career at some future point regardless of the negligence? What would their likely medical profile have been (i.e. *but for* the negligence).

- Their medical profile at the time of discharge – would your client have been able to continue to serve? Bear in mind, as mentioned above, that it is fairly common practice for Medical Boards to list all conditions at the time of discharge.

Experts with little or no knowledge of the PULHHEEMS system or military occupational health protocols are unlikely to be able to assist you or the court with these questions.

### 13.4.5 Instructing the employment expert

Where your client is pursuing a significant loss of career, you will probably need an employment expert to report. You will need to ensure that the expert is appropriately qualified. They will usually have a background in human resources and ideally would have served themselves. Marrying up your expert's own military background with your client's may add a further advantage to their evidence, but it is not strictly necessary nor will it always be possible. You might ask them to consider:

1. A military career forecast i.e. what military career would your client have had *but for* the negligence, to include likely promotions and likely termination date.

2. A post-military career forecast i.e. what civilian career might your client have enjoyed having served their military career.

3. Their civilian earning prospects now and into the future (if any and in the light of the medical evidence), to include any assessment of pension.

4. Whether and to what extent they are disadvantaged in the employment market (this may differ greatly depending on the available work near their home).

In completing their report, there will be a number of factors that may influence their view, including:

- Your client's background and education.

- Their military personnel file and appraisals.

- Their rank, trade and/or specialist skill set.

- Their family and personal circumstances at the time they were serving (evidence suggests that those service personnel from families with a tradition of service or whose spouse/partner also serves are more likely to serve a full career).

- Their medical condition and profile at the time they were serving.

- Their current medical condition and prognosis.

- Any work that they have been able to undertake since leaving service.

- Their motivations, goals and interests - they will invariably be more successful if they are able to find work that they enjoy and are good at.

The last factor should not be underestimated; most employment experts will tell you that, subject to any medical conditions, the length of a service person's career will depend primarily on their willingness to serve. Again, where the evidence is supportive, such aspirations should be borne out in the witness evidence.

In respect of your client's aptitude and ability to promote, this may be influenced by a number of factors such as manning considerations (i.e. whether there were positions open for them to promote into) and/or redundancy. Ultimately the expert will be led by your client's appraisals, and the more that are available to them the more accurate a picture they will be able to draw of the projected military career.

Another issue that is often underestimated is the likely post-military civilian career but for the negligence. Many service personnel are able to transition into lucrative roles given their specialist skill sets. This might involve consultancy work abroad which attracts tax savings. For example, the close protection (i.e. bodyguard) and maritime security industries have traditionally sought Army and Royal Marine personnel and offered lucrative contracts. Other industries will open their doors to service personnel only after they have enjoyed the benefits of a military career and developed necessary expertise, management and leadership skills as well as, importantly, those who are fit and healthy. These post-military careers may now be lost to your client because of their injuries. They may have a very good idea about these potential industries and may also be able to put you in touch with former colleagues who have gone on to make a success of themselves in these fields. Some examples of post-military careers include:

- Close protection
- Maritime security
- Off-shore industries
- Aviation
- Supply and logistics
- Police, fire and ambulance services

In some cases it may be beneficial to ask the expert to provide a 'desktop' report (i.e. on the basis of the papers only), for example when you need quick assessment of loss at an early stage. But a full assessment and meeting with the client is recommended; so much will depend on your client's character and motivations and the employment expert will need to assess these first-hand. This will also improve the report, because these human factors will personalise it and make it more convincing. Not every case will deserve the input of an employment expert and it can be an expensive and time-consuming process.

## 13.5 AFCS and abatement

The Armed Forces Compensation Scheme (AFCS) is a large topic and beyond this book. The following is a short summary of issues that may be relevant to your practice:

- The AFCS is a statutory 'no fault' scheme, which entitles service personnel to compensation for injuries suffered as a result of service. Any injury suffered prior to 6th April 2005 will be considered under the previous 'War Pension' scheme. The scheme is managed through Veterans UK, which is a part of the MoD and manages all compensation and pension payments to service personnel.

- Eligible service personnel will be awarded compensation according to the tariffs of the scheme, which are largely dependent on the nature of the injury and any disability caused. They must make an application using the requisite form (AFCS/WPS01) within seven years of their injury.

- Some injuries are not compensated under the scheme, such as slips and trips, self-inflicted harm and travel between home and work, to name a few.

- Awards under the scheme may include lump sums or Guaranteed Income Payments (GIPs), the latter of which can be very significant. Awards can be interim or temporary in nature, pending full resolution of treatment and a clearer prognosis. Decisions can be appealed, and often are. Appeals are heard by the War Pensions and Armed Forces Compensation Tribunal. Generally, awards under the scheme will pale in comparison to an award made in a civil claim.

- An application under the AFCS is now automatically made on behalf of service personnel who are medically discharged. There is nothing to preclude your client from applying for compensation under the scheme whilst also seeking compensation through a civil claim.

- If your client settles their civil claim or receives an award at court, their entitlement to AFCS may be affected. Paragraph 40 of the Armed Forces and Reserve Forces Compensation Scheme Order 2011/517 provides for this process, known as 'abatement'. Generally, this entitles the Secretary of State to reduce or stop benefits under the scheme where a claimant is compensated for the same injury in a civil claim (and so as to avoid double recovery). The regulations do not specify how abatement should happen, but a copy of MoD abatement policy is obtainable by request (unchanged since November 2011). Generally, the policy directs for AFCS awards to be reduced on a 'like for like' basis i.e. a GIP may stand to be reduced in the light of an award for loss of earnings, and the lump sum may be reduced depending on the level of PSLA.

- When settling a case you will be keen to avoid any adverse effect on your client's entitlement to AFCS. Whilst avoiding double recovery you must also seek to ensure that they are not under-compensated. In as far as possible, any settlement agreement should ideally be documented in a court order (a *Tomlin* order) which provides for a breakdown of the settlement in respect of individual heads of loss and expressly states that the settlement sum has taken into account any AFCS awarded. This will provide your client with evidence of what heads of loss have been compensated, which may protect them from excessive abatement of their AFCS awards. You may also consider including wording in your agreement either to expressly prohibit further changes to your client's AFCS award and/or for liberty to restore the case should awards be adversely affected.

- It is normal practice for solicitors acting for the MoD to report to Veterans UK about the conclusion of any civil proceedings and your client will also be obliged to disclose the terms of the settlement when making an application.

- You may be obliged to point out to your client that they have a right to claim under the AFCS and their deadline for doing so. Bear in mind that there is no entitlement to legal costs under the scheme, which can be complex and often riddled with delays.

- Your client's AFCS file will be disclosable and may include a number of documents relevant to their civil claim. You will need to check these documents to ensure congruence with the civil claim and, where there are discrepancies, seek instructions.

## 13.6 Points for practice

- Military claims require a huge amount of time and investment in the preparation of evidence, normally at the early stages of a claim. The importance of having a network of good experts cannot be underestimated, nor the need for early conferences and reports. This can result in expensive pre-action investigations.

- Try to establish your client's likely career path(s) early, not forgetting the potential civilian career that could have followed military service, and build *certainty* into the evidence. What you may think of as an 'open and shut' case of loss of military career may turn out very differently for all sorts of reasons that are not immediately apparent. Equally, just because your client's military career was not lost as a result of any negligence, does not mean that their claim will be of limited value. Review your arguments on loss at regular intervals.

- Your job is to consider your client as an individual rather than a statistical average. So much will turn on their intentions towards their military career, the good esteem that they were held in by their peers and managers, and those family and loved ones who were willing to support them in their military careers. These factors must be addressed comprehensively in the witness evidence.

- Be cautious when dealing with statistics thrown at you by defendants to undermine your client's claim for a lost career, particularly those provided in career forecasts. These statistics rarely show the complete picture.

- Your client may well be proud of their military service and the fact that it has ended will be a very raw issue for them. They may find digesting an employment expert's opinion difficult where this does not favour a long or successful career.

- Military claims are well disposed to a multiplicand/multiplier approach to the calculation of future loss and broad-brush awards should be resisted. The emphasis on career progression, regular testing, appraisals and promotional boards provide a clearer understanding of a potential lost career as opposed to many other industries.

- Establishing that your client is disabled, assuming the evidence supports this, may be determinative and might enable you to argue for enhanced losses. Focus on providing clear examples of how your client faces disadvantage in their day-to-day life. Focus on what they cannot now do.

- Your client may be entitled to an award under the AFCS, which will have to be made within seven years of their injury. AFCS awards must be credited in civil claims and may be abated after settlement or judgment.

'A Practical Guide to Noise Induced Hearing Loss (NIHL) Claims' by Andrew Mckie, Ian Skeate, Gareth McAloon

'An Introduction to Beauty Negligence Claims – A Practical Guide for the Personal Injury Practitioner' by Greg Almond

'Intercompany Agreements for Transfer Pricing Compliance' by Paul Sutton

'Zen and the Art of Mediation' by Martin Plowman

'A Practical Guide to the SRA Principles, Individual and Law Firm Codes of Conduct 2019 – What Every Law Firm Needs to Know' by Paul Bennett

'A Practical Guide to Licensing Law for Commercial Property Lawyers' by Niall McCann & Richard Williams

'A Practical Guide to Adoption for Family Lawyers' by Graham Pegg

'Essential Motor Finance Law for the Busy Practitioner' by Richard Humphreys

'A Practical Guide to Industrial Disease Claims' by Andrew Mckie & Ian Skeate

'A Practical Guide to the Law of Armed Conflict' by Jo Morris & Libby Anderson

'A Practical Guide to Redundancy' by Philip Hyland

'A Practical Guide to Vicarious Liability' by Mariel Irvine

'A Practical Guide to Claims Arising from Delays in Diagnosing Cancer' by Bella Webb

'A Practical Guide to Applications for Landlord's Consent and Variation of Leases' by Mark Shelton

'A Practical Guide to Relief from Sanctions Post-Mitchell and Denton' by Peter Causton

'Butler's Equine Tax Planning: 2nd Edition' by Julie Butler

'A Practical Guide to Equity Release for Advisors' by Paul Sams

'A Practical Guide to Unlawful Eviction and Harassment' by Stephanie Lovegrove

'A Practical Guide to the Law Relating to Food' by Ian Thomas

'A Practical Guide to the Ending of Assured Shorthold Tenancies' by Elizabeth Dwomoh

'A Practical Guide to Financial Services Claims' by Chris Hegarty

'The Law of Houses in Multiple Occupation: A Practical Guide to HMO Proceedings' by Julian Hunt

'A Practical Guide to Unlawful Eviction and Harassment' by Stephanie Lovegrove

| ‘A Practical Guide to Solicitor and Client Costs’ by Robin Dunne |
|---|
| ‘A Practical Guide to Wrongful Conception, Wrongful Birth and Wrongful Life Claims’ by Rebecca Greenstreet |
| ‘Occupiers, Highways and Defective Premises Claims: A Practical Guide Post-Jackson – 2nd Edition’ by Andrew Mckie |
| ‘A Practical Guide to Financial Ombudsman Service Claims’ by Adam Temple & Robert Scrivenor |
| ‘A Practical Guide to the Law of Enfranchisement and Lease Extension’ by Paul Sams |
| ‘A Practical Guide to Marketing for Lawyers – 2nd Edition’ by Catherine Bailey & Jennet Ingram |
| 'A Practical Guide to Advising Schools on Employment Law' by Jonathan Holden |
| 'Certificates of Lawful Use and Development: A Guide to Making and Determining Applications' by Bob Mc Geady & Meyric Lewis |
| 'A Practical Guide to the Law of Dilapidations' by Mark Shelton |
| ‘A Guide to Consent in Clinical Negligence Post-Montgomery’ by Lauren Sutherland QC |
| ‘A Practical Guide to Running Housing Disrepair and Cavity Wall Claims: 2nd Edition’ by Andrew Mckie & Ian Skeate |
| ‘A Practical Guide to Digital and Social Media Law for Lawyers’ by Sherree Westell |
| ‘A Practical Guide to Holiday Sickness Claims – 2nd Edition’ by Andrew Mckie & Ian Skeate |
| ‘A Practical Guide to Elderly Law’ by Justin Patten |
| ‘Arguments and Tactics for Personal Injury and Clinical Negligence Claims’ by Dorian Williams |
| ‘A Practical Guide to QOCS and Fundamental Dishonesty’ by James Bentley |
| ‘A Practical Guide to Drone Law’ by Rufus Ballaster, Andrew Firman, Eleanor Clot |
| ‘A Practical Guide to Compliance for Personal Injury Firms Working With Claims Management Companies’ by Paul Bennett |
| ‘A Practical Guide to the Landlord and Tenant Act 1954: Commercial Tenancies’ by Richard Hayes & David Sawtell |
| ‘A Practical Guide to Psychiatric Claims in Personal Injury’ by Liam Ryan |
| ‘A Practical Guide to Dog Law for Owners and Others’ by Andrea Pitt |

www.ingramcontent.com/pod-product-compliance
Lightning Source LLC
LaVergne TN
LVHW052252200926
848481LV00002B/347

*9781912687275*